Therapy Breakthrough

Other Books by Michael R. Edelstein, PhD

Three Minute Therapy: Change Your Thinking, Change Your Life (with David Ramsay Steele, 1997)

Stage Fright: 40 Stars Tell You How They Beat America's #1 Fear (with Mick Berry, 2009)

Rational Drinking: How to Live Happily With or Without Alcohol (ebook only, with Will Ross, 2013)

Other Books by Richard K. Kujoth, EdD

Job Placement of the Emotionally Disturbed (edited with Lawrence P. Blum (1972)

Chess Is an Art: Games, Notes, Problems, Drawings (1955, 1997, 2004)

Rational Power for Younger People: A Guide to Rational Emotive Education (with Jo Ellen Kujoth, 1983, 2006)

Other Books by David Ramsay Steele, PhD

From Marx to Mises: Post-Capitalist Society and the Challenge of Economic Calculation (1992)

Three Minute Therapy: Change Your Thinking, Change Your Life (with Michael R. Edelstein, 1997)

Atheism Explained: From Folly to Philosophy (2008)

Therapy Breakthrough

*Why Some Psychotherapies Work
Better than Others*

MICHAEL R. EDELSTEIN, PH.D.

RICHARD K. KUJOTH, ED.D.

DAVID RAMSAY STEELE, PH.D.

Open Court
Chicago

To order books from Open Court, call toll-free 1-800-815-2280, or visit
our website at www.opencourtbooks.com.

Open Court Publishing Company is a division of Carus Publishing Company,
dba ePals Media.

Copyright © 2013 by Carus Publishing Company, dba ePals Media

First printing 2013

Printed and bound in the United States of America.

ISBN: 978-0-8126-9686-8

Library of Congress Control Number: 2013941016

To the memory of Albert Ellis (1913–2007),
the Copernicus of Psychotherapy

Contents

Preface

This book will explain to you what different types of psychotherapy are trying to do, why there are hundreds of competing 'schools' of psychotherapy which don't agree with each other, and why, despite that, psychotherapy has made terrific progress, is way better than it used to be, and is better than drugs at helping you overcome your problems.

Therapy Breakthrough will inform you why most therapists sixty years ago were very interested in your dreams and your early childhood, whereas most therapists today are not very interested in those matters—and it will explain why, despite this change, most movies, novels, and TV shows, still present psychotherapy as it was sixty years ago. When you've read *Therapy Breakthrough*, you'll not only know that the New Therapy works better than the Old Therapy, you'll understand exactly why it does.

This book is aimed at thoughtful people who want to understand what psychotherapy is all about, how effective it might be, how it has changed, and why. It's also aimed at therapists and counselors who will find herein some fascinating bits of information about what psychotherapy is and where it came from. Many of the things we say here are already very familiar to specialists; we've put them together in one package for a wider audience.

Two of the authors of this book wrote an earlier book called *Three Minute Therapy: Change Your Thinking,*

Change Your Life, which explains the basic principles of our approach to psychotherapy in the simplest possible terms. *Three Minute Therapy* is one of those books that never make it onto the best-seller charts but never go out of print. It just keeps on finding thousands of appreciative new readers, and we often get questions about its broader implications. We therefore decided to write a further book—still intended to be readable for the complete newcomer to the topic of psychotherapy—looking at some of these ideas in a wider and more philosophical perspective.

While writing this new book, which was to become *Therapy Breakthrough*, we heard from Richard Kujoth, a psychotherapist who was also writing a book about the same kind of therapy and with a broadly similar purpose. Richard completely agreed with what we had written in *Three Minute Therapy* and what we planned for the new book. So we joined forces.

Richard Kujoth died while *Therapy Breakthrough* was nearing completion. His active role in contributing ideas and polishing the manuscript was taken over by his widow, Jo Ellen Kujoth, herself also an experienced and knowledgeable therapist.

In *Therapy Breakthrough* we argue for the New Therapy, Cognitive-Behavioral therapy, and against the Old therapy, Psychodynamic therapy. We're not concerned here to compare the merits of one form of Cognitive-Behavioral therapy with other forms. We do, however, believe that Albert Ellis's Rational Emotive Behavior Therapy (REBT) has the edge, in some respects, over other types of Cognitive-Behavioral therapy, though we also think REBT therapists will benefit from keeping up with what's going on in other forms of Cognitive-Behavioral therapy, and will sometimes find valuable new advances which they can incorporate into their own therapy.

The authors developed the ideas in this book in telephone seminars every two weeks for thirteen years. The actual chore of stringing words and sentences together fell to David Ramsay Steele.

1
What Happened to Psychotherapy?

Psychotherapy today is a familiar part of life for millions. Ten percent of people have been in therapy at some time in the past few years, and more than fifty percent will consult a therapist at some point in their lives.

Psychotherapy is everywhere, sometimes where most people don't expect it. For example, in discussions of policy regarding drug addiction, there is much talk about 'addiction treatment'. Most of the public don't realize that virtually all addiction treatment in the US today is psychotherapy and nothing but psychotherapy. Marriage counseling has become both the best hope for saving a relationship and a conventional accompaniment to the termination of a relationship. Marriage counseling (like most things described as 'counseling') is mostly psychotherapy.

Psychotherapy is overtaking religion. Most people with an emotional problem or facing the breakup of a relationship will now more readily turn to psychotherapy than to a minister of religion. But if they do go to the pastor of their local church, they will probably find that he has taken a course in psychotherapy, or will recommend them to a 'Christian therapist', who will turn out to be pretty much like a non-Christian therapist, with a few Biblical quotations thrown in.

Not only that, but much religious preaching today sounds increasingly like psychotherapy. The Reverend Joel Osteen's church has the biggest congregation of any church in America. His preaching to a football-stadium-sized audience is also televised, and he regularly brings out books which easily top the best-seller charts. Ninety-nine percent of the content of his preaching and writing is what psychotherapists might say in the course of therapy sessions. We don't mean to imply that psychotherapy can be done for a mass audience—it can't. And we don't mean to imply that we agree with everything Reverend Osteen says—we don't. But the influence is unmistakable.

The Revolution in Psychotherapy

In view of the central place of psychotherapy in modern life, it's remarkable that there has been a revolution in psychotherapy, *a revolution which most people just haven't noticed.* The revolution has not yet completely triumphed: the Old therapy and the New therapy exist side by side, and many psychotherapists mix elements of the Old and the New. But the New form of therapy did not exist at all sixty years ago, and it is now the major form of therapy. Year by year it keeps gaining ground, and the Old therapy is in retreat.

Here's what we're going to show you in this book:

- **The key differences between the Old Therapy and the New**

- **Where the Old Therapy came from and where the New Therapy came from**

- **How the Old Therapy is based on a whole slew of mistaken ideas**

- **Why the New Therapy works better than the Old Therapy**

The differences between the Old and the New therapies are not minor or superficial. They are fundamental. The Old and the New Therapy have very different approaches to solving your problems. Here are some of these different approaches:

OLD THERAPY: **Understanding what happened in your childhood is vital.**

NEW THERAPY: *No! Understanding what happened in your childhood may be fascinating, but is irrelevant to your current problems.*

OLD THERAPY: **You're bedeviled by hidden forces in the depths of your unconscious mind, which resist any attempt to be brought to light.**

NEW THERAPY: *No! Hidden or unconscious influences have no will of their own. In many cases, you can bring them to light quite easily. In many other cases, you can never bring them to light, but you don't need to.*

OLD THERAPY: **Repressed memories are the cause of your emotional problems.**

NEW THERAPY: *No! What you have forgotten has no power over you.*

OLD THERAPY: **Your dreams are a key to unlock your problems.**

NEW THERAPY: *No! Analyzing the 'meaning' of your dreams can be fun, but can contribute little to solving your problems.*

OLD THERAPY: **You should let out your anger and other feelings, because it's risky to bottle up your unwelcome or unpleasant emotions.**

NEW THERAPY: *No! In giving vent to an emotion, you're training yourself to keep on having that emotion. If you give vent to anger, in the long run you make yourself more prone to anger, not less.*

OLD THERAPY: **Once you have relived your past traumas, and gained insight, your problems are solved.**

NEW THERAPY: *No! You don't need to relive past traumas, nor do you even need to gain insight (helpful though that may sometimes be). What's needed is to train yourself to think and behave differently, so that you stop making problems for yourself.*

We see here that the Old and the New therapies have very different views of the human mind, emotional and behavioral problems, and the best way to treat these problems.

What we've been calling the Old therapy is more often called *Psychodynamic therapy*, and what we've been calling the New Therapy is usually called *Cognitive-Behavioral therapy*. Sixty years ago nearly all psychotherapy was Psychodynamic whereas today most psychotherapy is Cognitive-Behavioral.[1]

Psychodynamic therapists usually encourage their clients to go back to their childhoods and dwell on what happened to them then. Cognitive-Behavioral therapists understand that problems are created by *what people are telling themselves now.*

Take a woman who's depressed because she keeps telling herself that she is no good. We can suppose that she started telling herself she's no good because when she was a little girl, her parents kept telling her she was no good. This is very probably mistaken, because research indicates that in general people's personalities are *not* formed by their early interactions with their parents. But, true or false, it's not important now. What matters is that she train herself to stop telling herself she's no good. If she does that, then she will probably stop feeling depressed.

---

[1] We can't give percentages because so many therapists are eclectic (borrowing ideas from several different schools of therapy) and no one has undertaken the complicated job of counting all therapists' affiliations.

4

Living in the Past

Just imagine this. You live in a world pretty much like our world, with plenty of cars, trucks, and planes, but whenever you watch a movie or a TV show, all you see are horse and buggies. You never see a car, a truck, or a plane in a TV show. Crazy, right?

But this is just what we do experience, not with transportation but with psychotherapy. Whereas most real-life psychotherapy is Cognitive-Behavioral therapy, nearly all the therapy we see in movies and TV shows, or read about in new novels is Psychodynamic therapy.

Here are some examples of therapists as depicted in movies and TV shows.

Jennifer Melfi	
(Lorraine Bracco)	*The Sopranos*
Frasier Crane	
(Kelsey Grammer)	*Frasier*
Arnold Wayne	
(Andy Umberger)	*Mad Men*
Ben Sobel	
(Billy Crystal)	*Analyze This*
Paul Weston	
(Gabriel Byrne)	*In Treatment*
Susan Lowenstein	
(Barbra Streisand)	*The Prince of Tides*
Sean Maguire	
(Robin Williams)	*Good Will Hunting*

All these characters are Old-style therapists, Psychodynamic therapists.

You may think we're cheating just a little bit here, because *Mad Men* is set in the late 1950s and the 1960s, when the great majority of therapists really *were* Old Therapists. The revolution in psychotherapy is a bit more recent than the replacement of the horse and buggy by the automobile.

And we admit there are a few rare exceptions, movies where the psychotherapy shown is New therapy: we can think of only two examples in major movies: Bernie Feld (Steve Carell) in *Hope Springs* and 'Tanya' (played by the distinguished Cognitive-Behavioral therapist Penelope Russianoff) in *An Unmarried Woman*.

Psychotherapy in today's movies is nearly always the psychotherapy that predominated sixty, seventy, or eighty years ago, not the majority psychotherapy of today. There has been a revolution in psychotherapy but most people don't know it. They don't know it, in part, because popular culture nearly always portrays therapy as if the revolution hasn't happened.

Anyone watching therapists in TV shows or movies will get the idea that therapists are interested in their clients' dreams and early childhood (especially their relations with their mothers), try to recover long-buried memories, ask vague and undirected questions to help the clients 'discover themselves', and attribute to their clients bizarre hidden motives, which it is the task of psychotherapy to uncover. But the majority of psychotherapists in practice today have no truck with these notions, and neither do we.

It's not just popular fiction and drama. There are many popular books and articles criticizing the impact of 'therapy' on our society. In most of these writings, 'therapy' is discussed as if it were only Psychodynamic therapy, and Cognitive-Behavioral therapy is just not mentioned.

In *One Nation Under Therapy* (2005) by Christina Hoff Summers and Sally Satel, the authors attack the self-esteem movement and the way in which education is dominated by the conviction that children need to be protected against anything that might hurt their feelings. Summers and Satel blame what they call "therapy" but they mean only Psychodynamic therapy. The book reads as if Cognitive-Behavioral therapy did not exist. There is a passing reference to Albert Ellis, the originator of Cognitive-Behavioral therapy, but the context implies, falsely, that Ellis was partly responsible for the growth of the movement towards self-preoccupation and wallowing in emotions. The truth is that Ellis was objecting to this movement before Summers and Satel were born, and mostly in precisely the same terms.

These two authors (one of them is a psychiatrist) must know that Cognitive-Behavioral therapy exists and is out-competing Psychodynamic therapy. Why did they choose to paint such a misleading picture? No doubt partly because the pop-culture stereotype is so powerful it is easy to play into it. And no doubt partly because it makes a simpler, more dramatic, and therefore more saleable picture to depict all 'therapy' as the enemy. To admit upfront that what Summers and Satel are saying is just what leading psychotherapists have been saying for fifty years, and that the ideas they are attacking are promoted by social workers, schoolteach-ers, literary intellectuals, and politicians who have adopted old-fashioned and now largely abandoned concepts of psy-chotherapy—that would reduce the dramatic force of their argument.

An earlier book by Terence Campbell, *Beware the Talking Cure: Psychotherapy May Be Hazardous to Your Health* (1994), gives a similar misleading impression. It's an on-slaught on "traditional therapy," meaning mainly Psychody-namic therapy (which Campbell calls "Analytic therapy"). Campbell carefully avoids mentioning Cognitive-Behavioral therapy. He mentions "Behavior therapy," apparently favor-ably, though then dismissing it as "pseudoscience" (245). Like the work by Summers and Satel, Campbell's book sacrifices factual accuracy to the imperative of giving a crudely sim-plified picture of psychotherapy as almost all bad.

The late psychiatric gadfly Thomas Szasz is another writer who conveys the misleading impression that Cogni-tive-Behavioral therapy does not exist. In his entertaining and insightful book *The Myth of Psychotherapy* Szasz makes some sound criticisms of "psychotherapy," but he's talking only about Psychodynamic therapy. The book has detailed discussions of various Psychodynamic therapies, but never mentions Cognitive-Behavioral therapy, not even once. Szasz wrote many books, all of them on topics closely related to psychotherapy. He was also a professor of psychiatry and a psychotherapist in private practice. He never publicly revealed what type of psychotherapy he practiced, and never mentioned Cognitive-Behavioral therapy in print, despite being fully aware of its existence and growth—for example, Szasz had a well-publicized public debate with Albert Ellis.

Despite the systematic ignoring of Cognitive-Behavioral therapy, we can report a detectable shift in one area. Thirty years ago, we would often encounter some clients who would be strongly distrustful of the suggestion that *the way they think* could be at the root of their problem. Today this almost never happens. Clients today seem to more readily accept that thinking is basic. This may be due to the impact of such best-selling books as *Your Erroneous Zones* and *Feeling Good* (both of which we recommend) and perhaps also to the impact of motivational leaders like Anthony Robbins.

Out with the Old

There are many therapists who continue to practice Psychodynamic psychotherapy, yet their number is steadily dwindling. More and more, psychotherapists are rejecting the basic assumptions of Psychodynamic therapy in favor of Cognitive-Behavioral therapy. This is what we call the Revolution in Psychotherapy.

We're not the first to identify the revolution; it's well known to everyone directly involved with psychotherapy. But the fact of the revolution is not widely recognized among the broad public. Many people, including most media people, continue to talk as though all therapy is Psychodynamic. Meanwhile, the revolution has been going on all around us. Most therapy has been transformed. The last holdouts of Psychodynamic thinking are fighting a losing defense of shrinking territory.

One reason this revolution often goes unnoticed is that it is not a revolution from a single school of therapy, with one name and one leading thinker, to a single alternative school, with a different name and a different theoretical prophet.

That kind of simple combat between two armies is something that easily captures people's imaginations. If all Old therapists were followers of Freud and all New therapists followers of Ellis, this confrontation would be simple enough for journalists to grasp without doing any serious thinking: the pages of *Time* and *Newsweek* would be constantly updating us on the epic struggle between these two schools of thought. Since there are actually hundreds of schools of therapy, and most therapists are 'eclectic' (mixing ideas from more than one school), the revolution is harder for media folk to see. But the revolution is real.

The very profusion of hundreds of different schools of therapy, the very fact which makes the revolution easy to overlook or ignore, is itself part of the revolution. In the 1950s there was one dominant school of therapy: Freudian therapy, known as psychoanalysis. Even the small minority of therapists who were not Freudians shared most of Freud's broad assumptions.

Therapists who continue to accept these broad assumptions—the power of the unconscious mind, the decisive influence of early childhood—are Psychodynamic therapists. Other therapists challenged not only some specific ideas of Freud but also his broad assumptions. Most of these therapists are the ones we call Cognitive-Behavioral.

The revolt against the old Freudian school has taken three main forms:

1. **All the Psychodynamic therapies which are not strictly Freudian. These are the great majority of Psychodynamic therapies, since narrowly Freudian therapy is now embraced by only a tiny minority.**

2. **The Cognitive-Behavioral therapies, which reject the most fundamental assumptions of Freudianism: the importance of the unconscious mind, of repressed desires and repressed memories.**

3. The rejection of all psychotherapy in favor of a 'biological' approach which seeks to solve people's emotional and behavioral problems simply by giving them drugs or other physical treatments.

In this book, we will explain why we think Freudianism is mistaken, why all Psychodynamic approaches are mistaken, and why the purely physical 'drugs only' approach is also wrong—though drugs can have a place in helping some people with emotional and behavioral problems. The role of drugs may well expand as they become better designed; on the other hand, psychotherapy will also continue to become better designed.

We say that the (Old) Psychodynamic approach is fundamentally mistaken, while the (New) Cognitive-Behavioral approach is broadly on the right lines. There's a big difference, after all, between the horse and buggy and Psychodynamic therapy. The horse and buggy in its day was the most efficient means of transport available.

But whether we're right or wrong about that, we also point out a simple, demonstrable fact—that Cognitive-Behavioral therapy has been growing and gaining support, so that it is now the major broad type of therapy, while Psychodynamic schools of therapy have been shrinking and losing support.

The Breakup of the Freudian School

Sixty years ago, the vast majority of practicing psychotherapists were psychoanalysts—followers of Sigmund Freud. The entrenched orthodoxy of Freudian psychoanalysis was not overthrown by one new, completely worked-out type of therapy. Instead, what happened was that different therapists began to rebel against Freudianism in different ways. As a result, several new types of therapy appeared—eventually, hundreds of them.

Until the 1950s, nearly all therapy was indeed very similar. Therapy was therapy, and it was pretty much all based on 'psychoanalysis', often called just 'analysis', the official label for the ideas of Sigmund Freud. The few therapists who were not Freudians usually differed from Freud in comparatively minor ways.

This is the situation depicted in the TV show *Mad Men*, set in the late 1950s and 1960s. In those days, 'therapy was therapy' and that almost always meant Freudian therapy—psychoanalysis—or something very close to it. At that time, Cognitive-Behavioral therapy had just made a start, with the work of Albert Ellis, but had not yet become very widely known.

The proliferation of multifarious schools of therapy is due to the reaction against Freudian thinking, the slow, messy death of psychoanalysis. No single school of therapy yet commands enough assent to come close to the dominant position of Freudian psychoanalysis sixty years ago. However, year by year we witness a steady growth in several schools of Cognitive-Behavioral therapy and a steady decline in most schools of Psychodynamic therapy.

Why Did the Revolution Happen?

We can see at least six reasons for the success of the New Therapy in ousting and supplanting the Old Therapy:

1. **The theory of Cognitive-Behavioral therapy is true. The theory of Psychodynamic Therapy is false. It's factually incorrect to say that our emotional troubles are due to mysterious events in our unconscious minds, or that they can be dispelled by bringing back repressed memories of early childhood.**

2. **Cognitive-Behavioral therapy works well. It gets good results. Psychodynamic therapy does not work so well.**

3. **Psychodynamic therapy is traditionally slow: it promises results in the fullness of time. Cognitive-Behavioral therapy is much quicker: it**

often yields the key to the solution of a major problem in the first session.

4. Psychodynamic therapy tends to be mysterious and therefore makes the client (the person in therapy) dependent on the wisdom of the therapist. Cognitive-Behavioral therapy can be *fully explained* to the client, tending to make the client independent of the therapist.

5. By appealing to forces buried in the unconscious, Psychodynamic therapy conveys that the client has no immediate control over her problems, whereas Cognitive-Behavioral therapy shows how the client can always make *immediate* progress in tackling her problems.

6. Psychodynamic therapies rely on such far-fetched theories about the mind and behavior that they can easily lead to preposterous and dangerous practices. The 'recovered memory' craze of the 1990s led to the creation of 'false memories' and the persecution of entirely innocent people accused of incest, rape, and satanic ritual abuse. The death of a young girl during a 'rebirthing' episode in 2001 is another example of the hazards of the Psychodynamic approach. Although most Psychodynamic therapists are innocent of such appalling abuses, it's hard to imagine how such things could ever occur in Cognitive-Behavioral therapy.

The Quickness of Cognitive-Behavioral Therapy

One of the constant complaints about orthodox psychoanalysis (the Freudian method) is that it takes so long, with little sense of direction or achievement during the years of analysis. Nearly all Psychodynamic therapists who have departed from Freud have offered a system of therapy that would not take so long. A therapy that can make perceptible progress from the beginning, and can often bring about perceptible improvements within a few weeks, has obvious appeal.

Many therapists with a Psychodynamic orientation and training have seen that they will suffer financially if they cannot offer quick results, and so they borrow Cognitive-Behavioral methods for their limited-duration clients. They may reconcile themselves to this by telling themselves that Cognitive-Behavioral therapy is 'quick but superficial', and to get to the roots of problems requires more time and Psychodynamic methods. Having made this compromise, they may subsequently come to appreciate the power of Cognitive-Behavioral methods. In this way, Psychodynamic therapy is being taken over from within by the Trojan Horse of borrowed Cognitive-Behavioral ideas and techniques.

Psychotherapy Works!

Research is continually being conducted into the outcomes of psychotherapy. This research consistently and strongly indicates that psychotherapy does work, as a cure for emotional and behavioral problems, and works at least as well as drug treatments for most emotional problems.[2]

At one time there used to be people urging that psychotherapy be abandoned completely, and only drugs used to treat emotional problems, but you rarely hear this point of view any more. It can't be reconciled with the growing mass of research evidence. Furthermore, you can't discount this research evidence entirely, because it is conducted on the same lines, with just as much rigor and precision, as research into the effects of medications. So if you ignore the

---

[2] A good survey of what research tells us about the effectiveness of different kinds of therapy for different kinds of emotional problem can be found in *What You Can Change and What You Can't* (Seligman 2007 in the Bibliography at the back of this book). For discussions of the evidence, see Chambless and Olendick 2001; Hunsley and Di Giulio 2002; Epp and Dobson 2010.

evidence that psychotherapy works, you ought also to ignore the evidence that medications work.

Furthermore psychotherapy has three advantages over drug treatments:

1. **Psychotherapy does not have potentially dangerous physical side-effects (which virtually all drugs do, though probably only for a small percentage of persons treated, just like any other medications).**

2. **Psychotherapy does not have non-dangerous but inconvenient physical side-effects, which virtually all drugs do—causing many clients to stop taking their medications.**

3. **Psychotherapy provides the client with a technique she can use to tackle her problem, so it is less likely to come back later, and if it does, she has already been taught the way to fight it off. Long-term relapse rates are much higher for people treated with drugs than for those given psychotherapy.**

A busy psychiatrist today has a strong incentive to prescribe drugs for emotional and behavioral problems. After a ten-minute interview with a client, he can prescribe a medication. He can get through dozens of clients in the time it would take to give one client a course of psychotherapy. But taking everything into account, and looking at this from the standpoint of the person with a problem, Cognitive-Behavioral psychotherapy works out as ultimately more effective and less costly.

Some Psychotherapies Work Better than Others!

It's no longer controversial that psychotherapy provides genuine help to people. However, there is a school of thought which maintains that all types of psychotherapy work equally well. According to this point of view, yes, research shows that psychotherapy is effective, but the same research shows that *all types of psychotherapy are equally effective*. This is called the theory of 'psychotherapy equivalence'. Put crudely, psychotherapy's great, but any one type of therapy is just as great as any other!

This point of view was proposed in the 1961 book *Persuasion and Healing* by Jerome D. Frank. Frank maintained both that psychotherapy is effective and that its effectiveness has nothing to do with the various different theories held by rival schools of psychotherapy. Frank's book developed quite a following, despite the fact that Frank could offer no evidence (in 1961) for either of these assertions. The most recent edition of Frank's book is not quite so sweeping in its claims, and acknowledges the superiority of Cognitive-Behavioral therapy for some problems, but persists with his claim that the type of therapy makes little difference to the outcome.[3]

One way of describing this point of view is known as the 'Dodo Principle', named after the incident in *Alice in Wonderland*, where the Dodo announces the results of a race in which the contestants have all run in different directions, "All have won, and all shall have prizes."

How could that possibly be true, in view of the fact that different types of psychotherapy are so utterly different in their approach to people's problems? Following Jerome Frank, the people who argue for psychotherapy equivalence have an answer to that. They claim that most of the theories held by psychotherapists are irrelevant to the effectiveness of the therapy. What really matter are aspects of psychotherapy which are common to all types of psychotherapy, such as the relationship (or 'alliance') between therapist and client, and the acceptance by the client of the therapist's theory (right or wrong).

Right away we can point out one misleading element in this conclusion. It's supposedly based on research comparing

---

[3] Frank and Frank 1993.

the effects of different types of psychotherapy. But most types of psychotherapy are never considered in research studies. There are hundreds of schools of psychotherapy and most of them don't figure in any research. The research looks at major, accepted types of therapy. Typically a study will compare two or three types of therapy, selected from among the dozen or so most popular and reputable types. The smaller and less reputable schools of therapy, as well as the 'eclectic' approaches of many therapists, will usually not be covered at all. This makes perfect sense as convenient research procedure, but it does mean that (even if the studies did show that the types of therapy looked at had similar results) most therapy that is actually out there is simply not included in such studies. So the conclusion that 'any type of therapy is just as good as any other' would not follow.

However, there is very considerable evidence in these studies that Cognitive-Behavioral therapy works a whole lot better than Psychodynamic therapy. John Hunsley and Gina Di Giulio looked closely at some of the claims made for the Dodo Principle and found that these conclusions rest upon mistakes in the way the studies have been interpreted. After examining the various 'meta-analyses' of research studies, they concluded that

> there is no support whatsoever for the Dodo bird verdict. Psychotherapy equivalence, at least in its broadest form of general equivalence across all therapies, is most definitely a myth. (Hunsley and Di Giulio 2002, 12)

The evidence clearly shows that (for a wide range of emotional problems), Cognitive-Behavioral therapies are significantly superior to other forms of treatment, and so, say Hunsley and Di Giulio, "cognitive-behavioral treatments should be the treatment of choice for dozens of adult and child conditions."

That does leave the question of why Psychodynamic forms of therapy are helpful at all, even though provably less helpful than Cognitive-Behavioral therapy.

It's possible that some of the factors identified by Jerome Frank, such as the client's alliance with the therapist and giving the client a definite theory (true or false) to explain her problem, are in fact helpful. However, another possibility is that all major Psychodynamic therapies now include *some* Cognitive-Behavioral elements, and these alone may be responsible for the limited success of the more reputable Psychodynamic therapies. The fact that more and more Psychodynamic therapies have taken to borrowing ideas and techniques from Cognitive-Behavioral therapy means that the gap in performance between the two types of therapy has been reduced, though not eliminated.

Furthermore, it seems likely that these research studies tend to select those forms of Psychodynamic therapy which have incorporated the most Cognitive-Behavioral elements. This could occur for two reasons: by picking the most established and recognized schools of Psychodynamic therapy, and by limiting the length of therapy (to make the studies more manageable). As we will see later in this book (Chapter 6), some major figures in Psychodynamic therapy started incorporating Cognitive-Behavioral elements quite early, and many Psychodynamic therapists lean most heavily on Cognitive-Behavioral approaches when they do 'brief' or limited-term therapy.

2
Therapy Isn't Therapy!

Most people have no idea of the vast differences between different types of psychotherapy. They assume that all therapy is more or less the same, that 'therapy is therapy'. Someone who feels she has benefitted from therapy will often recommend 'therapy' to a friend, quite unaware that if the friend picks a therapist at random, this therapist will very likely have a very different approach.

In fact, there are hundreds—yes, hundreds—of different types or 'schools' of psychotherapy. Very often, two psychotherapists will give diametrically opposite advice in a similar situation—and a third will refrain from giving any advice at all.

Therapy is not like accounting, medicine, or law, where the vast majority of practitioners share a common body of agreed knowledge and generally advise roughly the same course of action in similar circumstances. Therapy is more like religion or popular diets: there's a great range of different schools of therapy, and not much consensus. In 1981, Raymond J. Corsini listed 241 different "systems" or schools of psychotherapy, and there were many others he didn't list. There are far more than that number active today, possibly close to a thousand, though many of these, of course, have a very small following.

In addition to the many different schools of therapy, there are 'eclectic' therapists, who borrow ideas from several different schools. A great many therapists—maybe the majority—call themselves eclectic, but this doesn't mean that they are all similar, as different eclectic therapists may borrow from different combinations of schools. One therapist who borrows from both Jungian and object-relations theories will be called eclectic, but so will a therapist who borrows from Gestalt therapy and Rogerian therapy, and a third who borrows from both Personal Construct Therapy and REBT. These three therapies, all labeled 'eclectic', won't have very much in common.

The wide and incompatible differences among types of therapy can be obscured by the fact that some therapists may borrow techniques from different schools of therapy without adopting the basic assumptions of those schools of therapy. For example, one type of therapy called Gestalt therapy originated the 'empty chair' technique, in which the therapist asks the client to talk to a part of himself, supposedly sitting in an empty chair. An object-relations therapist might use this technique to have the client talk to her mother, again supposedly sitting in the empty chair, while an REBT therapist might have the client talk to her 'irrational beliefs'. The technique looks the same in all three cases, but the point of it is somewhat different.

Whenever the topic of different types of therapy comes up in conversations with our clients, we nearly always find that they're unaware of such differences. Nearly all members of the public and even most persons in therapy do not know that psychotherapy is fragmented into a thousand different schools based on incompatible theories.

Some people find a therapist by going online or looking in the yellow pages. Others are referred to therapists by insurance companies, medical doctors, or courts. In most cases, these institutions also pay no attention to the divergent schools of therapy, but assume that 'therapy is therapy'. They may provide a list of different therapists, leaving the client to pick one, but these lists do not usually label the therapists by type of therapy.

You might suppose that the differences between therapists are trivial, and that they really all agree on the fundamentals, but you would be wrong. It's certainly possible to pick out a few general assertions about therapy that would be endorsed by the majority of therapists, but the differences are just as significant.

Some therapists firmly believe that emotional problems have their roots in early childhood, while others utterly reject this view. Some therapists hold that biological or genetic factors play a major role, while others repudiate this. Some maintain that the therapist should refrain from moral judgments on the client's conduct, while others say precisely the opposite.

Confronted with a problem involving anger, for instance, some therapists take the view that anger is healthy and ought to be vented, while others deny that expressing anger can be helpful. Faced with a problem of over-eating, some therapists say that willpower is entirely beside the point, and a harmful distraction, while others offer their clients exercises to build up their willpower.

At this point you may think that this extreme diversity of views about therapy is a sorry state of affairs. If there are a thousand schools of therapy which can't agree, then how can we trust any of them? You may also find the thousand-and-one types of therapy confusing. How can we make sense of this chaotic variety?

Surprisingly, the news is good. You will find as you read this book that most psychotherapy is way better than it used to be and is improving all the time. While there are a few schools of psychotherapy which we view as terribly wrongheaded and even hazardous, there are also broad, long-term trends among most schools of therapy which are at least roughly in the right direction. Free debate, openness to scientific research, and practical experience are together sifting out the worst kinds of therapy and expanding what is most valuable.

A Few of the Thousand-and-One Types of Therapy

Most of today's hundreds of types of therapy can be placed within one of two broad paradigms: Psychodynamic (Old) therapy and Cognitive-Behavioral (New) therapy.

There are hundreds of distinct types or schools of psychotherapy! Some of these are Psychodynamic therapies, others are Cognitive-Behavioral. A few of them are mixed, or difficult to classify. Here's a list of some well-known schools of therapy, mostly classified as Psychodynamic (Old), Cognitive-Behavioral (New), or a mixture of the two.

Adlerian Therapy	*Mixed*
Art Therapy	*Either or mixed, most often Old*
Behavior Therapy	*New*
Biocentric Therapy (Branden)	*Old*
Bioenergetic Analysis	*Old*
Body Therapies	*Either or mixed, usually mainly Old*
Buddhist Therapy	*New*
Cognitive Behavior Therapy (Beck)	*New*
Dance Therapy	*Most commonly Old*
Direct Decision Therapy	*New*
Existential Therapy	*Either, mostly Old*
Family Systems Therapy	*Old*
Feminist Therapy	*Mostly Old*
Gestalt Therapy	*Old*
Human Potential Therapy	*Old*
Hypnoanalysis	*Old*

A Few of the Thousand-and-One Types of Therapy

Hypnotherapy	*Either or mixed, mostly Old*
Interpersonal Therapy	*Old*
Jungian Therapy	*Old*
Logotherapy	*Mixed*
Meditation Therapies	*Either or mixed*
Mindfulness Therapy	*New*
Morita Therapy	*New*
Multimodal Therapy	*New*
Music Therapy	*Either or mixed*
Naikan Therapy	*New*
Pastoral Counseling	*Either or mixed*
Person-Centered (Rogerian) Therapy	*Hard to classify*
Personal Construct Psychotherapy	*New*
Positive Therapy (Peseschkian)	*Old*
Positive Therapy (Seligman)	*New*
Primal Therapy (Janov)	*Old*
Psychoanalysis (Freud)	*Old*
Psychodrama (Moreno)	*Hard to classify*
Rational Emotive Behavior Therapy (Ellis)	*New*
Reality Therapy (Glasser)	*New*
Reset Therapy	*New*
Rolfing (Rolfian Therapy)	*Old*
Sandplay Therapy	*Old*
Schema Therapy	*New*
Solution-focused Therapy	*New*
Transactional Analysis	*Mixed*
Twelve-Step Therapy	*New*
Vegetotherapy (Reich)	*Old*
Zen Therapy	*New*

Just because we classify a therapy as "New" in this list does not mean that we recommend it. Twelve-Step Therapy (Alcoholics' Anonymous, Shoppers' Anonymous, Gamblers' Anonymous) is "New" in that it aims at changing the addicts' thinking, but Twelve-Step Therapy holds that addicts need to acknowledge their own powerlessness and place their trust in a Higher Power (an 'anonymous' God). Not only do we disagree, we think these ideas can be harmful. But still, Twelve-Step Therapy attempts to eliminate harmful addictions by changing the addict's thinking, not by having the addict relive childhood traumas or explore her unconscious, and it therefore qualifies as a Cognitive-Behavioral (New) therapy.

You may be surprised to see that the types of therapy related to Buddhism are classified as New, since Buddhism is two and a half thousand years old! However, some of the basic ideas of Cognitive-Behavioral Therapy are prefigured in early Buddhism. The legendary Gautama Siddharta, the Buddha, may have been history's first recorded psychotherapist, and if his thinking can be gleaned from the Buddhist traditions, it seems to have been broadly Cognitive-Behavioral, definitely not Psychodynamic. The Buddha rejected even the existence of the self, and any talk about an unconscious mind would have given him a good belly laugh.

Today's New therapy, Cognitive-Behavioral therapy, is even more clearly prefigured in the Greek and Roman Stoic philosophers of two thousand years ago, especially in the *Handbook* of Epictetus. Cognitive-Behavioral therapy is Stoicism updated and scientifically refined.

Since the 1950s, when nearly all psychotherapy was Psychodynamic therapy, there has been a steady growth of New approaches to therapy. We adhere to the first Cognitive-Behavioral school, REBT, founded by Albert Ellis in the 1950s, but most of what we say in this book would be accepted by followers of other Cognitive-Behavioral schools of therapy, and would be rejected by all Psychodynamic schools.

"Psychotherapy is conversation," said the late Thomas Szasz, the famous libertarian critic of both psychiatry and anti-psychiatry, who himself started out as a psychoanalyst. People who disparage all psychotherapy in favor of treatment by drugs alone refer to psychotherapy dismissively as 'talk therapy'.

Of course, psychotherapy, like any form of counseling, for example financial planning, involves a lot of talk. But Cognitive-Behavioral therapy also involves homework exercises for the client—exercises which the client can do by herself, away from the therapist. This is one of the big differences between the Old and the New therapies: Cognitive-Behavioral therapy has a clear goal and a clear plan which the client can fully understand. There is no mystery about it. Cognitive-Behavioral therapy is not open-ended and interminable: it is quick and to the point. And so the client is expected to take on homework assignments which clearly help to attain the goals of therapy. Some of our clients comment that in therapy they feel as if they're back in school! Or, as we Cognitive-Behavioral therapists like to say among ourselves: We expect to get paid but we make sure that the client does most of the work.

Basic Assumptions of Old and New Therapies

Throughout this book we'll be examining both kinds of therapy and comparing them with each other in detail. But here we can give a quick idea of the fundamental difference in approach.

If you have an emotional problem (like anxiety or depression) or a behavioral problem (like overeating or procrastination), a Psychodynamic therapist will usually believe that the problem is caused by something going on in the hidden depths of your mind, your 'unconscious' mind. The therapist may or may not tell you that this is what he believes, but either way, it is what directs the therapy.

According to Psychodynamic therapy, not only is something going on in the hidden depths of your mind, something of which you are unaware and which is causing your problems, this something resists your attempts to uncover it: there is no way that you can determine for yourself what the underlying cause is, and if that underlying cause is suggested to you, you will be inclined to dismiss it. But by a long and arduous process of self-discovery, with the expert help of a Psychodynamic therapist, you may be able to recognize this hidden aspect of yourself, come to terms with it, and thus free yourself from its control over you.

The 'cure' for your problem is to uncover this underlying cause, which is usually some incident or incidents in your past, probably in early childhood. You must then revisit that experience, perhaps relive it. Most Psychodynamic therapists still emphasize 'reliving' past experiences, though some confine themselves to merely reconstructing and re-examining those experiences.

The Psychodynamic therapist is usually very interested in your childhood. This type of therapist believes that your problems stem from forgotten childhood incidents or phantasies. The Psychodynamic therapist might ask you about your dreams. Old-fashioned Psychodynamic therapy typically took a long time, and was therefore usually quite expensive. Several years in therapy would be perfectly normal, and more than half a lifetime was far from unknown. Recently various attempts have been made to come up with forms of Psychodynamic therapy which will make rapid progress, but these attempts always borrow heavily from Cognitive-Behavioral therapy.

The new Cognitive-Behavioral therapy rejects all the above and takes an entirely different approach. Cognitive-Behavioral therapists reject the theory that our emotional or behavioral problems are caused by mysterious hidden influences that we cannot easily identify.

According to Cognitive-Behavioral therapists, no useful purpose is served by trying to recall incidents from your childhood. Even if it did happen to be the case, in any particular instance, that the problems began with some particular incident in the past, this doesn't prove that recollecting and reliving that incident will do anything to make the problem go away. Furthermore, if you have difficulty remembering something from your early childhood, and make prolonged attempts to remember it, you will very likely produce a false memory, a memory of something which never really happened. In fact, much of what you already think you remember from your early childhood is very likely inaccurate, and there is no way to establish the truth by any mental operation (though you might establish it, for instance, by finding a video or a document contradicting what you thought had happened). According to Cognitive-Behavioral therapists, if some past incident is important in causing present suffering, it can only be because the sufferer makes it important by the way she thinks about it *now*.

According to Cognitive-Behavioral therapists, there are no hidden depths of the mind. We don't dispute that there are things going on in your brain which you're not aware of and which affect the way your mind works. But you can't get at these events going on in your brain by analyzing your dreams, by remembering your childhood, or by free-associating. And you don't need to get at them, because they are not the root of your problems.

What you have forgotten cannot be the cause of your present emotional or behavioral problems, and you will not make any progress by remembering it. Except in cases of literal, physical illness, you make your emotional and behavioral problems by the way you think, by what you keep on telling yourself in your ordinary thoughts. While it's true that a sufferer may not be sharply aware of what her ordinary thoughts are, she can quickly become aware of them: there is no 'resistance' to uncovering them, except the familiar 'resistance' of inertia and inattention.

There is also no merit in dwelling morbidly on memories of past suffering. On the contrary, it's only sensible to do precisely what the Psychodynamic therapists will tell you not to do: deliberately put those episodes out of your mind, and instead address your attention to practical solutions of your current problems.

The New therapy is much quicker than the Old: in many cases a few weekly forty-five-minute sessions may be all that is required. The average length of Cognitive-Behavioral therapy is around twelve forty-five-minute sessions.

Psychodynamic therapy is heavily influenced by ideas stemming ultimately from Sigmund Freud and his followers at the end of the nineteenth century. It became popular in the United States by the 1920s, expanded rapidly, and ruled without much serious challenge until the 1950s. Cognitive-Behavioral therapy was developed by writers like Albert Ellis in the 1950s and Aaron Beck in the 1960s, though they were following up some clues from earlier writers. Both Ellis and Beck started out as psychoanalysts—followers of the Freudian method—and became dissatisfied with this approach, before developing their own radically different approaches.

Debriefing Disaster

After the World Trade Center towers collapsed on September 11th, 2001, thousands of 'mental health workers' rushed to the scene to provide 'help' to those expected to be traumatized by the experience. The same thing happened after Katrina hit New Orleans in 2005 and Hurricane Sandy hit the Jersey Shore in 2012. It has become routine in cases of natural disasters or terrorist attacks, and even in smaller scale episodes. In fact it is mandatory, because federal disaster funding comes with numerous conditions which now include provision of 'mental health' treatment. After a school shooting, the students will be given several hours of counseling, and a police officer involved in a violent shootout will be required (in most cities) to undergo several hours or days of counseling by a psychotherapist.

Following 9/11 follow-up studies were done, trying to get at the impact of the psychotherapeutic help. The good news is that the therapists had a great time. They were working hard, using their expertise and obviously helping a lot of people in need. They felt really good about what they were doing.

But what about the supposedly traumatized survivors who were being helped? Research studies have now shown that in such cases, therapeutic intervention, on balance, made their mental and emotional condition *worse*.[1] This is exactly what we would have expected, given that most 'trauma therapy' is still heavily infected with Psychodynamic notions.

The great majority of people who go through a bad experience such as a terrorist attack or a natural disaster, no matter *how* very, very bad the experience is, will recover from it emotionally, without any professional help, within a few weeks. They will want to put it behind them, think about it very little, and get on with their lives. They will not be haunted or seriously troubled by it in later years. Most people are resilient and in no need of any counseling for a grueling experience they have been through. Post Traumatic Stress Disorder (PTSD)—what used to be called shell-shock—is not a risk for most soldiers or civilians.

The people who are still seriously troubled by the bad experience several weeks later are an exceptional minority. They disturb themselves by the way they think about their bad experience and they can be helped—not by painfully re-imagining and reliving the experience (which will make things worse for some and have no appreciable effect on others) but by learning new ways of thinking about the experience and about other bad experiences.

The standard method for counseling disaster survivors—sometimes called 'psychological debriefing'—is to encourage them to talk through the bad experience, blow by blow, dwelling particularly on their emotional responses. This approach follows from Psychodynamic theories, which suppose that emotions have a life of their own cooped up in the unconscious mind and will become vicious unless they are let out regularly and taken for a walk. In fact, people are generally not helped by reliving an unpleasant experience—for some people it's a problem that they find it difficult to stop

---

[1] Bisson et al. 1997; McNally, Bryant, and Ehlers 2003; Watson, Brymer, and Bonanno 2011.

themselves reliving it—and some people will be harmed.

Psychologists specializing in disaster trauma now recommend that psychological debriefing be scrapped in favor of 'Psychological First Aid' (PFA). Some elementary help will benefit all survivors: providing information to reassure them that things are back to normal and that they and their loved ones are now safe. Survivors can be contacted and observed; those few still troubled after one month can be given Cognitive-Behavioral therapy, changing the faulty thinking which prompts them to upset themselves.[2]

Shortly after 9/11 and before the above research findings were known, some office workers reportedly developed a fear of working in high buildings. An insurance company approached one of the authors of this book, Michael Edelstein, to provide counseling to such workers. The company representative explained that the objective was to get these office workers to vent their worries about planes crashing into buildings, and asked Michael: "Do you do this type of thing?"

Michael explained what he would do: identify the client's anxieties but not encourage them to wallow in these emotions, before dealing with the harmful thinking that gave rise to those. After some back and forth, in which Michael rephrased this in various ways without being untruthful, the representative was persuaded to find it acceptable, and Michael was hired.

Good Grief

What goes for disasters, involving thousands of people, also goes for smaller-scale disasters which impinge on one or a few people, such as a death in the family. So far, no research has been conducted on the actual results of 'grief counseling', so let us put it on record in advance of any such findings: if grief counseling is motivated by Psychodynamic theories, it will tend to worsen the mental state of the bereaved person.

---

[2] Harmon 2011.

The death of a loved one such as a spouse or a child is usually felt as a loss, followed by a period of grieving. Encouraging the grieving party to 'work through' their grief, repeatedly dwelling on the negative emotions associated with loss, is not helpful and may be harmful.

This is made worse because Psychodynamic grief counselors usually don't discriminate among different emotions. They believe that all emotion needs an outlet and therefore the expression of all emotion ought to be encouraged. However, in many cases, a person who has just lost someone dear to them has a mixture of emotions, some of which are unnecessary and potentially harmful. Along with their pain at the loss, they may have feelings of guilt, fear, hopelessness, anxiety, inadequacy, and insecurity. Psychodynamic therapists will often encourage the grieving person to express all these emotions. These emotions flow from specific thoughts, such as 'I don't deserve to live now that my loved one has died', 'I can't cope without my loved one', 'I needed my loved one, and can't face the world without him', or 'Who knows what frightful dangers are lying in wait, now that my loved one has gone?'. These unhelpful thoughts are faulty, and the emotions they give rise to are not healthy or appropriate responses to loss. The pain of loss itself is not harmful and can be allowed to run its course.

This failure to differentiate different classes of emotion, along with the view that all the emotions arising from loss need to be vented, interferes with the grieving cycle and tends to make it more painful and prolonged. Faulty thinking underlies unhelpful emotion. By encouraging the expression of such emotion, the Psychodynamic therapist reinforces and prolongs the suffering associated with loss.

Often this approach is based on the mistaken notion that if a client is encouraged to express her sense of loss, then despair guilt, anger, or fear are only natural and appropriate, and encouraging the client to express these emotions allows them to be released. But the human mind isn't built that way. Expressing an emotion, any emotion, is practicing having that emotion. Over the long haul, repeatedly expressing an emotion does not release that emotion, but builds up the disposition to have that emotion.

A typical 'grief therapy' session conducted by a Psychodynamic therapist may go something like this

> THERAPIST: How are you feeling about your loss?
> CLIENT: It makes me so mad, the unfairness of it all.
> THERAPIST: That's only natural.
> CLIENT: She seemed so healthy, it's plain unfair. The hospital killed her.
> THERAPIST: Don't hold back. Get that anger out.
> CLIENT: Those damn doctors don't know their ass from their elbows.
> THERAPIST: That's it. Now see if you can put more feeling into it.

In some cases, it's even worse than this, because Psychodynamic therapists often believe that there is unconscious anger where there is actually little or no anger, and they will work with a client who has little or no anger to begin to express some anger! Worse still, in some cases a Psychodynamic therapist will adhere to the theory that the grieving person is unconsciously angry at the departed one and such a therapist will try to stimulate a sense of outrage against the deceased, believing that this outrage is already prowling around in the client's unconscious. The theory is that the client needs to work through her anger at the departed loved one before she can come to terms with her loss. In our view, this theory is quite mistaken. In most cases, there is no anger at the deceased, but where there is, no good purpose is served by expressing it. This doesn't mean that we morally disapprove of anger or chastise our clients for being angry. It means that we help them to understand that their anger flows from faulty thinking, and we teach them techniques to change their thinking. If they do this, their anger will automatically terminate or greatly diminish.

One of this book's authors, Richard Kujoth, was called upon for crisis intervention in a bereavement. Among other things, he suggested that the bereaved person read Albert

Ellis's book, *How to Make Yourself Happy and Remarkably Less Disturbable.* The bereaved person was shocked and a family member was scandalized that a book with such an up-beat title should be recommended "at a time like this." They were both convinced that the fashionably appropriate thing to do was to be encouraged to wallow in their suffering.

In another episode where Richard was involved, a woman was upbraided by the pastor of her church for not displaying enough grief following the death of her sixteen-year-old son. She was handling it well, feeling deep sadness but containing it, not disturbing other people or crying in public. This appropriate and helpful behavior was unsettling to the minister, who felt that something must be wrong, and he clearly thought it was Richard's job to help generate more of a flamboyant display of emotion.

Emotions Hot and Cool

When gas heating and lighting were introduced in the nineteenth century, some people found it astounding that the pipes bringing the gas to the burners were themselves quite cold. They couldn't believe it and kept feeling the pipes to check and recheck this unbelievable fact.

Psychodynamic therapists are like that with respect to emotion. They think that emotion exists inside people, and when these people become emotionally worked up, that emotion has come to the surface. In reality, there is no emotion inside of anyone. The emotion is like the burning of the gas in the heating element of a gaslight: it only exists when it burns.

Psychodynamic therapists view emotions as elemental forces, like magma in a volcano being pushed to find an outlet. They see emotional problems arising because emotions are pent up. They see emotions as being largely independent of thoughts and somehow existing inside us, even if they're not currently showing themselves. They see the relief of emotional problems in allowing emotions to spill out, much as ancient physicians thought that causing patients to bleed would provide relief for almost any illness.

If a client is depressed, the Psychodynamic therapist will assume that the depression is anger turned against oneself. If the client can be induced to let the anger out, she will no longer turn it against herself and the depression will lift.

This way of looking at anger is fundamentally mistaken. There is no anger 'inside' someone who is currently not feeling any anger. Anger only exists in the feeling of it, as gaslight only exists in the burning of the gas and not in the gaspipes. A person may have, 'inside' them, a *disposition* to anger, but that disposition is largely activated by their thinking. When it's not being activated, it's not doing anything; it's not seeking an outlet. Every time a person expresses anger, he's learning to be more angry in future. He's not 'letting his anger out' because there is no anger apart from his expression of it.

A person will feel less angry just after an angry outburst than just before it, and this may mislead him into supposing that his outburst released some of his anger, causing him to become less angry. But, first, intense emotion tends to die down by itself, so he would also feel less angry now than he did a few minutes ago if he had *not* had an outburst. And second, there's a difference between the immediate effects and the longer term effects. If you've just eaten six donuts you'll probably be less interested in eating donuts than you were before you started eating them, but that doesn't mean you'll have a reduced appetite for donuts tomorrow. However, controlled experiments show that, even in the very short term, expressing or acting out anger makes people more angry, not less, and providing 'outlets' for 'aggression', such as having people smash things with a baseball bat, causes them to feel *more* aggressive, not less.

A person may feel angry and try to conceal it or to behave just as he would if he were not angry. In other words, he's suppressing the anger he feels. This may be harmful, but at worst it is no more harmful than outright expression of his anger. Better than either of these, however, would be for him to stop making himself feel angry in the first place, by changing his thinking.

Suppose someone is angry at an injustice committed by a government against some minority. The angry person may say: 'Yes, I am angry! Do you want me to condone that injustice?' The answer is: 'No, but you can be just as much opposed to the injustice without making yourself angry, and without anger you can make your opposition more effective.' Anger flows from the foolish thought: 'This injustice absolutely must not happen!' Non-angry opposition flows from the wiser thought: 'I passionately dislike the fact that this injustice has happened and I'm resolved to do what I can to make the continuation of such injustices less likely!'

Psychotherapy and Your Feelings

Cognitive-Behavior therapy often starts and ends with feelings. A client often comes to therapy because of feeling bad: depressed, anxious, stressed, panicky, phobic, guilty, or angry. Therapy is successful if the client overcomes these disturbed feelings. In our therapy practice, we focus on feelings to begin the first and end the last sessions with. However it's usually a waste of the client's time and money to spend much more time on feelings. Asking the client about her feelings is a bit like taking her temperature; it's occasionally informative but no more. To help the client with her self-defeating feelings, the proper task is to focus on her underlying unreasonable *thinking* creating these feelings, and then teach her how to identify this faulty thinking and change it to create more helpful feelings.

Some therapists talk a lot about helping clients 'get in touch with their feelings'. In our experience, the problems most clients have involve being *too* much in touch with their feelings. They dwell, ruminate, and obsess on their disturbed feelings. They hate themselves or life because they have these feelings. 'I *must* not be anxious or depressed otherwise I'm a loser', 'I *must* not panic or else life is awful', 'I *absolutely must* be relaxed and happy all the time otherwise I can't be happy at all' are common refrains among therapy clients. The solution involves calmly accepting their feelings, allowing themselves to feel the emotions all humans feel, and then moving on with life.

For most clients expressing their feelings is neither a problem nor a solution. Telling your wife, friend, or boss you're feeling anxious or resentful may be okay, but is not usually the first step in solving emotional problems. If you express this, you're usually still anxious or resentful. Expressing a feeling tends to reinforce it, rather than excise it. Since emotions are manifestations of our interpretations of events, the path to improvement involves changing our interpretations rather than expressing our emotions. And a key part of changing our interpretations is changing our habitual and routine thinking.

Self-Defeating Behavior

People who become psychotherapy clients (as well as people who don't) often engage in behavior which, to a friendly outside observer, looks to be clearly self-defeating or even self-destructive. Why do they do this?

The Psychodynamic therapist has a ready answer. They do this because they *want* to defeat or destroy themselves— even though they don't know it! They have an unconscious drive to punish themselves even to the point of destruction. The woman who enters a series of abusive relationships wants to be abused. The compulsive gambler wants to lose all his money. The self-condemning depressive wants to end up dead.

This theory explains any self-harming behavior very simply, but it does so at the high cost of supposing that there are long-term implacable purposes, systematically pursued, which the individuals concerned don't know about—and can't find out about by any quick and straightforward method. To offer therapy based on this theory, the therapist has to believe he can become aware of three things: the client's true unconscious motive, how to bring this unconscious motive to the client's attention, and how to change that motive and replace it with another. So what seemed very simple requires a complicated structure of theory—which turns out to be false.

The theory of Cognitive-Behavioral therapy avoids all this. We can convincingly explain why people act self-defeatingly without supposing that they unconsciously want to defeat themselves. They act self-defeatingly because of the faulty ways they think, and we have techniques for helping them to identify and change the ways they think.

In the next chapter, let's see how therapy works in practice.

3
The Old and New Therapies in Action

Just how different are the two broad approaches to psychotherapy? In this chapter we present, side by side, what might happen to the same person with the same problems, getting each kind of therapy. In each case, we give a description of the person and that person's problems, then we describe how that person might be treated by both a Psychodynamic (Old-style) therapist, and a Cognitive-Behavioral (New-style) therapist.

These stories reflect and combine numerous examples we have read about and heard about over the years, including what we have been told by our clients who have previously been in Psychodynamic therapy.

There is enormous variety among Psychodynamic therapists, and some variety among Cognitive-Behavioral therapists; some of these differences are reflected below. We are not at this stage criticizing the Psychodynamic therapies, nor are we discussing in this chapter how successful they might be. Nor are we trying to discredit all Psychodynamic therapy by giving a few examples of the strange forms it may take: we do this just because these kinds of therapy are out there and are taken seriously by millions of people. We simply want to contrast the two different types of therapy, so that the reader can see how different they are. Since we've included more than one style of Cognitive-Behavioral therapy, we don't completely endorse every detail of the Cognitive-Behavioral examples.

You should be warned that, just as watching a video of people strenuously working out will not cause you to lose weight, so, reading accounts of therapy will not give you the experience or the benefits of therapy. But it will help you to understand the aims and methods of different types of therapy.

Clarence

Clarence is a tall twenty-year-old with an athletic build. A few months ago he experienced a sudden panic attack which seemed to come out of the blue. He had all the physical reactions appropriate to the terror of facing a hungry tiger, but there was no tiger there. His heart raced, his throat tightened, his breathing became rapid, he had a dreamlike feeling of unreality and thought he might be about to faint.

After this attack he began to feel apprehensive about having further attacks, and sure enough he began to have them quite frequently. He worried that he might be going crazy, might become unable to breathe, or might lose control. For example, in a class, he felt anxiety rising as he imagined he might do something outrageous which would make him an object of ridicule or contempt by the professor or the other students and would lead to his being put in a mental hospital. He avoids situations where he feels that some kind of 'breakdown' would be especially embarrassing or dangerous, such as giving a presentation before a class or driving on the freeway. He begins to spend more time in the bar drinking, feeling that this will relax him and make an attack less likely. He visited the college medical facility hoping to get tranquilizers. The doctor prescribed a mild tranquilizer and also referred him to a psychotherapist.

Clarence, who hails from Atlanta, once dreamed of playing professional basketball and had shown promise in his first semester on the college basketball team. In the second semester, his girlfriend Yolanda terminated their relationship and his performance on the team nose-dived. His performance in the academic classes had been poor and now got worse. He is on the point of dropping out of college, and isn't sure what he'll do when he does drop out.

Clarence's Psychodynamic Therapy

The Psychodynamic therapist believes that panic attacks are caused by unconscious conflicts which refer back to interactions with primary caregivers. In this case, the attacks were triggered by Clarence's decline in basketball ability, arising from rejection by his girlfriend. The loss of Clarence's girlfriend Yolanda repeats two earlier experiences of abandonment and loss: the death of Clarence's mother when he was six, and the departure of his big sister who had mostly raised him, when he was fourteen. Clarence had never known his father, and as a result has a fragile ego, but the therapist perceives that in infancy Clarence resented the departure of his father.

The therapist concludes that Clarence is boiling with unrecognized anger: at the father he had never known, for deserting the family, at his mother for dying when she did, and thus also deserting the family, at Clarence's sister when she left to be with her boyfriend, and at his recent girlfriend for dumping him. Clarence is affectionate and outgoing to his friends and relations, a quality the therapist identified as 'reaction formation'—doing the opposite of what he unconsciously feels. The terror Clarence feels during panic attacks is the rage he feels at those who abandoned him, a rage turned inward against himself.

The therapist helps Clarence to recognize the way in which his early interactions with family members have structured his character. For example, Clarence is observably polite and gentle, a compensation for intense unconscious hostility. In the first few sessions of therapy, the therapist explores Clarence's unconscious feelings, and encourages him to express the hurt and anger he has so deeply repressed. Meanwhile, the therapist knows that Clarence will develop 'transference', a strong emotional bond with the therapist, who in turn will develop 'counter-transference', a strong emotional bond with Clarence. And so from the beginning of Clarence's therapy, the therapist is planning the final stage, in which therapy is terminated, echoing the termination of Clarence's relationship with his father, his mother, his sister, and Yolanda.

When the therapist finally 'dumps' Clarence, she will help him to understand how this repeats Clarence's being dumped by his father, his mother, his sister, and Yolanda, but now Clarence will appreciate some of the unconscious forces at work—especially the pain of loss which he had turned against himself in the form of unacknowledged rage, leading to panic attacks. By living through these partings and losses, while openly expressing terror and anger, Clarence will have recognized his unconscious hostile impulses and thus have removed the source of his panic attacks.

Clarence's Cognitive-Behavioral Therapy

The therapist explains to Clarence that thousands of people experience panic attacks for a while, eventually recover from them, and don't faint, collapse, die, horribly embarrass themselves in public, or go crazy. The therapist also tells Clarence that although panic attacks or anxiety sometimes seem to come from nowhere, without any cause, there is in fact always a specific cause. Once started, however, the person's fear of panic attacks often leads to heightened anxiety and further attacks. Physical symptoms of anxiety are misinterpreted as signs that the person may lose control or even die. The therapist asks Clarence to write down each of his physical symptoms, his fears about the dire consequences of each symptom, and the correct medical analysis of each symptom. For example, the feeling of unreality is a common accompaniment of anxiety and does not mean he will faint: quite the opposite, acute anxiety raises the blood pressure and makes fainting impossible.

After giving Clarence a better understanding of his panic attacks, the therapist pursues the anxiety that preceded them. Among Clarence's automatic thoughts are 'I'll *never* find another girlfriend like Yolanda'; 'Now that I've had some bad games, my basketball career is over'; 'If I'm not the best player on the team, I'm nothing'; 'Unless I'm an athletic superstar, I don't belong in college'. The therapist helps Clarence to challenge these thoughts and replace them with more realistic and appropriate thoughts. Clarence thinks in 'catastrophizing', all or nothing ways, and by Socratic questioning, the therapist brings out the superior realism of more moderate alternatives. For example, instead of 'I'll never find another girlfriend like Yolanda', Clarence writes down the thought 'Breaking up is painful, but I'm resilient and will get over it in time. At some point in the next six months I'll probably start a new relationship with someone who won't be exactly like Yolanda but may be slightly less appealing in some ways, slightly more appealing in others'. Clarence performs numerous written exercises to make the more realistic thoughts become second nature.

The therapist has Clarence write out all the advantages and disadvantages of trying to stay in college until graduation, and after thoroughly exploring all these pros and cons, Clarence makes an informed and firm decision.

Mary and Ray

Mary is a thirty-year-old tropical fish curator. Ray is a thirty-two-year-old landscape architect. They have been married for three years before seeking couples counseling. Their disagreements often escalate into heated, vituperative arguments.

Mary says that Ray gets angry and picks on her, hurting her feelings. "I gave him an ultimatum to leave or come for marriage counseling." Mary and Ray continually disagree about money management. Mary is depressed much of the time, and Ray criticizes her for not being more cheerful. Ray will bring home his job stress, then criticize and nag Mary for the late dinner or the messy house. Mary complains that Ray is autocratic. Rather than work out problems with her collaboratively or show any interest in her opinion, he tells her how she should act.

Ray explains that Mary spends money unwisely, is a sloppy homemaker and is often depressed and sullen for no good reason. He adds that he has lost interest in her sexually since she has put on weight.

After the first session, Mary moved out of their apartment. Mary and Ray continued in therapy but with different addresses. They would alternate between seeing the therapist together and individually.

Ray and Mary's Psychodynamic Therapy

The Psychodynamic therapist concludes that Mary and Ray are each reliving their early experiences with the opposite-sex parent. Mary adored her father, and admired him for being so devoted to her mother. The therapist concludes that Mary's admiration for her father is a reaction formation to contain her hostility, caused by her jealousy of her mother.

Mary reports a dream in which she is attending the funeral of an aunt. The casket is lowered into the ground, and dirt thrown on top, with the words 'Ashes to ashes'. Then the coffin begins to shake and someone shouts 'It's an earthquake!'. The body emerges from the coffin and turns out to be, not the aunt but Mary's mother, who wakes up and says 'I was just resting. Now I have to get to work.'

Following Jung's theory that dreams give us important constructive messages from our unconscious minds, the therapist interprets this dream as a representation of Mary's marriage. The message might be that Mary should escape from her marriage in order to get on with her life, or alternatively that she can view the marriage as not really oppressive but something to take advantage of. More dreams will be needed to achieve clarity on this issue.

Ray remembers his childhood as being permeated with bitter resentment at his father's dictatorial and inflexible style. The therapist is able to show Ray that he actually identified strongly with his father, and is striving to replace him as head of the household and possessor of his mother, now symbolized by Mary.

Ray dreams that he is fleeing across the rooftops of a city, jumping or gliding from one rooftop to the next, pursued by some powerful evil enemy whom he is not able to name. He feels that the enemy is right behind him, but whenever he looks back, he cannot see him. Then he comes to the Statue of Liberty, which starts talking with a heavy French accent. At a moment when he isn't looking, Liberty turns into an ordinary woman of normal size and appearance speaking without an accent. Ray accepts this as perfectly normal, just what he was expecting. Then he suddenly remembers the evil enemy and asked the woman, 'Is he still coming after us?' An anguished look appeared on her face, she says something he can't make out, and he wakes up sweating.

The therapist explains that the enemy is Ray's Shadow— the embodiment of everything about Ray that is unacceptable to his own concept of himself, and the generator of everything disorderly and dirty. The woman symbolizes Ray's feminine side, his Anima, suggesting that the best hope for keeping evil at bay is to respect his Anima and he would then be able to respect Mary.

These are the first of many dreams to be recorded and analyzed over the next several years. The therapist also draws upon some of his own dreams about Ray and Mary, and upon fairy tales like Jack the Giant Killer (applicable to Ray) and Rapunzel (applicable to Mary).

Ray and Mary have embarked upon an open-ended journey of self-discovery, filled with bracing adventures and fascinating stories. The therapist's hope is that they will become more fully individuated, and consequently better able to relate to each other.

Ray and Mary's Cognitive-Behavioral Therapy

After asking Ray and Mary some basic questions, getting a sense of each of their perspectives on their problems, the therapist briefly explains the Cognitive-Behavioral approach;

that our feelings and our behavior flow in part from our habitual and usually unexamined thoughts, and that these thoughts can be identified, questioned, and perhaps found to be faulty. If so, they can then be replaced with more helpful thoughts, which are usually more logical and more accurate in reflecting reality.

The therapist questions Mary and is able to identify her demanding thoughts or 'musts'. These demands include: 'I *must* not be criticized by Ray. If he does criticize me, I'm worthless'. 'I *must* not disappoint Ray, or if I do, I'm a failure as a wife'. 'I *must* be understood and validated by Ray's sympathy or support, and if I don't get this from him, I'm a cipher'.

The therapist is also able to elicit some of Ray's demanding thoughts: 'Mary *must* consider my suggestions relating to her financial irresponsibility', 'Mary *must* keep the house perfectly clean and neat', 'Mary *must* cheer up and not look like a sourpuss'.

The therapist then explained the Problem Separation Technique to Mary and Ray. The idea behind this technique is to separate each personal problem into a *practical problem* and an *emotional problem*. In this case, Mary and Ray had emotional problems of hurt and anger, and practical problems because of poor skills in communication and assertiveness. These distinct problem areas can be addressed separately: their emotional problems of hurt and anger can be tackled by countering their demanding thoughts, and their practical problems of poor communication by communication skills and assertiveness training.

The therapist gives them written Three Minute exercises to help them replace their demanding thoughts with more helpful thoughts. For instance, Ray's thought, 'Mary *must* keep the house perfectly clean and neat', is replaced with 'I would prefer it if Mary were to keep the house perfectly clean and neat, but I can survive quite well if she doesn't'. And Mary's thought, 'I hate to be criticized by Ray. If he does criticize me, I'm worthless', was replaced with 'It would be better if Ray did not criticize me, but if he does, I am quite capable of carrying on, without feeling too bad about it'.

The therapist also gives them exercises to help communication. For example, when making requests of one another, they are asked to frame these not as demands, but to begin with 'I would prefer it if . . .'

Colette

Colette is a bright, twenty-eight-year-old IT project manager in a large biogenetics company. She describes herself as "an anxious person" and says her anxiety has been intensifying of late and her panic attacks have been increasing. In addition, her relationship with Trevor, her boyfriend, has been deteriorating due to her preoccupation with her deteriorating emotional state.

She had her first panic attack in college and has been on anti-anxiety meds since, prescribed by a psychiatrist. Her sixty-nine-year-old father is recovering from an auto accident two months ago, which almost killed him. She began dwelling on her father's mortality at which time her anxiety increased. At times, her heart starts racing, she feels very scared, a feeling of doom comes over her, and she experiences feelings of depersonalization.

When asked what it is that she's anxious about, Colette replies 'Nothing in particular'. She is one of many people commonly thought to be suffering from 'free-floating anxiety', anxiety without any definite object.

She recently took a leave of absence from work. One day she googled "psychotherapy help father anxiety panic" and then scrolled down until she came to the name of a therapist in her city, with whom she then made an appointment.

Colette's Psychodynamic Therapy

Colette's Psychodynamic therapist calls himself an existential-humanist therapist and believes that most emotional and behavioral problems are due to deep-seated anxieties about the ultimate existential concerns: fear of death, fear of isolation, fear of a life without meaning, and fear of being free. This therapist holds that free-floating anxiety arises from inner conflicts relating to one or more of these four unavoidable and tragic 'givens' of human existence.

To the therapist, the fact that Colette's problems got worse following her father's accident is a dead give-away. The therapist elicits the facts that Colette's mother died in Colette's early childhood, and her father's second wife died shortly after Colette went to college. The therapist's diagnosis is confirmed when Colette reports a dream about kayaking in dangerous rapids (she had gone kayaking a few times with friends in college), as a river is a symbol of death.

In response to questions, Colette readily admits that when she thinks about death, she doesn't consider the prospect appealing. The therapist explains that the root of her problems is a deep-rooted terror of death. The therapist believes that fear of death is ever-present and can never be overcome, but it's possible to replace terror at the prospect of death with controlled anxiety.

Guided by these insights, the therapist helps Colette to explore her early relationships, especially with her father and her step-mother. Her problems began shortly after she moved away to college, so her fear of death is also linked with her fear of being alone. The therapist's plan is to encourage Colette to understand that, though she will always be alone and mortal, she can develop relationships which provide some consolation. The therapist also offers explicit philosophical arguments, such as 'For millions of years before you were born, you didn't exist, and death can be no worse than that', and 'Death is so terrifying because life is so precious, therefore best to make the most of every minute of your life'.

Colette's Cognitive-Behavioral Therapy

The Cognitive-Behavioral therapist explains the major concepts they will be working with to help Colette with her problems. These consist of the notion that emotions are generated by our thinking, not by internal or external events. Further, disturbed emotions such as anxiety and panic come from a particular kind of thinking, thinking in terms of absolutistic demands, *musts, shoulds, supposed tos, have tos.*

He then asks Colette to get in touch with what she tells herself during these episodes of intense anxiety. She identifies her thoughts, which include: 'I *must* not spiral into a panic attack', 'I *have to* get to a safe environment', 'I *gotta* feel better tomorrow,' 'I *must* not freak out at work', 'I *should* be normal', 'this *shouldn't* be happening to me', 'I *must* have a guarantee I'm not going crazy'.

The therapist explains to Colette she has a severe case of *secondary disturbance.* She makes herself anxious *about* being anxious and having a panic attack. Doing this exacerbates her anxiety, *increasing* the likelihood of worse anxiety and panic attacks. She dwells on her anxious feelings thereby magnifying them. This creates a vicious circle: the more she tells herself, 'I *absolutely must* not feel anxious', the more she dwells on it. The more she dwells on her anxiety the worse it feels. The worse it feels, the more desperate she makes herself about ridding herself of the feelings, and on and on until she has whipped herself up into a panicked frenzy and gets emotionally paralyzed.

He then explains the paradoxical solution: allow and accept her uncomfortable feelings rather than desperately attempting to squelch them. The more she allows them to come and go, the less power she'll feel they have and consequently, they will diminish. He teaches her the Three Minute Exercise in which she identifies irrational thoughts about her anxiety and then confronts, challenges, and contradicts them. He assigns her the homework to regularly write out these exercises a few times daily in order to develop a more reasonable philosophy about anxiety and to reinforce this view many times to build new pathways in her brain. The goal is to make a profound cognitive change to overcome her intolerance of emotional pain. As she accomplishes this, it is expected that her anxiety will subside.

This therapist, like most Cognitive-Behavioral therapists, believes that there is no such thing as objectless anxiety.

Most apparent cases of free-floating anxiety are really cases of secondary disturbance. The person had some anxiety about some specific thing at some point in the past, became alarmed at the symptoms of that anxiety, then became fearful at the prospect of renewed anxiety attacks, viewed these attacks as painful experiences that came from nowhere, and then began to bring on these attacks precisely because of her fear of them.

Megan

Megan, a twenty-five-year-old sales rep for an international marketing agency, engages in a number of compulsive behaviors, but only when she's drinking. She flirts with the husbands and boyfriends of co-workers, picks up strangers in bars for brief sexual flings, and uses cocaine. She misses days of work due to morning hangovers, and just before entering therapy, she had driven home from a party having consumed a couple of bottles of wine, and only just managed to talk herself out of a likely DUI citation after being stopped by a policeman. Megan's father, one of her grandparents, and two of her uncles, had been violent drunks.

Megan's Psychodynamic Therapy

Megan's Psychodynamic therapist decides that Megan's self-destructive conduct was probably set in motion by the immature behavior of her parents, who in all likelihood had been sexually dysfunctional. The therapist concludes that because the parents could not relate to each other in a satisfying adult relationship, they used alcohol to cover up their depression, caused by a lack of real love in their marriage. Megan's father had probably been sexually seductive toward her, but whether or not he had actually molested her is irrelevant, because she obviously yearned unconsciously to be his lover.

The therapist takes the view that because Megan has been raised with a conventional religious morality, she cannot respond as her father's sexual partner. Instead she experiences guilt feelings, which she has repressed, and has redirected her desire for her father onto the male mates of co-workers, using alcohol to suppress her guilt about these overtures. The repressed guilt feelings make themselves visible by causing Megan to punish herself by excessive drinking and risking jail for drunk driving.

Megan is encouraged to free-associate about the events that concern her, using dream analysis to access her hidden fantasies about lusting after her father. The therapist refrains from actually pointing out the real root of her seductive behavior, but over a couple of years of free-association and dream interpretation, he gives only occasional hints to encourage Megan to gain insight into the incestuous nature of her actions. In the course of this therapy, he avoids her inevitable seductive behavior directed at him, the well-known process called 'transference', by trying to act as the good father Megan never had.

Megan's Cognitive-Behavioral Therapy

Megan's Cognitive-Behavioral therapist agrees with Megan that her problem is compulsively acting on an impulse to do things that she subsequently wished she hadn't done—actions that are momentarily pleasurable and yet create bad consequences later.

The therapist believes that when people create such problems for themselves, they're doing it because of distorted thinking: they keep telling themselves things that are inaccurate and unhelpful. The therapist tries to identify these 'automatic thoughts' or 'self-statements' and then help the client train herself to replace these thoughts with more accurate and more helpful thoughts.

The therapist questions Megan about the thoughts that go through her mind immediately before drinking, taking cocaine, or seducing her co-workers' husbands. On reflection, Megan is able to identify insistent, repetitive thoughts such as 'If I don't have a lot of fun I'll be a party pooper', 'If I'm a party pooper I'll have no friends', 'After a hard day's work, it would be *unbearable* if I couldn't unwind', 'I can't unwind if

I don't seize every opportunity to give myself immediate pleasure', and 'I *can't* unwind if I sometimes feel awkward or embarrassed by social interaction'.

The therapist encourages Megan to view these thoughts as hypotheses—possibly true, possibly false. For example, 'Is it really true that I'll have no friends if I don't drink, snort cocaine, and have sex with co-workers' spouses?' 'Would it really be unbearable if occasionally I didn't unwind?' Among homework exercises, the therapist asks Megan to list the good and bad things (benefits and costs) of her behavior.

Megan's faulty thinking stems from general beliefs which color much of her thinking. She feels that she would be unable to stand it if an acquaintance viewed her as not a fun person, that something terrible would happen if she became stressed out and couldn't immediately take solace in something thrilling. The therapist gives Megan exercises to counteract these more general faulty beliefs.

The therapist explains David Burns's concepts of 'fortune telling' and 'mind reading', and shows Megan how to avoid these errors. 'Fortune telling' is assuming without evidence that the future is fixed and that certain things, actually changeable, can never change. 'Mind reading' is assuming the worst about what other people are thinking, again without sufficient evidence.

Ursula

An executive assistant at a large health care agency, Ursula often feels tired and unmotivated and has recently even thought about suicide. She has never known her biological parents and recalls being a childhood victim of sexual abuse committed by her foster father. She's now twenty-eight and noticeably overweight. Though occasionally attracted to men she meets, she had never had an extended intimate relationship, and for the last several years, no relationships at all. Her foster parents continue to be involved in her adult life, and Ursula contributes to their financial support.

Over time Ursula has gradually come to spend an increasing proportion of her evenings and weekends lying on the sofa or in bed, watching TV. She turns down invitations to go out for drinks with co-workers after work. She has recently got a new boss at work, who will sometimes yell at her and belittle her for failing to accomplish things which she feels are actually beyond her control. When it occurs to her that she is suffering from depression she feels worse, because she considers that only pathetic losers get depressed or turn to therapy.

Ursula's Psychodynamic Therapy

Ursula's Psychodynamic therapist concludes that Ursula had felt rejected at an early age. Her depression was rooted in the fierce but unconscious anger she feels for the biological parents who had abandoned her and the foster parents who denied her any real love. The molestation by her foster-father might or might not be genuine, but in either case it represents her passionate fixation on him as the hoped-for lover and provider. His failure to fulfill this role, despite her attempts to buy his favors, means that she wants to be rejected and abused, as befitting the bad person she is.

The foster father's place was taken by Ursula's boss at work. The therapist's plan is that it will in turn be taken by the therapist himself, who will show kindness to Ursula, and exhibit intense interest in minute details of her life, expecting that this will lead to a transference crush by Ursula on the therapist, who will then contrive a scene in which Ursula will become aware of her dysfunctional needs.

In the sessions prior to the emergence of the transference, the therapist questions Ursula closely about her relations with her foster parents and how she imagines she might have related to her biological parents. The therapist gently prompts Ursula to come to an understanding that her boss's verbal abuse is a substitute for her foster father's physical abuse.

The therapist also anticipates that he will begin to feel intense emotional concern for Ursula (counter-transference), and that he should keep this in check, otherwise it will reinforce her pathology.

The therapist purposely does nothing that might encourage Ursula to distance herself from her foster parents or her boss, as a termination of these dysfunctional relationships would make it harder for Ursula to work through them and thus gain insight into the way she had related in infancy to her foster parents.

Ursula's Cognitive-Behavioral Therapy

The Cognitive-Behavioral therapist explains to Ursula that she is adding to her sense of helplessness by beating herself up about being depressed. After discussion, she agrees that depression is very common in the population, that some very famous and capable people have been depressed, and that many people with depression, even lasting for years, do completely recover and become permanently undepressed. She writes these points down and reminds herself of them every time she feels sad.

The therapist focuses Ursula's attention on her automatic thoughts, such as 'No matter what I do, no one appreciates me'. The therapist encourages Ursula to question these assertions, recalling that there have been occasions when someone has appreciated her, and that sometimes she has experienced enjoyment whether appreciated or not.

After careful assessment, the therapist concludes that Ursula's core belief is 'No one will ever love me because I am a worthless person'. Following more questioning and discussion, Ursula begins to realize that this judgment is too sweeping and it would be more accurate to say 'I have strengths and weaknesses like everyone else. People no better than me are often liked and occasionally loved'.

Ursula is given specific, easy assignments to work on, like finding out about a local theater group and saying yes the next time a co-worker asks her for drinks. She is also given written exercises to do every day, designed to replace faulty thinking with more helpful thinking.

Ursula also performs self-assertion exercises, training herself to resist people's demands, firmly yet calmly and pleasantly. She begins to practice these exercises on her foster-parents and on her boss, priming herself in advance to continue being politely firm if she meets any unpleasant or discouraging response. Later, she registers with an Internet dating service.

Brett

Brett, aged forty-three, is a systems analyst for a major airline. His problem, as he sees it, revolves around his relationship with his wife, Millie. Though generally reserved and easy-going, he has become increasingly worked up about Millie's annoying, irresponsible, and sometimes incomprehensible behavior. Millie has a twenty-year-old smoking habit, drinks frequently to alleviate her feelings of stress, and is habitually late for deadlines and appointments. At different times, Brett feels anger, resentment, guilt, hopelessness, and worry. He is interested in whether there is anything he can do to help Millie with her emotional problems.

Brett's Psychodynamic Therapy

Brett's Psychodynamic therapist soon concludes that Brett and Millie's marriage should probably be ended, because Brett has sought a mate who punishes all that he stands for. Divorce is expected to occur as soon as Brett's ego is able to handle it. The most likely hypothesis is that Brett, a neat and orderly person, has been attracted to an incompatible person whom he unconsciously wishes would punish him for his anal fantasies. However, this therapist holds the view, common among Psychodynamic therapists, that he should not give advice or recommend any course of action to his client.

Over the course of numerous sessions, involving chiefly free association, the therapist hopes that Brett will come to see that his attraction to Millie lies in bringing his rebellious id under control by making himself suffer frustration and difficulty. Brett will free himself from Millie's alluring ways and look for a mate who is uninhibited yet more controlled in her behavior.

The therapist decides that though it might be all right for Brett to stay with Millie if she herself were to receive the right kind of therapy, he would refuse to treat her, suggesting to Brett that he look for another therapist for his wife.

Brett's Cognitive-Behavioral Therapy

After briefly questioning Brett, the Cognitive-Behavioral therapist decides that Brett's demanding thoughts include: 'I *should not* have to put up with such an irresponsible mate', 'Millie *must* not be so unreasonable', 'I *must* not be inconvenienced by Millie's lateness', 'I *must* avoid an explosion with Millie,' 'I *should* be a perfect husband'.

Brett applies the Problem Separation Technique, understanding that he can stop disturbing himself by philosophically granting Millie the unconditional human right to be wrong, before attempting to influence her to change her behavior.

Brett worked on ABC exercises to dispute and undermine his demanding thoughts, replacing them with more reasonable thoughts. He wrote out several ABC exercises daily. He also adopted the goal of giving Millie some positive feedback each day.

Emma

Emma is an attractive, somewhat overweight twenty-seven-year old marketing consultant with a lively, upbeat manner. Her problem is that she is a long-time moderate smoker (a pack a day) who has tried many times to quit and always gone back to smoking. She has had several romantic relationships over the years, and is now interested in a man who is a non-smoker and somewhat repelled by the smell of cigarette smoke. Emma recently learned that her mother, also a long-time smoker, has been diagnosed with lung cancer.

Emma admires her mother as someone who was independent, worked hard, and knew how to have fun.

Questioning reveals that Emma likes to spend a lot of her time socializing and drinks alcohol in greater quantities than she really thinks appropriate, drinks four cups of coffee a day, and occasionally with close friends smokes marijuana or snorts cocaine, though none of these drug habits cause her serious concern as smoking does. She also wishes she could get her weight down, but does not care too much about that. She says that she will occasionally go for days without drinking alcohol, but finds she cannot get through a day without smoking cigarettes and drinking coffee. She believes that if she did quit smoking, she would automatically become even more overweight.

Contemplating the shock of her mother's diagnosis and her own possible marriage with her non-smoking boyfriend, Emma has become increasingly anxious about her enslavement to the smoking habit.

Emma's Psychodynamic Therapy

The therapist recognizes Emma's addictions as a form of 'oral fixation', stuck in the two-year-old pattern of relating to the world through the mouth. Emma was bottle-fed and put into daycare by her hard-working and party-going mom. As a child Emma was encouraged to act grown-up and look cute to entertain her mother's boyfriends. Emma looks back on these episodes as highly enjoyable, which the therapist interprets as a sign of repressed hostility and anger against her mother.

The therapist encourages Emma to recall episodes of resentment toward her mother, the goal being for Emma to recognize her domination by 'the bad breast' and her need for liberation by finding the 'good breast'.

Emma's Cognitive-Behavioral Therapy

After discussing Emma's various addictions and identifying some of her automatic thoughts, the therapist points out to her that she is convinced she *must* feel good all the time, and if she does happen to feel stressed out or uncomfortable, she *needs* to make up for it by letting her hair down and really unwinding.

At one point Emma starts wandering from the subject and then comments happily: "You see, I'm such a scatter-brain—I'm ADD." Emma had gone to college aiming to become a research psychologist, but had then had to drop out because she didn't complete assignments.

Emma has a problem even more serious than her addiction to cigarettes: unreasonable procrastination. But while Emma had viewed smoking as something to see a therapist about, it had never dawned on her that she had a more serious problem with unreasonable procrastination, and that unreasonable procrastination might be a problem suitable for treatment. Emma's workday is a perpetual cycle of leaving things to the last possible minute, then rushing to get them completed—then rushing round to the bar for a drink and a smoke with friends. The therapist teaches Emma ways to combat unreasonable procrastination, including the No Future Regrets method and the Three Minute Procrastination Buster.[1]

Emma's problem is not ADD—she easily read *The Girl with the Dragon Tattoo* in three sittings one weekend—but *low frustration tolerance*, a type of faulty thinking that can lead to both procrastination and substance addiction. Low frustration tolerance, identified by Albert Ellis, comes from the deep conviction that every moment *must* be comfortable or thrilling, and if it turns out not to be, then a person *must* get immediate enjoyment or escape to make up for the disappointment.

After the therapist has questioned Emma about her various forms of drug consumption and her preferences and goals, the therapist and Emma together determine that her immediate objectives are to quit smoking altogether, to reduce her alcohol consumption to a permanently lower level, while leaving her consumption of coffee, marijuana, and cocaine unchanged.

---

[1] Edelstein and Steele 1997, 78–87.

Emma begins to monitor her smoking and drinking, keeping a careful record of every cigarette and every drink, the goal being to gradually reduce the daily quota—to zero in the case of cigarettes. As frequently occurs, Emma finds that the simple act of monitoring causes her to reduce her consumption of cigarettes and alcohol.

The therapist gives Emma exercises to combat her smoking and procrastination, both of which arise from the thought 'I *can't* go a moment longer feeling so uncomfortable'. This demanding thought can be replaced with more helpful thoughts, such as: 'If I don't have a cigarette now, I will feel some discomfort, but I can survive that, and know that I am putting long-term benefits in the bank', and 'Trying to finish that report while I feel a bit tired is not a delightful prospect, but I can do it, and in a few minutes' time I will feel some satisfaction that I have made progress with it'.

Eric

Eric's Road Rage

Eric is a driver given to "road rage." He becomes furious at other drivers' behavior, shouts abuse at them, makes his passengers nervous, and turns every trip into an ordeal for himself and his family and friends.

Eric's Psychodynamic Therapy

The Psychodynamic therapist explains Eric's problem by his resentment toward his father. This is eventually traced back to an incident when Eric, at the age of three, opened his parents' bedroom door to witness them having sex. The treatment was for Eric to spend many sessions with the therapist, reliving the rage he had experienced as a child and finding new ways to let out his pent-up anger.

Eric's Cognitive-Behavioral Therapy

The Cognitive-Behavioral therapist asks Eric about the thoughts that go through his mind immediately prior to his outbursts of rage. These are such thoughts as: 'Other drivers *shouldn't* be so inconsiderate', 'They *shouldn't* cut me off', 'I *can't stand* how badly, and how dangerously, they drive', 'That guy's an idiot—he *shouldn't* be on the road', 'He's deliberately slowing me down and making me late for my appointment— that's *awful*', 'I *should* be able to turn right now, and I *can't stand* waiting'.

The therapist then challenges these thoughts, to get Eric to question their reasonableness, and to think about other drivers differently. In response to the therapist's questions, Eric comes up with alternative, more reasonable thoughts: 'I don't know that other driver's life—maybe he has a serious health or emotional problem that's distracting him', 'It's not very likely that that driver is deliberately trying to slow me down, but if he is, he's just a jerk and that's no big deal', 'I'm too mature to get upset about the existence of such people, who will not magically change their behavior if I become angry about them', 'I don't run the universe and can't control other drivers', 'Those other drivers have choice and free will—they'll do what they decide to, and that won't always be what I think they will do or ought to do'.

Eric is given homework to write down these more helpful thoughts several times a day.

Allan

Allan is an extremely bright thirty-year-old male with an MBA. He says he feels empty, hopeless, and useless. He has been a PR consultant in a high-tech field, but was laid off when his company downsized. He came into therapy because he is deeply depressed over his jobless state.

He explains that depression 'runs in his family'. He also discloses that he has been unemployed once or twice before, and has always suffered bouts of severe depression at these times. Each episode of depression had lasted from the point of losing his job until he was well into making a success of the next one. He knows his depression places an emotional burden on his wife, and it makes him less effective in seeking new employment.

Allan's Psychodynamic Therapy

The Psychodynamic therapist quickly arrives at the conclusion that Allan's problems began with very early experiences in which he disappointed his mother. This could very likely have occurred during potty training, as producing feces is symbolic of making money in a job. As an infant, then, Allan had sometimes been unable to produce feces, or produced insufficient, making his mother unhappy.

The Psychodynamic therapist does not rely on mere guesswork, however shrewd and well-trained, but tests his hypothesis by analyzing Allan's dreams and by having Allan free-associate. Both these approaches dramatically confirm the therapist's professional hunch. For example, Allan has a dream about pushing coins into a vending machine and not being able to get a chocolate bar in return, clearly symbolizing anxiety over passing feces. And, if further proof were needed, in response to the word 'dirt', Allan free-associated to the word 'clean'.

After a couple of years of regular weekly sessions, largely consisting of dream analysis and free association, Allan learns to relax his anal sphincter and general genito-urinary tract, so that he can more readily have good bowel movements.

In this way, Allan is able to overcome anal-retentive traits associated with tying job success to primary pleasures. It's expected that he will then become better able to continue to function in a healthy and normal heterosexual relationship with his wife, despite economic hard times.

Allan's Cognitive-Behavioral Therapy

After questioning Allan for a few minutes, the therapist explains that the immediate goal is to be able to be undepressed even while unemployed. Instead of waiting until a new job is under way, it would be an improvement if Allan could be free of depression even before he finds the new job.

Allan's demanding thoughts are easy to spot: 'I *must* find a job, but it's impossible,' 'Since I'm a good, hard-working, and qualified person, the universe *must* guarantee me what is due to me: security and serenity', 'I *must* prove myself in my next job, so that I am never laid off again', 'I *must* not be so hard on my wife,' 'I *must* have clear goals right now, because I *can't stand* the uncertainty', 'I *must* not be so self-absorbed and petty about my problems', 'I *must* be happy, but I'm totally miserable'.

The therapist asks Allan to try various exercises to eliminate and replace, not the contents of his bowels, but these harmful demanding thoughts. For example, the demanding thought, 'I *must* not be so self-absorbed and petty about my problems' is successfully replaced with the more reasonable thought: 'It would be an improvement if I were not so self-absorbed and petty about my problems, and I would therefore prefer that'.

After learning Three Minute exercises, Allan is quite conscientious in writing out three per day. But after he has observed how effective they are, he ups his average to five per day. In cases where the E's in the Three Minute exercises seem hollow and phony, the therapist teaches him the Debating Till You Win technique.[2]

When Allan states that he's totally miserable, the therapist asks him to draw up a list of simple, fleeting pleasures that he was deriving from life. At first Allan insists that there are none, but when pressed he comes up with quite a long list, including taking a shower, watching *The Simpsons*, eating dinner, getting into bed at night, and having sex with his wife.

After a few sessions, Allan comments that he's not deriving any benefit from the therapy. The therapist is able to quote back at him earlier comments he had made about feeling better, and to point out that he now smiles and chuckles occasionally, which he had not done at first. The therapist asked Allan to make a list of signs of his recovery, and somewhat to his own surprise, he quickly came up with nine, including 'sleeping better' and 'feeling like playing the piano again'. On the therapist's recommendation, Allan began adding to this list over time, and reading it over every day.

---

[2] Edelstein and Steele 1997, 98–101.

Steven

Steven is a twenty-nine-year-old, handsome, muscular model, actor, and male escort. One day he phoned a therapist in a condition close to panic. He becomes agitated as an image keeps on passing through his mind, repetitively and apparently uncontrollably: 'Someone taking an ax and slicing my penis off'.

As a result of this recurring image, he finds himself temporarily impotent during his daily grind of having sex with clients. Even worse, the horrible image keeps on intruding while he's driving, distracting him from the road and causing him to have several near misses.

Despite the fact that he seems unable to stop these images from appearing, Steven blames himself for having such 'ridiculous' thoughts. When the nightmarish picture begins to play out, he feels he has to grab his crotch to protect himself from the ax. He feels very silly doing this, and this makes him even more ashamed of his predicament. At other times, he desperately tries to ignore the vision of impending amputation, and act just as if nothing untoward is happening. But this merely has the paradoxical result that he feels out of control and even more humiliated.

Steven's Psychodynamic Therapy

Steven's Psychodynamic therapist concludes that Steven suffers from a Castration Complex, arising from fears that he lusted after his mother, and therefore assumed that if his father should ever learn of these guilty desires, he would kill Steven. Of course, these facts are not known to Steven, and are unaffected by the fact that Steven's parents are both deceased.

It would be quite mistaken, and possibly dangerous, to explain these findings to Steven, who must instead be encouraged to discover them for himself, by free-associating and reporting on his dreams. Gently guided by the therapist, who interposes the occasional question, Steven will eventually arrive at the source of his anxiety, probably in some recollected memory from infancy.

For Steven to achieve this understanding will probably take years of weekly sessions, and for many months at a time, it will appear that no progress is being made. This unhurried pace is essential if Steven is to discover the real origins of his emotional problem. The therapist advises Steven against reading any psychoanalytic or psychiatric literature which might prematurely set him speculating as to the roots of the problem.

Steven's Cognitive-Behavioral Therapy

The Cognitive-Behavioral therapist briefly explains the principles of Cognitive-Behavioral therapy, and helps Steven to identify his demanding thoughts. These included 'I *shouldn't* have this disturbing image because I'll lose money', 'I *must* not experience ridiculous mental pictures', and 'I *must not* sabotage the great time I am having, and I'm a total loser if I do'.

The therapist teaches Steven the ABC Exercise developed by Albert Ellis. Once the unreasonable demanding thought has been identified, it is written down, and then actively disputed, by writing down arguments against it. The unreasonable thought is then replaced with a more reasonable thought. 'I must not experience ridiculous mental pictures' could be successfully replaced by 'It's a bit distracting having these ridiculous mental pictures, but it's not the end of the world and I can easily cope with them'.

The therapist also teaches Steven the technique known as *paradoxical intention*, developed by Viktor Frankl. This consists of *deliberately trying* to bring about some behavior (such as a stammer) or experience (such as a mental picture of having one's member detached with an ax), which one would normally struggle to escape. Often, the deliberate effort will fail to summon up the intended behavior or experience, and this will help the client to quell his fear of it. The practice of paradoxical intention also gives Steven the experience of having control and helps him to see the humorous aspects of his fear.

The therapist explains that reinforcement through practice is most effective at dislodging faulty thinking and replacing it with more helpful thinking. Just as, in studying for an examination, writing out notes on the material is more reinforcing than simply reading it through, so with Cognitive-Behavioral therapy. The therapist asks Steven to write out his ABC exercises daily.

In contrast to many Psychodynamic therapists, Cognitive-Behavioral therapists believe that the more the client knows, the better. Steven's therapist encourages him to read *A Guide to Rational Living* by Ellis and Harper.

4
Where the Old Therapy Came From

In the 1997 movie *Titanic*, set in 1912, the heroine, Rose, played by Kate Winslet remarks that Dr. Freud has an explanation for men's preoccupation with size. The clear implication is that the man she is addressing, the Director of the White Star Company which developed and owned the *Titanic*, had authorized the production of this gigantic ship because he was anxious about the small size of his penis.

That this idiotic notion was presented by screen writer and director James Cameron not as a piece of silliness but as a superb put-down, or at least as the healthy irreverence of youth, is a tribute to the enormous influence of Freudian ideas. And yet it is certainly not something that Freud would have approved of.

The assumption that men do things, even things apparently unrelated to sex, because of anxiety about penis size is very widespread. On the TV talk show *Politically Incorrect*, the subject of hunting animals as a pastime came up, and host Bill Maher commented that this was something done by "men with small penises."

Now, in fact, contrary to Rose, Dr. Freud had nothing to say about men's concern with the size of their penises, but he quite seriously maintained that women—all women without exception—harbor something called 'penis envy', an unconscious preoccupation with their unconscious belief that their penises had been pruned at an early age.

The real Dr. Freud would also have had no trouble in diagnosing Rose's pathological urge to make a nuisance of herself by being insolent to the older male Director, clearly indicating that she was unconsciously in love with him and, without knowing it, ardently wished to give him oral sex.

This incident from the *Titanic* movie thus illustrates some facts about the current state of popular belief about psychology. According to this popular consensus, Freud was a great scientist who discovered things about human beings previously unsuspected. He thought in terms of 'phallic symbols' and discovered that we are generally unaware of the true motives for our actions and that these true motives are predominantly concerned with sexual urges we had, without knowing it, in childhood. But often, as with the *Titanic* incident and forgotten penis envy, the precise details of what Freud believed are forgotten, so in effect Freud's 'discoveries' are edited to make them comply with currently fashionable notions.

In the *Doctor Who* episode, 'The Curse of the Black Spot' (2011), The Doctor, an alien who looks human and has been everywhere in time and space, remarks to a belligerent pirate:

> You're big on the gun thing, aren't you? Freud would say you're compensating. Ever met Freud? (*Doctor Who*, New Series 6, Episode 3)

One of The Doctor's regenerations must have clouded his memory, for Sigmund Freud would never have said anything like that. Alfred Adler might have, but not with the implied phallic reference.

People who are meticulous or perfectionist are often described as 'anal-retentive' or simply as 'anal'. The other day one of the authors heard a colleague say "I'm sorry to be so anal." She was apologizing for her concern to make sure that some minor detail of a project was carried out precisely.

Freud maintained that people's concern for order and detail stemmed from their potty-training in infancy. Probably many people who now use the term 'anal' in some such way don't think much about this Freudian theory, but they may vaguely suppose that there is *some* causal connection between potty training and a concern for order and method. This widespread supposition is clearly derived from the great influence of Freud. If it were not for a century of public indoctrination with Freudian formulas, we would surely all view any such suggestion as totally daft, as indeed it is.

Many of Freud's own specific ideas are now distinctly unfashionable. It's no longer considered quite the done thing to suggest that an assertive career woman is betraying the fact that she feels most acutely the lack of a penis. Penis envy, that key tenet of traditional Freudianism, once accepted by smart people at every cocktail party as an obvious truth, is now neglected, though when Ellen Degeneres published a book entitled *My Point—And I Do Have One*, even such hard-bitten skeptics as ourselves had to wonder momentarily whether there might, after all, be something in it.

The Freudian view that homosexuality and oral sex are always pathological symptoms of traumatic early development have similarly died away.

More important than the fate of these specific Freudian doctrines is the widespread acceptance of some very general theories which owe their popularity to Freud's influence:

- **Your interactions with your parents in early childhood have a major impact on the kind of person you grow up to become**

- **It's hazardous to bottle up your feelings: bottled up emotions will seek an outlet**

- **If anyone does anything notable, especially anything that superficially looks fine and good, this must be because of some quite different motive, usually of a mean and nasty quality**

- People are somehow able to 'repress' (willfully forget) memories they find too horrible to contemplate, and these memories, unrecognized, may appear later in disguised form to make their lives miserable.

All of these ideas are still quite popular, and they were made popular by the Freudian movement. Though they are now believed by many people who would not call themselves Freudians, they came from Freud.

The Sigmund Freud Story

Once upon a time, the Old therapy was new. In 1882, Sigmund Freud became a doctor in Vienna, specializing in nervous disorders. He coined the term 'psychoanalysis' for his evolving theories in the 1880s, but these theories took the distinctive form in which 'psychoanalysis' was to conquer the world in 1897–1899.

Many of Freud's cases are famous: they have been mulled over and argued over many times. It's only recently that new scholarly research has demonstrated that Freud systematically misrepresented these cases, so that much of what is 'known' about them is distortion or fabrication. We'll look at some of the new findings on Freud in Chapter 7. Here we'll stick fairly closely to the standard and traditional account.

Many people in the nineteenth century were fascinated with hypnosis and with attempts to extend and develop hypnosis in new directions. There was great speculation on what hypnosis could tell us about the nature of the human mind. Freud and his colleague and senior partner Josef Breuer were doctors who joined the European fashion for treating people's emotional problems with hypnosis. But then they began to develop their own approach which did not rely on hypnosis.

Breuer had a patient given the fictitious name 'Anna O.'. Anna appeared to suffer from various physical symptoms and emotional problems which were at that time described as 'hysteria'. Physicians disagreed about whether the causes of hysteria were purely physical, purely mental, or a mixture of both. We now know that hysteria was a bogus disease. Doctors came up with the term because they did not yet know much about some real diseases such as epilepsy, multiple sclerosis, asthma, or syphilis. Symptoms of all these diseases might be taken as symptoms of hysteria.[1] When doctors don't know what's troubling the patient, they're always tempted to blame the patient instead of their own ignorance.

In 'treating' Anna O., that is, feeding her narcotics and talking with her, Breuer observed that sometimes if she told stories she would feel better afterwards. This observation later morphed in Breuer's mind into the notion that if she related incidents connected with the onset of her symptoms, the very act of talking about these incidents would give some relief from the symptoms. *Reliving is relieving.* Anna O. herself called this "chimney sweeping" and Breuer called it "the talking cure." This idea was probably suggested by the spectacle of stage acts involving hypnosis.[2] At any rate, it was to become one of the most powerful ideas of the following century: *When you can recall and relate what caused your disturbance, then—and only then—will you be cured!*

According to the story, the emotional problems of Anna O. went through various stages until Breuer helped her to uncover a painful memory. Once this memory was recovered, all her symptoms vanished and she soon overcame all her emotional troubles.

Although Freud was never involved in treating Anna O., and broke off relations with Breuer before the launching of psychoanalysis, this story became a classic legend of psychoanalysis. It was endlessly retold and was taken to show that:

1. **The cause of a person's emotional problem is that person's buried memory of something painful.**

---

[1] Webster 1995, 71–89.
[2] Borch-Jacobsen 1996, 64–75.

2. **As soon as the buried memory is uncovered, and the person relives that painful memory, but not before, the emotional problem goes away.**

This approach was expounded by Freud and Breuer in a book they jointly published in 1895, *Studies on Hysteria*. They developed the method known as 'free association', encouraging the patient to express any random thought that came to mind. It was the belief of Freud and Breuer that words uttered in this way gave clues as to what was going on in 'the unconscious'. The unconscious was already a familiar notion among writers and psychiatrists; it was not invented by Freud, though he did develop a peculiar theory of the unconscious. What Freud did was to replace more or less accurate notions of the unconscious with disastrously mistaken ones.

Freud began to develop new ideas about his patients' behavior and their 'unconscious minds'. For example, if the patient stammered or suddenly ran out of things to say, Freud interpreted this as 'resistance'. This means that something in the unconscious mind is struggling very hard to get out and the patient, or some part of the patient's mind, is struggling very hard to stop it coming out—thereby demonstrating that this something is of vital importance.

From Imagined Real Sex to Imagined Imagined Sex

Freud also came up with the idea that emotional problems were caused by sexual experiences between birth and age six. These experiences had been 'repressed'—forgotten because they were so deeply upsetting—but they came back in disguised form to haunt the patient in adult life.

For slightly more than a year, from 1896 to 1897, Freud thought that these sexual experiences had really happened, and argued strongly and publicly for the theory that all 'neuroses' (emotional and behavioral problems) were directly caused by forgotten incidents of childhood 'seduction'. In 1897, Freud changed his mind, though he would not publicly acknowledge that he had abandoned the seduction theory for several more years.

Freud concluded that the incidents of childhood sex were not genuine memories but false memories, or as he later called them, 'screen memories'. The reality, according to this new theory was that these patients had *not* been 'seduced' in childhood, but had *wanted* to be seduced. What they had 'repressed' was not that they had had sexual experiences but that they had had phantasies about a particular type of sexual experience.

Notice the spelling 'phantasy', not 'fantasy'. We all have fantasies. A fantasy is a conscious thought process. It is no more 'unconscious' than reading a poem or solving a math problem. You can't have a fantasy without knowing you're having it (or at least, without knowing that something's going on in your mind). A 'phantasy', according to Freud, is something going on in your mind that you don't know about.

Freud's theory now took on the outlines of psychoanalysis as we know it today. Freud decided that domination by sexual longings and phantasies was universal in *all* children, up to the age of six. Every little boy wants to kill his father and have sex with his mother—the 'Oedipus Complex'. Strangely enough, he attributed the same desire to little girls, all of whom have a homosexual pash for their moms. (Freud was compelled to take this course by his theory that little girls start out with boys' minds and only become 'female' later.) Freud came to see the Oedipus Complex as universal in all human adults whatever their circumstances, as the source of all emotional problems, and as the true foundation of all science, art, and civilization.[3] It also became the acid test of Freudian orthodoxy: anyone questioning the centrality of the Oedipus Complex in all human affairs could not be a psychoanalyst and would be booted out of all psychoanalytic organizations.

Every boy is haunted by the fear that his penis will be cut off—the 'Castration Complex'. Every girl is deeply upset

---

[3] We're not making this up.

about already having had her penis cut down to size—'penis envy'. At age five, boys and girls diverge psychologically—boys become afraid they will be castrated, girls are disappointed to find that they have already been castrated and are therefore inferior. From age five, girls want to have a child by their fathers, this child being a replacement for their lost penis. All these little girls and boys are unaware of these wishes, desires, and terrors, and cannot become aware of them. They exist in the unconscious mind.

Freud did not, of course, dispute that there are actual cases of sexual molestation of young children, but, after 1897, he considered these exceptional. Sexual wishes and phantasies by young children, however, are universal, he claimed.

The Oedipus Complex, Freud believed, becomes fully focused between the ages of three and six. The child's first sexual stirrings are, in Freud's view, more diffuse. The child first goes through an oral stage, in which sexual pleasure is focused on the mouth, then an anal stage, in which the focus is on defecation, and then a phallic stage. What Freud is doing here is taking familiar facts about children, and describing as 'sexual' desires which, before Freud, were well-known but not necessarily always labeled 'sexual'. Freud holds the theory that all pleasure is sexual.

In well-adjusted people, those without neuroses, people who have achieved, as Freud put it, "normal unhappiness," these exciting adventures in the unconscious are somehow sorted out without too much damage. But in neurotic people, something goes wrong. When that has happened, the cure for a patient's problem is to get her to dredge up the phantasies of her own unconscious from the first six years of life and to relive these phantasies and other memories. The cure thus necessarily includes accepting the theories of psychoanalysis and their application in the patient's own life.

As long as a man maintains that he never wanted to kill his father, he must be 'resisting' and is therefore in trouble. If he accepts the reality of his infantile wish to murder his father, then this is at least progress. To complicate matters, however, it is considered useless or even harmful for the psychoanalyst to directly inform the patient that his troubles stem from wanting to make love to his mother and kill his father. This will only arouse resistance. The patient must discover for himself this curious fact about his early childhood wishes. In practice, of course, the psychoanalyst gently, or not so gently, nudges the patient in the direction of discovering this 'fact' for himself, and without the guidance of an analyst committed to this belief in advance, the patient would never come up with it.

To avoid possible misunderstanding about Freud's theory of the Oedipus Complex, we should state that there have undoubtedly been some individuals, among all the billions of humans throughout history, who have wanted to kill their fathers and have sex with their mothers, and, no doubt, a much smaller number who have been successful in one or both of these projects. These cases would absolutely *not* be examples of the Oedipus Complex. First, they would actually have happened, instead of being unconsciously imagined; second, they would probably have occurred later than the age of six, third, the persons in question would have known perfectly well what they wanted to do (these would not be unconscious phantasies but calculated aims), and fourth, these persons would remember what they had done (even filial ingratitude has its limits).

Dreams and the Unconscious

From 1897 on, Freud decided that dreams were a fruitful source of knowledge about the unconscious. His book, *The Interpretation of Dreams*, which bore the date 1900, is often considered his greatest work. All dreams, he claimed, are wish-fulfillments. Dreams are symbolic representations of achieving our deepest wants. For example, if we dream that we're shooting at a cow, this obviously represents our wish to have sex with our mother. This dream enables us to fulfill our wish, but in disguised form so that we don't recognize it as something we need to feel guilty about.

In *The Interpretation of Dreams*, Freud made five claims about dreams:

1. **All dreams mean something; they can all be interpreted.**

2. **The correct interpretation of a dream is absolutely strict and must involve every detail of the dream. The dream is like a jigsaw puzzle in which every part fits uniquely with every other part.**

3. **Dreams are symbolic. For instance, a gate or a flower symbolize the female genitalia, a train symbolizes the penis, climbing stairs symbolizes sexual intercourse, gold coins symbolize feces, and so on.**

4. **The hidden message or 'latent content' of a dream is always a wish: dreams are always wish-fulfillments.**

5. **Always, or almost always, the wish relates to sexual urges going back to infancy, urges which the patient is not aware of, but which help to explain all his thoughts and behavior.**

6. **The real meaning or latent content of a dream can be accurately recovered by the technique of 'free association'.**

The real meaning of the dream, what Freud calls its 'latent content', is disguised by symbolism, so that the apparent storyline of the dream, its 'manifest content' has to be decoded. By having the patient free-associate on each element of the dream's manifest content, it is possible, Freud believes, to reverse the process by which the dream was created, and to trace the dream back to the hidden wishes that gave rise to it.

After that, Freud turned his attention to slips of the tongue and slips of the pen. According to Freud's account, these are never really accidental, but always motivated by unconscious wishes. Here again, Freud's theories have passed into everyday language, and such errors are still sometimes called 'Freudian slips'. Freud applied the same analysis to jokes: humor owes its force to the release of unconscious strivings. Slips of the tongue and jokes are analyzed in basically the same way as dreams. Accidents, like falling off a ladder or dropping your fork at dinnertime, are also seen as symbolic expressions of unconscious motives.

Until 1920, Freud took sex to be the all-important drive, but in that year he developed his Dual Instinct Theory. He now saw aggression, or the Death Instinct, as equally important with sex, or the Life Instinct. In his book *Civilization and Its Discontents* (1930), Freud argued that life in civilized society is inherently unsatisfactory: in order to get the benefits of civilization, we have to submit to the irksome curbing and control of our deepest desires.

Toward the end of his life, Freud modified his model of the mind. Instead of just the Conscious and the Unconscious, Freud divided the mind into three: 'it', 'I', and 'above-I'. For some reason, when Freud's original German was translated into English, these terms were translated into Latin: 'id', 'ego', and 'super-ego'. The id or 'it' ('I couldn't control it', 'It came over me') is the boiling mass of raw urges, blindly seeking satisfaction. The ego or 'I' is the self which attempts to organize and control the id. And the super-ego is the moral sense or conscience.

In the science-fiction movie *Forbidden Planet* (1956), the deaths of astronauts and other disasters on the planet Altair IV have been caused by enormously powerful yet invisible monsters. It appears that a highly advanced civilization was wiped out by these mysterious creatures thousands of years earlier. This civilization left behind an underground installation which one of the astronauts now tries to use, followed by further destructive attacks from the monsters. It turns out that the installation was designed to materialize any object that could be imagined. Its inventors had foolishly overlooked that the equipment would materialize what was in their unconscious minds, "Monsters from the Id! Monsters from the Subconscious!" These materialized monsters are so powerful that there is no hope of saving the planet from destruction.

Growth of the Freudian Church

Following the publication of *The Interpretation of Dreams*, Freud gradually acquired a reputation and attracted a small but devoted following among young doctors. Psychoanalysis was launched as a new product on the market.[4] Whereas Freud's early patients had come to see the doctor for what they thought were medical problems, now people came looking for 'analysis', sometimes because of an emotional problem and sometimes because they wanted to discover themselves by diving into their own unconscious depths.

Psychoanalysis was expected to take years. The patient would see the analyst four or five times a week. The patient would lie on a couch and say whatever came into his mind, while the analyst would sit behind the patient with a notebook and pencil. There were often long periods of silence. A useful skill for a psychoanalyst was to be able to take naps without snoring.

Psychoanalysis quickly became popular in the prosperous United States, a country Freud despised. Freud and his then close friend and heir Carl Jung made an American lecturing trip in 1909. Practicing psychoanalysts soon found hundreds of clients, who had to be at least comfortably off to afford years of psychoanalysts' fees. This was the beginning of psychotherapy as a major American profession. Though there had been psychotherapists before Freud, they were very few compared with the growing numbers of psychoanalysts who emerged early in the twentieth century.

Psychoanalysis had its own institutes which organized training and accreditation for practicing psychoanalysts.

---

[4] Szasz 1988, 113–15.

These were completely controlled by orthodox Freudians, and ideas which departed from Freud could lead to expulsion. Through their networks of contacts, the psychoanalytic organizations were able to point promising candidates in the direction of lucrative careers as practicing psychoanalysts.

Many hospital psychiatrists became psychoanalysts by persuasion and tried to treat mental patients with Freudian methods. (A psychiatrist is a medical doctor who specializes in mental illness.) Psychiatrists who were not convinced by the new Freudian theories were mostly 'biological' theorists. They viewed mental illness as physical in origin, and treated patients with drugs, vapors, hot baths, and sometimes with very crude brain surgery or with electric shocks to the brain.

And yet the biggest impact of psychoanalysis was outside psychology, psychiatry, or psychotherapy. Scholars in subjects like literature, anthropology, and sociology became converts to psychoanalysis. So did creative artists: novelists, painters, and poets. Reference works such as encyclopedias and textbooks increasingly came to describe the theories of psychoanalysis as though these were scientific findings. Literary people, ignorant of science, came to think of Freud as a great theorist comparable with Einstein. Psychoanalysis was also disseminated to a much broader public via popular culture, for example through Hollywood movies such as *Carefree* (1938), *Lady in the Dark* (1944), and *Spellbound* (1945).

These insistent messages from popular culture have acquainted everyone with the outlines of Freudian theory. We all know in our bones that mental problems are due to horrible upsets in childhood, that memories can be forgotten because they are painful, and then recovered years later as though preserved on videotape, that our dreams provide clues to powerful forces at work in our unconscious minds, and that any adult problems with excessive or insufficient orderliness are due to childhood problems with potty-training.

We 'know' these things in the same sense that we know that vampires really hate garlic and have to be in bed by sunrise: they are a part of our culture—both the culture of the educated elite and the pop culture of the masses. Nevertheless, these prevalent ideas about the unconscious mind and the decisive impact of early childhood, which many people seriously believe, are just as out of touch with reality as prevalent ideas about vampires, which everyone understands are pure fiction.

Narrow Freudianism and Broad Freudianism

Between 1910 and 1940, when psychoanalysis had a huge impact on American thinking, the official organization of psychoanalysis, represented in the US by the American Psychoanalytic Association and its affiliates such as the New York Psychoanalytic Institute, grew steadily. At first all of organized psychoanalysis worldwide was very tightly controlled by a handful of Freud's closest associates. But from the beginning there were splits and dissenters within the movement. All the people who started out agreeing with psychoanalysis and then broke off because of differences continued to maintain some of the more general ideas held by Freud. Even though they were denounced and demonized by official psychoanalysis, they were still spreading broadly Freudian ideas.

And so we can distinguish between narrow Freudianism—ideas held by Freud and by the majority of psychoanalysts and psychodynamic therapists until the 1940s—and broad Freudianism—general ideas which came from Freud and which continued to be popular among people who had rejected narrow Freudianism. Today, narrow Freudianism has few remaining believers, while broad Freudianism is still tremendously powerful. Broad Freudianism is what we have been calling 'Psychodynamic' thinking, now the most popular name for it.

Here are some examples of *narrow* Freudianism:

- **According to Freud, all paranoia is due to unconscious homosexuality. A person becomes morbidly afraid that other people are out to get him** because, says Freud, he wants to make love with people of the same sex, though he is completely unaware that this is what he wants to do.

- People sometimes suffer from agoraphobia (fear of open spaces). Freud believed this was especially common among women, and attributed it to women's phantasies of being prostitutes. In other words, the fact that some women are scared of open spaces indicates that, unknown to themselves, they want to be prostitutes. He didn't explain why men are sometimes agoraphobic.

- A woman anxiously made a special point of removing all clocks from her room before she went to sleep. According to Freud, the reason she did this was that the ticking of the clocks symbolized the throbbing of her clitoris. (Just as we might expect, the woman rejected this suggestion, but in Freud's judgment her rejection merely constituted further evidence that he was right.)

- Another female patient dreamed that she went to the market to buy meat, but couldn't find the meat she wanted. She then went to the vegetable-seller, but couldn't recognize the peculiar vegetable, tied up in bundles, that she was offered. So she refused to purchase it. Freud's interpretation of this dream was that the patient was phantasizing that he (Freud) had made an improper sexual advance to her, which she had rebuffed. This would mean that she wanted Freud to make advances to her. (Freud routinely had the conviction that his female patients were, unbeknownst to themselves, madly in love with him.)

We've picked out here a few of Freud's interpretations which are decidedly odd. These inadvertently hilarious ideas were all propounded by Freud and believed in by thousands of faithful Freudians in the great days of classic psychoanalysis. These ideas today have far fewer believers than they did sixty years ago. There are however some broader ideas which also stem from Freud, and these ideas are still accepted by all the therapists whom we're calling Psychodynamic therapists. These ideas are 'Broad Freudianism' and though somewhat weakened compared to sixty years ago, they are still powerful:

- **Cure requires insight. You can only be cured of your emotional problem if you understand how it originated.**

- **Bottling up memories, emotions, or desires is hazardous. If you bottle them up, instead of giving vent to them, you may feel better for a while but they will later squirt out somehow and give you a hard time.**

- **What happens in the first few years of your life, especially your relationships with your parents, is supremely important in forming the kind of person you are.**

- **If you have emotional or behavioral problems, their roots must lie buried in your childhood. So it's important to find out just what happened in your childhood.**

- **Your conscious intentions and deliberate actions are at the mercy of hidden forces deep in your unconscious mind, forces which you can't get at without great difficulty and only with expensive specialized help.**

We see the influence of these ideas, not only in Psychodynamic therapy, but also, for example, in government policies requiring that people who have experienced a severe trauma should spend hours dwelling on it, talking it through, and reliving it. We see this influence in movies like *The Prince of Tides* or TV shows like *Dexter*. We still see it (although the tide began to turn for the better in the 1990s) in popular advice on child-rearing practices. Where we don't see it is in university departments of psychology, and where we see far less of it than we used to is in actual psychotherapy.

Broad Freudianism is Psychodynamic thinking. Among therapists Psychodynamic thinking has been losing out to Cognitive-Behavioral thinking. But among literary intellectuals—often people who have majored in subjects like modern languages, film studies, culture studies, and the like—and therefore among journalists and TV and movie scriptwriters who are recruited mainly from this group, complete ignorance of psychology and of scientific psychotherapy prevails, and popular culture tends to be heavily weighted with Psychodynamic thinking.

Those who accept all of narrow Freudianism are now a small sect whereas we hear from broad Freudianism all the time. But narrow Freudianism does not consist entirely of very weird claims like the ones listed earlier. Take, for instance, the claim that depression is anger turned inward. A depressed person suffers because she harbors pent-up unconscious rage, which having no outlet is turned against herself.

This is not as strange as the earlier examples we gave. It does not outrage common sense in the way that those examples do. Idly reflecting on it for the first time, you may well consider there may be something in it. But it is just as false as the more bizarre examples. Depression is not caused by redirected anger, and will not be cured by encouraging the depressed person to vent her anger. Treating people for depression by trying to get them to let their angry feelings out will do more harm than good. The depressed person's own feeling that life is so empty and hopeless it's not even worth getting angry about anything is much more indicative of what's going on with depression.

Despite the fact that few people now believe in narrow Freudianism, narrow Freudianism is worth thinking about because it shows the kind of thing that people have been inclined to believe and provides us with concrete examples of the broader Freudianism which is all around us. Narrow Freudianism consists of specific claims about what's going on in our unconscious minds, and thinking about whether these claims are true or false helps us to clarify whether *any* claims about unconscious influences might be true.

Nathaniel Branden, Prisoner of Freud

Numerous pop psychologists and psychotherapists have rejected narrow Freudianism only to double down on broad Freudianism. We can illustrate the power of broad Freudianism in our culture by the case of Nathaniel Branden.

The 1970s witnessed the explosive growth of 'self-esteem' in pop psychology. At the head of this movement was Nathaniel Branden, with his best-selling book *The Psychology of Self-Esteem*. This book contains some quite scathing criticisms of Freudian thinking. Branden points out that Freudians tend to suppose that undesirable feelings and motivations can either be 'repressed' or acted upon, ignoring the possibility that a person might have an emotion they consciously choose not to act upon, without any repression, because to do so would not be in their best interests.[5]

Yet despite his demonstrated readiness to attack narrow Freudianism, Branden never questions broad Freudianism: that emotional problems are rooted in childhood interactions with parents, that these problems cannot be tackled without revisiting the childhood events that caused them, that problems arise because we 'repress' our feelings, pushing them into our unconscious from which hideaway they later come crawling back to bite us, and that therapy involves getting clients to relive these events, or their responses to these events, accompanied by the arousal of strong emotions. These erroneous Freudian principles are reiterated uncritically in *The Psychology of Self-Esteem* and in all Branden's

---

[5] Branden 1971, 20-21, 23, 87, 166.

subsequent books. Essentially then, Branden replaces 'fearing castration because you phantased sex with your mother' by 'having your mother make you feel bad by undervaluing you'. The type of childhood trauma is different but the broadly Freudian framework of assumptions remains completely unchallenged.

Irvin Yalom, Another Prisoner

One of today's best-known writers on psychotherapy is Irvin Yalom, author of *Love's Executioner*. All the familiar Freudian trappings re-appear: repressed memories, traumatic childhood experiences, fears and motives we're not aware of, the unconscious speaking through dream interpretation. Instead of Oedipal or self-esteem issues, the buried horrors relate to the four 'existential concerns': death, isolation, meaninglessness, and inescapable freedom.[6] At least these are not things we can blame Mom and Dad for.

---

[6] Yalom 1980, 8–9.

5
Psychoanalysis . . .
Testing, Testing

Duncan believes that he ought to go to the dentist, but he keeps putting this off. Duncan's very busy and honestly believes that he repeatedly postpones going to the dentist because he can't spare the time.

As friends of Duncan, we may conclude that, although he is indeed very busy, and might go to the dentist sooner if he were not so busy, the chief reason he procrastinates about dental care is that he shies away from the discomfort of dental treatment. So we accept the possibility that Duncan could have made a mistaken judgment about his own actual motives. This kind of incomplete awareness of one's real motives has always been familiar to everyone and Freud sheds no light on it.

Now along comes a psychoanalyst and tells us that the true reason for Duncan's procrastination is castration anxiety. When told that Duncan has no recollection of any anxiety about the possibility of being castrated, and in any case understands perfectly well that having his teeth maintained is nothing like castration, the psychoanalyst responds: 'Exactly! What more proof could you possibly want?'

To the psychoanalyst, the mere fact that a person rejects some explanation of his own behavior is evidence that this explanation is true. The unconscious mind is fiendishly clever at disguising its own intentions and 'resists' these intentions being made conscious.

But wait, there's something not quite right here. For any human behavior, we can think of thousands of possible explanations which are not true and which the person concerned would reject as untrue. For instance, let's propose that the real reason Duncan puts off going to the dentist is because he unconsciously believes that he's about to visit the Moon, where the king of the Moon Men will use his advanced powers to give Duncan a perfect set of indestructible teeth. Duncan would reject this explanation too, but it doesn't follow that there's any truth in it.

Resistance Proves Existence

Most people, when they first hear some of the Freudian explanations, are inclined to be skeptical. But this very fact is taken as evidence for the truth of psychoanalysis. According to psychoanalysts, the fact that we tend to reject psychoanalytic explanations simply reveals that we harbor 'resistance' to them, and this resistance shows that the explanations are true, because unconscious ideas 'resist' coming into consciousness.

We can show that we are, comparatively speaking, mentally healthy and free of hang-ups, by accepting psychoanalytic theories, or at least keeping an open mind, which in this case means an uncritical mind. On the other hand, if we disagree with such theories, this probably indicates that we have serious emotional problems.

The Freudian stratagem of persuasion is similar to the one in the story, 'The Emperor's New Clothes', where the emperor and his courtiers pretend to see the magnificent new clothes because they accept the theory that those who cannot see the clothes are fools. No one wants to be thought a fool, and no one wants to be totally 'lacking in insight' into his own unconscious motivations.

If a person has been 'in analysis' (treated by a psychoanalyst) a long time and after rejecting an explanation comes to accept it, especially if the person does this while experiencing a powerful emotion, psychoanalysts will often say that this proves the explanation to be correct. But can we really take this as evidence? And if we do, why shouldn't we take it as much weightier evidence *against* psychoanalysis that most people never come to accept the explanations for their problems offered by psychoanalysts?

People are suggestible. Psychological experiments have shown that if a suggestion is repeatedly made to a person, he will be more inclined to accept it. False memories can be implanted in this way. There are cases on record of individuals confessing to crimes after prolonged questioning by the police, when it later turned out that they were innocent. There are also cases of religious indoctrination: we wouldn't suppose that just because a person has been converted to a particular religious outlook, this shows that the outlook must be true.

Not everyone, even under tremendous pressure, would come to believe they had committed a crime when they had not done so. Not everyone succumbs to the persuasive efforts of a religious cultist. Individuals vary in how credulous or how suggestible they are. But the mere fact that someone has shelled out repeatedly for years to pay a psychoanalyst demonstrates that she cannot be among the more critical-minded or skeptical members of the population, and also indicates that she's particularly inclined to vest her hopes in psychoanalysis. Despite this, it should be noted, many people in analysis, perhaps most, never do come to accept the analyst's explanation of their problems. For example, the great majority of Freud's patients, including his most celebrated landmark cases, always rejected his explanations.

If someone disputes the truth of a psychoanalytic explanation, psychoanalysts count this as evidence that it is true. And if someone accepts the truth of the psychoanalytic explanation, this also counts as evidence that it is true. This is not a real test of the theory behind the explanation. So what would count as a test?

When talking about suggestion in psychoanalysis we have to bear in mind what is possibly being suggested. 'Persuasion' might be a better word than 'suggestion'. We might imagine a patient in analysis, after thirty or forty years of five-times-a-week sessions, suddenly exclaiming:

It all comes back to me now! As I was swallowing blue jello at my fourth birthday party, I suddenly had this powerful feeling that Mom looked even tastier than the jello, and I immediately realized I'd need to apply Dad's chainsaw to his neck. And the amazing thing is, I had these feelings and thoughts without being aware I was having them. Wow! Who'da thunk it! Can you believe, I suddenly feel like a load's been lifted off of my mind. . . .

Analytic sessions are not subjected to systematic archiving and statistical scrutiny, but from what we can gather from psychoanalytic scuttlebutt, that kind of thing never happens. If it did happen, even once, we would never hear the end of it, like a Mormon missionary discovering a remote Amazonian tribe that spoke Hebrew. The 'best' that ever happens is that the patient becomes convinced of the general truth of the claims of psychoanalysis and therefore infers that he 'must have' unconsciously harbored Oedipal feelings at the age of four or five, much as a fundamentalist Christian becomes convinced that the reason he is tempted to sin 'must be' that Satan is always whispering in his ear.

Doubtful Interpretations

There's no decisive test of the claims of psychoanalysis, and it therefore belongs with other doubtful theories, such as the following:

- **A clairvoyant, who looks in a crystal ball, and tells us our future**

- **A tarot reader, who tells us what the tarot cards mean for our lives**

- **A tea-leaf reader (who, in the days before tea bags, would tell us about our life's decisions by** examining the shapes of the tea leaves left at the bottom of our tea cup)

- The *Yijing* (formerly called the *I Ching*), a Chinese method of consulting the meaning of various randomly generated patterns

- An astrologer, who informs us that our life is governed by the influence of heavenly bodies such as the Sun, Moon, and planets

These theories don't lay themselves open to testing. They do not make definite predictions that might turn out wrong, so that we could then say the theory was proved to be false. They don't take the risk of being falsified by observed facts, because they are compatible with any observed facts. Put another way, every conceivable observed fact *confirms* these theories.

Confirmations Prove Very Little

A major mistake in evaluating claims, whether of tea-leaf reading or of psychoanalysis is to be impressed by some striking event that seems to 'confirm' the theory of tea-leaf reading or the theory of psychoanalysis. *Observations that 'confirm' a theory, no matter how spectacular or striking, prove very little.*

This point was a great breakthrough in understanding how to evaluate theories. It was identified by Karl Popper around the beginning of the twentieth century. Popper, then a young teacher in Vienna, found himself confronted by four systems of ideas which were comparatively new and very fashionable, though also controversial: Freudian psychoanalysis, Adlerian psychology, Marxism, and Einsteinian physics (relativity theory).

Popper wanted to find out which, if any, of these theories was worth accepting, and also which, if any, could truly be called 'scientific'. Popper was closely in touch with some of the ablest proponents of these theories: in the case of Adlerian psychology, he had discussions with Alfred Adler himself, and in the case of Marxism, he was in touch with some of the leading Marxist theorists in Vienna. Popper was inclined to be sympathetic to all four theories: they all appealed to him and he felt that they might well be on the track of important truths.

Popper noticed that there was something about Einsteinian physics which sharply contrasted with Freudism, Adlerism, and Marxism. The Freudians, the Adlerians, and the Marxists were full of anecdotes which were well explained by their theories, and which therefore seemed to confirm their theories. If pressed to defend their theories, they responded by citing these impressive confirmations.

In sharp contrast, Einstein did not look for confirmation and did not care about it. Instead, Einstein was quite happy to specify, very precisely, those possible observations which would *disconfirm* and therefore *disprove* his theory. He announced that he would withdraw his theory and abandon it if certain tests were made and turned out negative for the theory.

The mistake of looking for confirmations tends to go along with another, related mistake: asking whether the theory 'explains' the observations that need to be explained. Since any observation can easily be explained by thousands of different theories, nearly all of them false, this approach is also no way to test a theory. It's better to compare the theory with some alternative theory, especially one that is more simple or straightforward, and ask whether the first theory can explain something the alternative theory cannot explain. (Einstein made clear that the alternative to his own theory was traditional Newtonian physics: the tests of his theory were predictions of observations contrary to the predictions of traditional physics.)

Popper's general approach is called Critical Rationalism. According to Critical Rationalism, if we hear any claim that something is true, instead of asking ourselves *How can we be sure that this claim is true?* we would do much better to ask ourselves, *What difference would it make to the world if this claim were false?*

Popper on Freud

Popper maintained that the key tenets of psychoanalysis are unfalsifiable, meaning that, unlike scientific theories, we cannot submit them to any test by comparing them with observations. Psychoanalysis does not run the risk of being refuted by observations, because it does not commit itself to any specific predictions which might turn out wrong. Whatever conceivably might happen, it would never require that psychoanalysis itself must be false.

As an example, Popper looked closely at Freud's claim that all dreams without exception represent the fulfillment of wishes. This looks promising, because science makes progress by finding universal laws, sweeping generalizations that have no exceptions. But how does Freud deal with possible falsifications—cases of dreams which don't appear to be wish-fulfillments, such as nightmares and 'anxiety dreams'? At times Freud recognizes that this is a problem for his theory and promises to address it more fully but never does. Freud alternates between accepting that this is an unresolved problem and curtly dismissing it as already answered. *Some* of these dreams, says Freud, can be explained by saying that they fulfill the 'wish' to make the psychoanalyst appear to be wrong, thus confirming his theory. Nonetheless, those dreams motivated by the wish to make the analyst appear to be right are not withdrawn as support for the theory. They too confirm the theory. The result is that no possible dream would be allowed to contradict the theory that all dreams are wish-fulfillments. Freud's theory that all dreams are wish-fulfillments is not scientific, because no conceivable example of a dream could ever be accepted as showing it to be false.[1]

For forty years the late Sidney Hook took every opportunity to ask psychoanalysts the question: How could we tell if a child did not have an Oedipus Complex? (He could have asked: How could we tell if an adult had not gone through

---

[1] Popper 1983, 163–173.

an Oedipal phase?) The numerous psychoanalysts queried were all at a loss to give a sensible answer to this simple question, some of them responding by attacking Hook as a peculiarly twisted person for asking it.[2]

The Method of Free Association

The standard method in psychoanalysis is to ask the patient to relate a dream, and then to ask the patient to say the first word that springs to mind when an element of the dream is mentioned. When the patient says this word, the analyst asks the patient to say the next word that springs to mind, and so on, for as many stages as the analyst wishes. This is the method of free association.

For example, a patient dreamed of a pair of horses. Asked to free-associate on the word 'horses', the patient produced the word 'whores'.[3] The patient was then asked to free-associate on the word 'whores', and came up with another word, which was in its turn free-associated on.

Let's consider just the first step in this free association. If 'horses' means 'whores', then this indicates that there had been an unconscious thought of whores which had gotten transformed into a dream image of horses. An unconscious thought of whores caused horses to appear in a dream. (This hackneyed psychoanalytic idea was copied in the notorious dream in *The Sopranos*, Season Five, where Tony Soprano dreams he's riding a horse inside his house, and his wife Carmela tells him he can't keep bringing his horse into the house.)

Does the production of 'whores' by free association show that the dream horses were transformed whores? In other words, if someone says 'whores' when asked to free-associate on the word 'horse', does this show that this person's dream of horses was caused by his unconscious thought of whores? If the answer to this question is 'No', then psychoanalysis is on a level with the tarot, the *Yijing*, or tea-leaf reading.

---

[2] Hook 1959, 214–19.
[3] Kahn 2002, 159.

Just consider one implication of a 'Yes' answer: that if we had done the free association an hour earlier or later, the word 'whores' would have been provided just the same. We can't directly test this possibility, but it doesn't seem self-evidently true. It surely seems reasonable that the same person has dozens of different possible associations with the word 'horse', and which of them arises on any particular occasion may depend upon various minor circumstances.

One sign of a problem is that different psychoanalysts will get different results with similar patients. You might wonder how this can be, if the psychoanalyst merely allows the patient to free-associate and does not direct the patient. In practice, though, the individual psychoanalyst's outlook affects the situation in two ways. First, the patient usually knows something in advance about the particular psychoanalyst's approach. Second, even an unusually scrupulous psychoanalyst does direct the patient, for example, by remaining silent or sounding encouraging, by stopping with a certain word, or by asking the patient to free-associate again on that word.

To a non-Freudian therapist, the patient would not be so ready to come up with 'whores', with its sexual meaning. The patient might come up with 'courses' (from 'horses for courses'), and this might indicate that the patient unconsciously felt himself to be ill-suited to some college course he was enrolled in. The patient might come up with 'carriage', and this easily leads to marriage or the idea of convenient transportation (and therefore of leaving his current situation). The patient might say 'race', and according to the predilections of the analyst, this might lead to ethnic groups, or gambling, or electoral politics.

Early in the history of psychoanalysis there were breakaways from the movement. Adler and Jung both broke with Freud, and both denied Freud's theory that unconscious ideas are generally related to infantile sex. Adler developed a theory that the unconscious ideas were related to feelings of inferiority, while Jung developed a more spiritual conception, according to which the unconscious is filled with age-old symbols signifying what Jung called 'archetypes'.

It was soon noticed that patients who went to see Adlerian analysts had Adlerian dreams, patients who went to see Jungian analysts had Jungian dreams, and patients who went to see Freudian analysts had Freudian dreams. The problem is that no independent, objective method exists for comparing the merits of the three systems of dream interpretation. There are also thousands of other possible ways, in addition to those of Freud, Adler, and Jung, in which any dream might be interpreted. It's even conceivable (not our view, but it is conceivable) that there is an unconscious mind which does affect all our actions and cause us emotional problems, and no one knows anything about it—no one has yet figured out what's in the unconscious mind and how it affects us. The practical result of that for psychotherapy would be the same as the conclusion that there is no unconscious mind.

Adlerians, Jungians, and Freudians all had plenty of confirmation of their theories. Yet if any one of these three theoretical systems is true, the other two must be false. And since it is certain that at least two of the three must be false, it becomes easy to see that all three might be false. How would we know?

Furthermore, even two psychoanalysts of the same school, two Freudians or two Jungians, for example, may well arrive at quite different interpretations of the same dream. The situation is very different from physics or chemistry, where an experiment can be done by thousands of different scientists, and the result will be the same. It's a requirement of experiments in physics and chemistry that they must be reproducible. If occasionally an already known experiment doesn't turn out the way it's expected to, it can be done again, probably with closer attention to all the conditions and controls, and usually then the expected result will occur. (If it doesn't, we may begin to wonder whether the earlier and now expected results were correct after all.) In sciences where controlled, reproducible experiments are not feasible, like astronomy, most observations have to be reproducible. Anyone can get a telescope and check that the planet Jupiter is just where the theory says it should be, and that it has several moons, just as earlier observations had claimed.

If a large-scale study of human beings is conducted, to decide whether a new drug works, whether left-handed people are more intelligent than right-handed, or whether redheads are more hot-tempered than blondes, the precise details of the study can be reported, and someone else can later try to do a similar study, perhaps fine-tuned to remove any flaws that critics might have pointed out in the first study. Usually the results of such studies are not accepted and written into textbooks until they have been repeated several times, by several independent teams of researchers.

In the world of psychoanalysis, there's nothing like this. A psychoanalyst listens to a patient, several times a week over several years. The analyst and the patient together explore the patient's unconscious mind (by discussing the patient's dreams and having the patient free-associate) and eventually decide what was troubling the patient. This can't be reviewed or checked in any way. If the patient never comes to accept the psychoanalyst's conclusions, this merely shows the patient's resistance; it does not put psychoanalysis in doubt, or even that particular psychoanalyst's opinions. We have to trust the conclusions of the analyst. The qualification for you to become a psychoanalyst is to be analyzed yourself by a psychoanalyst. (In the early days of psychoanalysis, even this requirement was not always imposed: the only qualification was that Dr. Freud liked you.)

No one can become a qualified psychoanalyst by passing a blind-graded test or by demonstrating any kind of skill. No one could ever become a psychoanalyst while proclaiming that psychoanalysis is pure bullshit, while there is nothing to stop anyone becoming a nuclear physicist, a medical doctor, or an accountant, proclaiming that these areas are pure bullshit. In these fields, it is possible to measure people's competence without paying any attention to their beliefs.

One psychoanalyst may arrive at a conclusion about a patient which would be entirely different from the conclusion that would be reached by another psychoanalyst. How can we devise some test which will enable us to say that the one conclusion is true and the other is false? It's difficult to come up with such a test, because both theories are based on free association and the analysis of dreams in terms of symbols; both experience and common sense tell us that this whole approach can lead in many different directions. As a result, and quite inevitably, the results of 'analysis' will confirm the beliefs of the analyst, whatever these may be. Freudians, Adlerians, Jungians, Reichians, Rankians, Kleinians, and Horneyites will all say that the conclusions were arrived at by considering the results of free association. But the vastly different conclusions show that the personal convictions of the analyst are decisive in determining what is concluded from the experience of free association.

This line of criticism was made early in the history of psychoanalysis, especially after Adler and Jung had each gone their separate ways. The general response was twofold:

1. **The people who follow that other school of so-called psychoanalysis are mentally ill.**

2. **We know our brand of psychoanalysis is correct because of its clinical results.**

'Clinical results' means whatever happens in the sessions involving analyst and patient. It suggests that the psychoanalytic method has been successful in some way that can be shown from these sessions. How can we test this claim? Analysts may get the impression that they have been successful, but the history of quack medicines, faith healing, and other ineffective treatments shows many times over that practitioners of ineffective healing methods may easily convince themselves that they have had successes. Some apparent 'successes' will occur anyway, as a substantial percentage of emotional problems go away by themselves after a while, with or without any form of treatment (it's called 'spontaneous remission'). As the testing of new drugs illustrates, to show that some treatment is effective requires a fairly elaborate statistical test: if you merely listen to anecdotes told by sincere enthusiasts for the method you can easily go astray.

Freud and his followers resisted the suggestion that psychoanalysis should be subjected to rigorous outcome studies. But proponents of the new non-psychoanalytic therapies that began to emerge in the 1940s through the 1960s were usually strongly in favor of such studies. Many such studies have now been done, and are being done all the time, and they consistently show that, while all major forms of psychotherapy (including even psychoanalysis) do some good, psychoanalysis and methods of psychotherapy closest to psychoanalysis have the least beneficial impact.[4]

Slips of the Tongue

After explaining dreams, Freud went on to explain slips of the tongue and other mistakes. We sometimes mis-speak, and Freud argued that such cases are never random or accidental: they always say something about our true thoughts or feelings. Just like dreams, their true meaning can be uncovered by the method of free association.

He gives the example of someone who goes up to a grieving widow at her husband's funeral and says "Please let me offer my congratulations." This, mistakenly substituting "congratulations" for "condolences," might in some circumstances be an embarrassing indication of the speaker's real thoughts. Just such occurrences have become known as 'Freudian slips', and it is supposed that they do reveal something about unconscious thoughts.

However, when the slip has an embarrassing message, we tend to remember it. If the slip has no such implication, we forget it. It's a bit like the case of psychics who predict events such as the assassination of a president. Such things are predicted by psychics all the time, and are most often untrue, but by coincidence they will occasionally be right. The occa-

---

[4] See footnote 2 to Chapter 1.

sional correct predictions are impressive when taken in isolation. Similarly, most slips of the tongue do not have any clearly identifiable hidden or embarrassing meaning. But by chance some will have such a meaning and these may stick in our minds; this does not show that the embarrassing or hidden meaning caused the slip of the tongue.

Since only a few slips of the tongue have an immediately recognizable 'hidden' meaning, it shouldn't be supposed that the great majority of slips, which have no such meaning, are dismissed by Freud as irrelevant. Freud maintains that all slips in every case have a dangerous hidden meaning caused by 'forgetting'. Precisely the cases where no such hidden meaning is apparent, Freud analyzes to show that there is a hidden meaning, which is almost invariably sexual.

When one of the authors was aged about eighteen he bought a coffee in a cafeteria where, it turned out, there were no free tables. But there was one large table with only one occupant, an attractive young woman. He approached the table and said: "Do you mind if I sleep here?" We pounce on this example, and remember it, as a 'Freudian slip'. Yet the vast majority of slips have no such obvious explanation in terms of sex or of plausible hidden motives. Furthermore, even cases like this do not corroborate the Freudian theory because the motive is not hidden from the person who makes the slip; there is no resistance and no repression; the person is quite ready to acknowledge the motive 'revealed' by the utterance. The tiny minority of cases where there is an obvious sexual meaning are used as evidence for the vast majority of cases where there is no obvious sexual meaning. And yet the 'obvious' examples don't really count, because if the meaning is readily apparent, it can't have been repressed.

Freud Slips Up

Let's now take a look at Freud's most famous analysis of a slip of the tongue. It's in Latin, but you don't have to know any Latin to follow this discussion.

Freud cites the case of a young man he once met who quoted a line of Latin poetry, but got it wrong, omitting the Latin word 'aliquis' (someone). Convinced that the omission or 'forgetting' of this word had to mean something important, Freud asked the young man to free associate on the word 'aliquis'. The young man came up with the German word 'Reliquien' (relics), which sounds a bit like 'aliquis'. (The young man, like Freud, was a native German speaker.) He was then asked to free-associate on 'Reliquien', and this process was taken through several more stages. The result was that, by a series of connections, the young man was led from the word 'aliquis' to his fear that a young woman he had recently been with might have missed her period, probably making him a father.

Freud claimed that this was a demonstration of the cause of the slip in dropping the word 'aliquis', and Freud also showed that we could move by stages from 'aliquis' to the feared missed period *by several alternative routes*. To Freud, these additional routes constituted further proof that anxiety about a missed period was the cause of the slip.

This example has been criticized ever since it was first published, and in the 1970s these criticisms were summed up by the Italian linguist, Sebastiano Timpanaro.[5] Timpanaro pointed out that we could, by Freud's technique of association, move from one word to the next in a number of different ways: similarity of sound, similarity of meaning, or abstract connection. (As an example of abstract connection, Freud takes the alleged miracle in which the blood painted on the church statue of a saint is supposed to periodically liquefy, causing the statue to 'bleed', and links this with menstruation.)

Now, if we can get from one term to another by these different methods, and each time move freely from one language to another, then it ought to be obvious that we can easily get from any one idea *to any other idea* in a few steps. The fact that we can do this in several different ways ought to alert us to the totally bogus nature of what we're doing.

---

[5] Timpanaro 1976. See Macmillan 1997, 569–570.

101

Timpanaro then takes in turn each word (other than 'aliquis') in the line misquoted by the young man, and asks us to suppose that this other word had been dropped from the quotation. He shows that we can get just as quickly and just as 'convincingly' from each of these words to the notion of a missed period.

Since any of the words could get us to the missed period—or the planet Mercury, or a pink monkey, or a rainbow, or eternal torture in Hell—why was the word 'aliquis' dropped and not one of the other words? Here Timpanaro points out that there's an obvious explanation for the omission of the word 'aliquis' (obvious to those who know Latin). The correct Latin line[6] is unusual, odd, and difficult to translate, whereas omission of the word 'aliquis' leaves a very ordinary Latin line, which translates quite naturally into German. Timpanaro points out that this process, called 'banalization', turning a strange or difficult-to-interpret series of words into a much more ordinary and easy-to-remember phrase, is very common in the history of documents that were copied down repeatedly before the invention of printing.

This case is given pride of place in *The Psychopathology of Everyday Life*. It's Freud's Exhibit A; he devotes an entire chapter to it. He's obviously very pleased with himself for being able to do this analysis, and he thinks that it's irresistible evidence for his theory of slips. (Being inordinately vain, he is also delighted to show off the fact that he can read several languages and recall entire lines from the classics.) Yet the example doesn't bear out Freud's theory. Obviously, the young man, worried about the possible pregnancy of his lady acquaintance, has not *forgotten* this possibility. Why would the young man's unconscious go to such ingenious lengths to disguise some topic, when it is at all times bathed in the bright light of his conscious awareness?

---

[6] "Exoriare aliquis nostris ex ossibus ultor." 'Let someone, an avenger, arise from my bones.' As well as dropping the word 'aliquis', the young man got the words 'nostris ex' in the wrong order. We won't pursue this detail here.

In fact, we could go further: couldn't the likelihood of words thrown up in free association be influenced by current, conscious preoccupations? Isn't it possible that whatever happens to be currently weighing on your mind might cause you to throw out a related word in free association? There would then be a tendency for *any* free association, beginning with *any* word, to move toward the issue that was consciously preoccupying you—exactly the opposite of Freud's theory of repression.

The other curiosity is that recent scholarship indicates that, almost certainly, the incident never occurred, or never occurred to a young man Freud had met.[7] In other words, Freud very likely invented the incident (as we know he habitually fabricated such accounts), perhaps by ruminating on an episode in his own life, in which he was afraid a romantic partner might have become pregnant (both Freud and the young man in the story were Jewish Austrians). So even an anecdote that Freud made up, a piece of fiction designed to provide the best possible proof of his theory, doesn't really corroborate the theory at all.

Why We Make Slips

Why do we make slips of the tongue or slips of the finger on the computer keyboard? Freud assumes that the mind operates with perfect efficiency unless some specific, powerful influence causes it to malfunction. But the human mind is imperfect and prone to error. No special explanation is necessary for mistakes. Perhaps some of them are random.

In most cases, however, we can see quite clearly why we make slips, and there's no mystery about it. This is an odd thing about Freud's theory of slips: he doesn't offer a false hypothesis to account for something puzzling. He offers a false hypothesis when we already know the correct explanation! When we speak or type, we are calling upon certain skilled routines we have learned. These routines operate

---

[7] Swales 1982, Sections III–VI.

'on automatic pilot'—we don't carefully plan out most of the sentences we utter, for example; we compose them freely, utilizing certain learned skills, and *loosely monitoring* our exercise of these skills. This is like the way a pianist plays scales. When she was learning the scales, she paid attention to which finger was hitting which note, but now that she has learned the scales, she doesn't think about this, but she does loosely monitor her playing of the scales, so that if she makes a mistake (for example, playing a note with a wrong finger), she notices it, then deliberately pays more attention, and corrects herself.

When we speak, we speak in sentences, yet we don't rehearse these sentences in our minds before we speak them; we make them up as we go along; we start sentences without knowing exactly how they will end. But we do loosely monitor ourselves. This loose monitoring is not perfect, and occasionally an error gets through, just as some spelling mistakes get through our computer spell check: if we type 'plaice' when we mean 'place', our spell check will not alert us, and neither will our grammar check, since both words are perfectly good English nouns. Just as word-processing programs have an automatic spell check and an automatic grammar check, so we, when we are speaking or writing, have an automatic 'intelligibility check', programmed into our brains by years of familiarity with the language (and before that, by millions of years of natural selection of hominid language use).

Suppose that we change our phone number. Then someone asks us for our number, and 'without thinking' we give our old number. Surely this is straightforward enough: we have got the habit of giving our old number, and we need to train ourselves to replace that habit with a different one.

Another influence favoring slips of the tongue is immediately prior mention. For example, if a group of people have been discussing Tom Cruise and then the conversation turns to Matt Damon, it's almost certain that one of the participants will soon say 'Tom Cruise' when she really means Matt

Damon. It's as if the preceding mentions of Tom Cruise have fooled the intelligibility check, by signaling that the words 'Tom Cruise' have earned a pass.

The 'prior mention' may, however, be something general in the culture. During President Clinton's second term, there was considerable media discussion of the Whitewater scandal, involving alleged wrongdoing by Clinton and his wife when he had been Governor of Arkansas. On numerous occasions, TV talking heads would say 'Watergate' when they evidently meant to say 'Whitewater'. 'Watergate' is the name of a scandal twenty years earlier, which led to the resignation of President Nixon. Sometimes this would be noticed and would prompt amused comments, other times it apparently passed without the discussants noticing it at all.

A Freudian would say that the substitution of 'white' for 'gate', and its move from after water to before water, signified something about a phantasy in the minds of these TV pundits, dating back to their first six years of life. Since a gate symbolizes the female genitals, water can often mean vaginal fluid, and in front and behind have many sexual associations, it's simple enough to come up with something sufficiently tasty for a psychoanalyst.

But surely there's no mystery about why people would sometimes say 'Watergate' when they intended to say 'Whitewater'. Watergate and Whitewater are both three-syllable names, including the component 'water', denoting locations, and both signify presidential scandals leading to long-drawn-out inquiries involving congressional hearings, and possible impeachment. Furthermore, Watergate was far more notorious than Whitewater, preceded it in time, and became such a by-word for any kind of governmental scandal that the suffix '-gate' was routinely added to subsequent scandals by journalists. Given all these circumstances, it was inevitable that many people would make the slip of the tongue of saying 'Watergate' when they meant to say 'Whitewater'. A Freudian explanation, apart from being excruciatingly silly, is entirely unnecessary.

The dropping of the word 'aliquis' can be fully explained by the well-known phenomenon of banalization. Before the invention of printing, books and other documents had to be copied out by hand, by professional scribes. Sometimes scribes would make errors. But they do not make these errors completely randomly. One common pattern is that the scribe would change a phrase to make it less odd, more ordinary. When scholars have two different readings of an ancient manuscript, they often use their knowledge of this process to help decide which is the earlier or more authentic version. A scribe will comparatively often make the mistake of changing a strange phrase to a common phrase, far less often changing a common phrase to a strange one.

We can see this process of banalization at work all the time. For instance, 'Kashmir', a well-known song by Led Zeppelin, has the line "I am a traveler *of* both time and space'. But most people if asked to remember the words, will remember this as "I am a traveler *in* both time and space', since this is the more common way of expressing that approximate idea in English. Shakespeare has the famous line, "We are such stuff as dreams are made *on*," but most people will remember this as "We are such stuff as dreams are made *of*."

Banalization is just one of the processes involved when mistakes arise in the copying of texts. Among those mentioned by Timpanaro (whose scholarly background was the study of ancient texts) are the influence of context (where a word is changed to be more like a word that accompanies it, similarity in the mistaken word for the original word, such as the same number of syllables, 'polar errors', where a word is replaced by one meaning the opposite, and repeating something that originally was stated only once.

Sometimes, the resemblance may not be immediately obvious and may relate to the personal knowledge of the individual making the slip. Recently the 1950s TV series, *Have Gun, Will Travel* came up in conversation. One person referred to the actor playing the main character as "Jack Palance." Then this person (who is not a psychologist and not especially interested in verbal slips) immediately saw his error and diagnosed why he had committed it. The name of the hero of *Have Gun, Will Travel* is Paladin. Both Jack

Palance and Richard Boone, who actually played Paladin, were notable for being ugly. They were actors of roughly the same generation, who often played in westerns. Jack Palance was much better known—and even uglier—than Richard Boone. Boone is an easily forgettable commonplace name, Palance more distinctive, as well as having a similarity to 'Paladin'. In examples like this, we see that the slip can be explained without bringing in unconscious desires or repressed memories.

Free association is the method by which Freud attempted to diagnose the underlying meaning of dreams, slips, and neurotic symptoms. Only if free association is reliable can there be any validity to psychoanalysis. Freud makes a connection between an occurrence in a dream, a slip, or a piece of behavior, and some supposed unconscious thought. The connection is a chain of associations. The only way to uncover this chain of associations is free association. But free association is, we believe, seriously unreliable. It is not objective, since it is always directed by the psychoanalyst's expectations. It does not give the same results when it is used by different psychoanalysts. We doubt very much whether it would give the same results with the same patient on different occasions.

In the early years of psychoanalysis, it was common to explain all mistakes or accidents, such as cutting your finger when you're chopping onions or running over a dog with your car, as meaningful slips that must have an unconscious motivation rooted in childhood sexuality. This theory seems to have died away without much discussion, presumably because psychoanalysts are just as accident-prone as anyone else.

Objections to Narrow Freudianism

Orthodox Freudian psychoanalysts insist that everyone above the age of six, without exception, has an Oedipus Complex (wanting to bump off Dad in order to have more fun with Mom). These complexes must have arisen toward the end of the first six years of life—later phantasies, experiences, or desires don't count. Any man, for example, who recalls wanting to have sex with his mother at the age of ten, has not got to the root of his Oedipus Complex, but is being fooled by his unconscious, which has thrown up this screen memory to shield him from the horrific reality of his true Oedipal phantasy.

For this theory to be true, every child, aged from three to six, must:

1. **understand what the sex act is**

2. **understand what killing someone is**

3. **spontaneously feel that wanting sex with a parent is unbearably shameful**

And these three thought processes must be going on in the unconscious mind, which, the psychoanalysts assure us, is the realm of 'primary process', a type of illogical, associative thought (though the unconscious mind must also have an IQ of 200 and a doctorate in classics). But some six-year-olds don't have much of an inkling of what the sex act is. They haven't had the opportunity to pick up that information. And children are not born with a moral sense that would tell them that sex with a parent is wrong; morality is acquired gradually. Six-year-olds do understand something about death, and do sometimes wish people dead, without feeling in the least bit guilty about that wish, and Freudians accept that. The Freudian claim is that the arousal of sexual desire is what evokes shame. The psychoanalysts claim that the kids spontaneously feel so horribly guilty that this stamps them for life. But why would a five-year-old, feeling sexually aroused by the thought of Mom's body, feel at all guilty about that? That it is somehow inappropriate to be sexually aroused by certain classes of people is something that has to be learned, picked up from the culture, and it's doubtful that all five-year-olds without exception have learned it. (G.K. Chesterton made this point against psychoanalysis in the early 1920s.)

A psychoanalyst might respond to the above by saying: The four- or five-year-old does not need to have developed a moral sense. He merely needs to be afraid that he will be castrated by his father as punishment for desiring his mother. This fear of castration is the basis of the sense of morality that develops later. But this interpretation merely shifts the problem. Why would a four-year-old jump to the conclusion that wanting sex with his mother would be punishable by castration? Why would this thought occur, not just to some children, but to every single human child without exception?

Freud's writings are filled with examples in which he surmises that someone in their early childhood witnessed their parents having sex, or witnessed the genitalia of someone of the opposite sex, or was threatened with castration. Freud seems to suppose at times that such experiences account for adult disturbances, yet his theory requires that everyone must have had such experiences. But what of children who completely miss out on any of these experiences? What about a child who, by the age of six, knows nothing of the sex act or of the anatomical differences between the sexes, and has never heard a threat of castration? What about a girl raised entirely by women, without ever seeing a male before puberty? Where did all these people get their Oedipus Complexes? Freudians absolutely insist that every human has had an Oedipal phase, but how is that possible? Freudians wouldn't accept that the Oedipus Complex is genetically programmed.

At the very least, we might expect that people who missed out on any or all of these experiences might show some difference in personality. But as a matter of fact that's false. Persons reared by a single parent, or by siblings without parental involvement, or by two or more caregivers of the same sex (either sex), turn out just the same, as far as anyone has been able to observe, as persons reared in a classic nuclear family.

Early in the history of psychoanalysis, critics pointed out that children don't display any signs of anxiety when their parents are affectionate with each other. Quite the contrary, they look pleased. When Mom and Dad kiss and cuddle, the little ones clap their hands with pure delight. This makes evolutionary sense, because if the parents get on well, the child's future is likely to be more secure. We might expect the kids' Oedipal jealousy to make them anxious, but we observe the opposite. Freudians must conclude that the anxiety is there, though repressed. But there's no way to test this by observation.

Broad Freudianism

We have noted the weirdness of Freud's interpretations. But more recent psychodynamic therapists may keep the basic Freudian model of the mind, while coming up with much less bizarre or sensational interpretations. For instance, a man might fall in love with a woman, and the therapist might say that he chose this particular woman because she reminded him in certain respects of his mother. The client may dispute this, but the therapist may say that being reminded of his mother is unconscious, and the client's rejection of this suggestion only goes to show that it is true. Eventually, the therapist may even convince the client that it's true.

Unlike Freud's typical interpretations, this one is not at all bizarre; it's very ordinary, and would not have shocked any dramatist during the last thousand years. It might even be true in some cases. It's obvious and undisputed that a man may be drawn to a specific woman because she reminds him of his mother, and the man might be unaware of this, as we are all unaware of some of the past influences that affect our current preferences. There is, however, no particular reason why the man in question would 'resist' this explanation once it occurs to him. And, after all, it might not be true. Guessing whether this kind of thing is true or not in individual cases is an uncertain business.

Furthermore, we would expect a man to be attracted to someone like his mother, for reasons other than his infant interactions with her: we're attracted to people who look like us because they share our genes. A person might be attracted to someone like his mother because of this genetic affinity (even if, for example, his mother died in giving him birth, and he was raised by someone who looked and acted very differently). Here, as in many attempts to account for individual behavior, an observer might be in no position to decide between parental influence, genetic affinity, some third possibility, or a combination of any two or all three of these.

Perhaps the broadest of all broad Freudian ideas is the theory that the way our parents treated us has played a major role in giving us the kind of personality we have, that the interaction of parents with young children is crucial for the children's mental health when they have become adults. This idea has become so widespread that many people don't even know that it came to us from Freud, and even many people who think of themselves as solidly anti-Freudian continue to accept it without question. Yet there's now plenty of evidence to show that this idea is one more Freudian blunder. The way parents relate to their children in the years from three to six has very little impact on the way the children will turn out as adults.[8]

---

[8] For a good summary of the evidence on this, see Paris 2000. If you're still not convinced, read Rowe 1994 or Harris 2009 and you will be.

6
Therapy Before Ellis

Down through the millennia, as long as there have been walking, talking humans, there has been psychotherapy. Some humans have wanted to help other humans with their problems. People's problems may be of a purely practical nature, like how to get enough food to stay alive, but they may sometimes be emotional or behavioral: this person sits around all day feeling sad and moping, that person always wants to pick a fight. This person is terribly afraid of something that other people don't usually find so very frightening, that person never gets around to doing what he believes he had better do.

We've already mentioned the pioneering psychotherapy of Buddhism in ancient India and Stoicism in ancient Greece and Rome. But we will skip over most of the psychotherapy that was done prior to the end of the nineteenth century. The reason is simple: in this book we're trying to give you an idea of what present-day psychotherapy is like and where it came from. Present-day psychotherapy begins with Freud. All the many schools of psychotherapy you are likely to run into originated with Freudian psychoanalysis. Most of them reacted against psychoanalysis and rejected it but they were nearly always led and promoted by people who began as psychoanalysts. They paid almost no attention to pre-Freudian psychotherapy.

From 1909 to 1930, psychoanalysis grew very rapidly in the United States. It was like an avalanche which completely engulfed all the pre-existing types of psychotherapy still being practiced. Anything that survived from pre-Freudian psychotherapy had a comparatively tiny following, and anyway, if it did survive at all, its practitioners soon started talking about Freud and how they related to Freud, often absorbing large elements of Freudian theory.

When Freud, Jung, and Ferenczi visited the US together in 1909, the newspapers were paying more attention to the Emmanuel movement, a program of psychotherapy promoted by people within the Emmanuel Episcopalian church in Boston. This kind of thing was already called 'psychotherapy'—Greek for 'mind treatment'. Although conceived within the Episcopalian church, the therapy itself was not primarily religious, but quite objective and sensible. The Emmanuel movement was mainly concerned with problem drinking, but it dealt with other emotional and behavioral problems too. Freud was asked by an American reporter what he thought of it and gave a dismissive comment. Those working in the Emmanuel clinic did not design their program of treatment on Freudian lines, but they were aware of Freud and began to refer to Freud more and more.

Earlier, in the mid-nineteenth century, American philosophers like William James and Josiah Royce were developing methods of psychotherapy. As you will have guessed, having gotten this far in *Therapy Breakthrough*, these pre-Freudian forms of psychotherapy were superior to Freudian psychoanalysis: their theories of the mind were sounder and we have no doubt that their effectiveness at providing real help to clients was better. Albert Ellis more than once remarked that Freud put back the development of psychotherapy by fifty years.

Schisms in the Freudian Church

Throughout his life, Sigmund Freud repeatedly had associates whom he admired and shared ideas with, then fell out with and denounced. In the 1890s he quarreled with Dr. Josef Breuer, formerly his close friend and co-author of his first book, *Studies on Hysteria* (1895). The chief reason for the breach was that Breuer, while lavishing praise on Freud and showing him great personal kindness, would not agree with Freud's claim that virtually all neuroses are due to sexual upsets.

As Freud broke with Breuer, he developed a close friendship and collaboration with Dr. Wilhelm Fliess. Freud and Fliess ceased to be friendly in 1900, when it became clear to Freud that Fliess's theories were incompatible with his own.

With both Breuer and Fliess there was the same pattern: Freud maintained some of the ideas that his collaborator had contributed, and made them part of his subsequent thinking, but attacked the collaborators for disagreements. Freud diagnosed the persons with whom he had serious disagreements as mentally sick, and relied on this diagnosis instead of seriously analyzing their arguments. And Freud repeatedly adopted a posture of vilification toward his former friends, refusing to communicate with them or grant them even routine courtesy.

From 1900 on, Freud was the celebrated author of *The Interpretation of Dreams*. Freud now attracted disciples. Freud and a small group of his followers began meeting regularly for Wednesday evening discussions, starting in 1902. Freud dissolved and then re-instituted this "Wednesday Society" in 1907–1908, making acceptance of Freudian theory a condition of membership. It was renamed the Vienna Psychoanalytic Society.

As with the origin of many ideological movements, political or religious, the little band of followers were filled with enthusiasm, with a sense of the importance of their new discoveries, and with burning admiration for their leader. But what would happen when some of the individuals involved began to think for themselves and develop ideas contrary to those of the leader? Would free debate and a diversity of views prevail? This might have led to the voluntary and amicable separation of the group into several smaller groups with partly overlapping interests and some differences in fundamental theory. Or it might have led to the evolution of the group into a broad forum not attached to any single doctrine. Alternatively, would deviations in theory be met with hostility and slander against the innovative thinkers? Unfortunately Freud's cult followed the latter, more common pattern.

The Expulsion of Adler

The first big rift in the Psychoanalytic movement was the expulsion of Alfred Adler. Adler's thinking at first seemed to be compatible with Freud's. He made innovations which Freud accepted. Freud considered him the best psychoanalyst, aside from himself, in Vienna, and sent his brother's wife to Adler for treatment.

In 1906 Adler began to develop his theory of 'organ inferiority'. He noticed that some great orators had suffered speech defects as children and that other outstanding achievers sometimes suffered from defects related to their area of achievement. He generalized this into a theory that individuals strive to overcome feelings of inferiority, and coined the well-known term, 'inferiority complex'.

Adler's rejection of Freud's ideas became gradually more conspicuous. Adler emerged as an independent theorist, prepared to disagree with the leader. This could be because he unconsciously wanted to kill his father.[1] Adler propounded a theory of 'masculine protest': that boys exaggerate aspects of culturally defined masculinity, as a defense against feelings of helplessness, perceived as feminine. In 1910 Adler openly questioned Freud's view that all neuroses must be rooted in sexual problems. He also suggested that if a patient came to fully recognize his Oedipus Complex, this would not guarantee any improvement. Although Adler never questioned Freud's view that emotional problems are rooted in early childhood, he placed more emphasis on the way these prob-

---

[1] Just kidding.

116

lems play out in the here-and-now, and he was more ready than Freud to take the patient's conscious thoughts seriously.

After some acrimonious discussions, Freud had Adler and his followers kicked out of the movement. Although, technically, Adler left voluntarily, Freud wrote to his then loyal follower Carl Jung: "yesterday I forced the whole Adler gang . . . to resign from the Society."[2] Adler's sins were attributed to his insane ambition, his mental disorders such as paranoia, his "resistance" to Freud's contention that all neuroses are exclusively sexual in origin, and his quarrelsome nature. The truth is that Adler was never given to quarrels and co-operated very well with many diverse people during his unusually active life, whereas Freud rarely had a serious disagreement with anyone without (sooner or later) quarreling with them, and was forever conducting a vendetta or purge against some heretical individual or group whom he wanted to hound out of his movement.

Unlike Freud, Adler was never a polished writer. Even the most formal of his expositions have something of the character of hurriedly prepared talks. Unlike the always conceited Freud, Adler was unpretentious and informal. Since his ideas were more commonsensical and closer to everyday observation, it was easy for Freudians to portray Adler's theories as 'superficial'.

Adler's influence did not end with his expulsion. Although for a long time his movement, called Individual Psychology, could not seriously challenge official psychoanalysis, it has steadily recruited support over the decades and has survived to see the once-mighty Freudian movement crumble away discredited.

Sticking It to Stekel

Following the break with Adler came the breach with Wilhelm Stekel. Stekel was a closer follower of Freud's ideas than Adler, though at the time of the Adler expulsion he

---

[2] Webster 1995, 360.

agreed with Adler in arguing for open debate within the movement.

Freud and Stekel disagreed on masturbation, Freud maintaining that masturbation leads to physical and mental deterioration, Stekel arguing (as Adler did) that masturbation is harmless. Freud never abandoned his conviction that masturbation, any form of oral sex, homosexuality, and all other 'perversions' are seriously harmful. Prior to Freud, the leading authority on varying sexual practices was Richard Krafft-Ebing. In early editions of his *Psychopathia Sexualis*, Krafft-Ebing took the view that homosexuality is a disorder, but in the last edition he acknowledged that homosexuality is normal. At that point the anti-homosexual Freud had become fashionable, and Krafft-Ebing's change of opinion therefore had little influence. Freud also bequeathed to the psychoanalytic movement (and thereby to conventional thinking in the United States) his unfortunate theory of the 'vaginal orgasm', as contrasted with the 'immature' clitoral orgasm.

Freud drove Stekel out of the movement. When he could not remove Stekel as editor of the psychoanalytic journal, he persuaded all the other analysts associated with the journal to resign, leaving Stekel with an empty position, and then founded a new journal.

The same pattern occurred with Adler and Stekel as earlier with Breuer and Fliess and subsequently with all later heretics: 1. Freud turned against them when they contradicted him on a point of theory, which he saw as a threat; 2. He broke off all connection, vilified the person, and rejected any friendly overtures; 3. He blamed the breach entirely on the other person, and ascribed it to that person's mental illness; 4. In denouncing the other person's views, he made almost no attempt to refute them by reasoned argument, but did little more than point out that they disagreed with official psychoanalytic doctrine; 5. He continued to maintain some of the views first proposed by the other person, though playing down his indebtedness to that person; 6. He or his supporters disseminated misleading claims about the other person and misrepresented the character of the breach.

In Stekel's case, the original ideas were those on dream symbolism which Freud incorporated in *The Interpretation of Dreams*. Freud's later advocacy of a 'death instinct' was lifted without acknowledgment from Stekel. The possibly true though unproven claims, spread by Freud's loyal soldier Ernest Jones, were to the effect that Stekel had fabricated case histories.

The Secret Committee

Freud and his loyal disciples had got rid of Adler and Stekel. We see here the clear pattern of the growth of a cult. The un-talented disciples perceive an advantage to themselves in sniffing out misguided, dangerous ideas, and at the same time, any impulses toward independent critical thought are discouraged by the spectacle of what could happen to heretics.

The disciples therefore have a dual motive in flattering the leader rather than criticizing him, and in conducting witch hunts against dissidents, especially more talented dis-sidents: fear of expulsion and desire for advancement. In re-turn for attacking the heretics, the disciples' position in the movement is made safe—they gain status and therefore perks because of their reliability—and they will be promoted in return for blind kowtowing to the leader's dogmas.

As soon as Adler and Stekel were out of the way, the Freudians could see the signs of other menacing challenges to the pure Freudian doctrine. A clash with Carl Jung loomed on the horizon. Encouraged by Freud, the cult-followers Jones, Ferenczi, and Rank organized a Secret Committee to control the psychoanalytic movement. Freud arranged for each committee member to wear a ring with a specially de-signed insignia. This covert body was the real government of the movement, and acted to root out all threats to orthodox ideas and to the unchallenged supremacy of the leader. Ex-actly the same pattern can be seen in the history of many re-ligious cults and in secular movements like Communism in the 1920s.

The Secret Committee ruled psychoanalysis with an iron grip from 1912 until 1927. It controlled the membership of all psychoanalytic societies, and determined, behind the scenes, exactly what could be published in psychoanalytic journals. The committee comprised Jones, Ferenczi, Rank, Abraham, Sachs, and Eitingon. As generally happens in such cults, two members of this inner circle were themselves eventually purged: first Rank, with Ferenczi yapping at his heels, and then Ferenczi.

The Break with Jung

For eight years, Carl Jung was the second most important figure in the psychoanalytic movement. Freud addressed him in letters as "My dear friend and heir," and declared that when he died, Jung (nineteen years younger than Freud) would take over as leader. The two men felt a close bond of friendship, which in the standard, fanciful manner of psychoanalysts they both interpreted as being unconsciously homosexual. From the beginning, Freud also perceived Jung as extremely useful to the movement. As an established psychiatrist at a prestigious clinic in Switzerland, and with a Christian background, Jung was a professional of acknowledged competence who helped to rescue psychoanalysis from being almost exclusively Viennese and Jewish, and to give it an international public image.

Gradually Jung's ideas began to depart openly from Freud's. Jung treated many individuals diagnosed as schizophrenic, which Freud never did. Jung tried to understand their delusions in terms of symbols, and began to doubt that these symbols always represented sexual drives or that the schizophrenic's 'loss of reality' always resulted from repressed sexual desires. Jung also questioned Freud's claim that nearly all anxiety in men could be traced back to parental threats of castration.

While fully accepting the existence of the Oedipus Complex in all males without exception, Jung came to dispute Freud's theory that little girls also have the Oedipus Complex, because of their homosexual lust for their mothers, leading them, just like the boys, to want to kill their fathers. Instead, Jung maintained the much more wholesome opinion that little girls want to kill their mothers and have sex with their fathers—the Elektra Complex. Freud always rejected this, continuing to maintain that girls up to age five lust after their mothers.

Jung's 1911 book, *Symbols of Transformation*, foreshadowed the future of the Jungian method. Jung looked at myths, folk-tales, and religious traditions in order to find universal symbols which also appeared in dreams and the delusions of schizophrenics.

Freud personally broke with Jung in 1912. The Secret Committee orchestrated the demonization of Jung. He was forced out of the presidency of the International Psychoanalytic Association and made to resign as editor of the leading psychoanalytic journal, the *Jahrbuch*.

The Collective Unconscious

The Jungian movement continues to grow even today. Some of Jung's own writings, such as *Memories, Dreams, Reflections*, have sold millions of copies. The movement now attracts popular interest through such books as *Women Who Run with the Wolves*, *Iron John*, and Joseph Campbell's works on myth. Jungian thought influences many writers of fiction, like Ursula LeGuin and Richard Adams, and movie makers like George Lucas. Today Jungian analysis has a far bigger following than orthodox Freudian psychoanalysis.

Jung claims that there is a collective unconscious as well as a personal unconscious. As with Freud, the personal unconscious consists of material not accepted by the conscious mind and is, of course, different for each individual. According to Jung, the collective unconscious is a common store of material tapped by all humans; we can find out about it by examining myths and fairytales, which can therefore be helpful in therapy.

The collective unconscious consists of archetypes, or fixed patterns, which govern our unconscious thoughts. Examples of common archetypes are the Dark Father, the Great Mother, the Wise Old Man, the Witch, and the Eternal Child. Jungians often talk as if individuals can draw upon the memories of the human species, in much the same mysterious way that the clones in Hollywood movies somehow manage to come up with memories from the life of the person they were cloned from. But some Jungians describe the archetypes in a more scientifically defensible way, as those images or patterns we find it easiest to think of, for both genetic and cultural reasons.

Jungians (like Freudians) make a distinction between 'analysis' and 'psychotherapy'. Analysis is considered far more important and more profound. Analysis requires "intensive work involving patient and doctor over a long period of time with frequent sessions."[3] Four or five times a week for several years would be quite normal. The goal of analysis is not very precise or concrete: enhanced wholeness through greater awareness of the unconscious. Jungian analysis appears designed for people with time on their hands and money to spare. The methods employed include dream analysis, and 'active imagination'.

Whereas for a Freudian, dreams are always full of incestuous urges, castration fears, phallic symbols, symbols of feces, and the like, the Jungians find hallowed archetypes, echoing the great themes of art, literature, and folklore. Parallels can be drawn from dreams to various myths and folktales. This is a refreshing change from the Freudian landscape but it is no more true. Jungians, however, can do a better job than Freudians at casting their client's life as a heroic struggle, and by contrast with Freudians, we can say that Jungians have generally treated their clients with respect and genuine empathy.

Jungian analysis doesn't appear to have any practical benefits, beyond the regular ones that may accrue from any shoulder to cry on. It is an essentially religious 'inward jour-

---

[3] Stein 1995, p. 16.

ney' in search of one's own true self. Unfortunately, it belongs with tea-leaf reading, tarot cards, the *Yijing*, ouija boards, the Bible Code, and Freudian dream interpretation: we can read into the various symbols what we choose to find there. There is no objective test of the 'findings'.

The Jungians delude themselves that they are exploring an inner reality, when in fact they are arbitrarily making up a story as they go along. It is all based on the fallacy that we can find out and describe what is in the 'unconscious mind' in terms that make sense to the conscious mind.

In Jungian dream analysis the dreams of the analyst ('doctor') are considered relevant, as well as those of the analysand ('patient'). Like Freudians, Jungians see analysis as an interactive process, involving 'transference' and 'countertransference'. Transference is the patient's emotional response to the analyst, often a crush, sometimes hatred, countertransference the analyst's response to the patient.

'Active Imagination' is a technique unique to Jungian analysis. It begins with a kind of meditative technique for reducing the dominance of the ego and paying attention to the unconscious. Building on unconscious promptings, the patient uses some artistic medium, such as painting, dance, storytelling, or modeling in clay to create a work that embodies insight into the unconscious.

In recent years a popular form of Active Imagination has been sandplay: the patient uses a sand tray with models of little people, small blocks, rocks, and other props, and arranges a tableau that 'tells a story'. First developed for use with children, sandplay is now popular for therapy with adults.

Jungian 'therapy', as contrasted with 'analysis' is more problem-focused and more in the nature of counseling. It is often eclectic, drawing sometimes upon the more 'practical' aspects of Adlerian therapy.

The Later Adler

A look at the early discussions involving Adler and Freud shows that Adler was never really a convinced

Freudian.[4] As Adler elaborated his own theories, they increasingly clashed with Freud's. Adler continued to agree with Freud's emphasis on the importance of early childhood and the importance of dreams, but he didn't embrace the Freudian insistence on infantile sex as the root of all emotional and behavioral problems.

In his later writings, Adler made more explicit his rejection of the entire Freudian conception of the unconscious, even going so far as to write:

> The unconscious . . . is nothing other than that which we have been unable to formulate in clear concepts. These concepts are not hiding away in some unconscious or subconscious recesses of our minds, but are those parts of our consciousness of which we have not fully understood the significance. (Adler 1979, 93)

While coming to reject the Freudian unconscious, Adler never questioned the other main dogma of psychoanalysis: the decisive influence of early childhood. Unlike Freud or Jung, Adler was always intensely interested in how the individual could best interact with the community. Adler saw the family as a kind of dress rehearsal for life in society, and therefore he placed great emphasis on birth order: whether a child is an only child, or first, second, or third among the children, and other conditions such as the age gap between the children, would set the individual's pattern for his subsequent relations with other people.

If early childhood had a lot of impact on the development of personality, then it would seem likely that birth order, one of the big systematic differences in the constellation of experiences of children in the same family, would have to be tremendously important. However, we now know that birth order actually has no measurable effect on adult personality, and even the difference between being an only child and having siblings has no or negligible

---

[4] Handlbauer 1998.

effect.[5] These findings put in question the assumption that early childhood has a lot of impact on the development of personality.

Otto Rank

After the excommunication of Carl Jung, the highly talented Otto Rank became Freud's favorite son, heir, and right-hand man. In 1924 Rank published *The Trauma of Birth*, where he maintained that being born is a catastrophic ending to a hitherto blissful existence, a trauma which scars us for the rest of our lives. Freud at first accepted this work, with reservations, as a legitimate contribution to psychoanalysis.

In other writings, Rank criticized psychoanalysis for its lack of interest in emotion and its preoccupation with childhood at the expense of the "here and now." The neurotic, argued Rank, does not suffer primarily because of what happened in his past, but because of the persistence of past influences into the present. Rank's capable writings on art and creativity helped to establish the popularity of psychoanalysis with literary people. Today his direct influence is most noticeable in the continuing popularity of Ernest Becker's book, *The Denial of Death*, heavily indebted to Rank.

Rank's theory of the birth trauma could be seen as undermining the importance of the Oedipus Complex, and some of Freud's fanatically orthodox disciples made the most of this.[6] Responding to accusations of heresy, Rank vacillated between abject submission and playful defiance. Eventually Freud

---

[5] Harris 2009, second appendix; Harris 2006, Chapter 4.

[6] Rank was outdone by Hans-Otto Zweitel, who published his daring *The Trauma of Conception* in 1926, just before his tragic and mysterious death at the age of twenty-eight. Zweitel explained how two individuals who don't see eye to eye about anything are brutally fused into one makeshift organism at the moment of conception, a profound shock from which neither of them can ever fully recover. Zweitel's epochal work was not only ignored by other psychoanalysts, but all traces of it and of Zweitel himself have been expunged from libraries and archives, a tribute to the fierce resistance aroused by his unbearably disquieting thesis.

cast him out, and the Secret Committee was abandoned. Sandor Ferenczi replaced Rank as favorite son but later he too became an apostate and had to be excommunicated.[7]

Rank and Ferenczi, like Adler and Jung before them, were viewed by Freud's loyal supporters as sufferers from serious mental illness. Just as we might wonder why so many of Stalin's associates were revealed to be traitors and fascist spies, and why almost everybody who knew Ayn Rand was ultimately exposed as viciously immoral, so we might speculate as to why nearly everyone who knew Freud (and absolutely everyone with any talent) eventually turned out to be a dangerous psychotic.

The Sexual Revolutionary

When psychoanalysis became well-known in the early years of the twentieth century, many people assumed it was against 'repression' of our 'instincts' and therefore would be in favor of 'free love'. In 1930 Freud published *Civilization and Its Discontents*, maintaining that repression is essential to the survival of civilization, and we'd better learn to live with both. Yet there was always a current of sexual liberation within the psychoanalytic movement. The most independent-minded and influential of the sexual liberationists was Wilhelm Reich.

As a young man, Reich fought in the Austrian army in World War I and then attended medical school in Vienna. He met Freud and became a devoted disciple. Very quickly, when Reich was aged twenty-two, Freud developed such trust in Reich that he referred patients to him. In treating patients' 'resistance', Reich paid more attention to what would later be called 'body language', and developed the theory that patients had built up a 'character armor', a pattern of tense muscles. Later he came to see the capacity to enjoy sex as a sign of mental health, though he defined enjoying sex rather

---

[7] Webster 1995, 398–340.

demandingly as full and satisfying orgasms, or as he termed it 'orgastic potency'. Reich held that most people are orgastically impotent because although they do have orgasms, their tense muscles prevent the fullest satisfaction. Reichian therapy came to encompass the analyst massaging the muscles of the unclothed patient.

Reich allied his sexual revolutionism with revolutionary socialism, trying to work with the Communist Party, who wouldn't put up with him because of his insistence on sexual as well as political revolution. He soon came to despise the Communist Party while remaining a revolutionary socialist.

Later, Reich came to see the entire universe as suffused with something he called 'orgone energy', which is experienced in orgasm, which can be seen in the aurora borealis, and which when blocked gives rise to diseases like cancer.

Reich moved to the United States in 1939. He developed the orgone energy accumulator, a box which patients could sit inside, with therapeutic results. These accumulators were manufactured and sold commercially. Reich wrote to Albert Einstein, trying to convince him of the existence of orgone energy. Reich claimed that the higher temperature measured inside the orgone box showed the reality of orgone energy. Einstein (who was quite open to alternative medical practices) tested the accumulator and concluded that the higher reading was an indirect result of temperature gradient (the temperature in a room is lower near the floor). In vain did Reich explain in meticulous detail why, properly interpreted, the readings still supported his theory. Einstein stopped answering Reich's letters.[8]

In 1951 Reich designed a 'cloudbuster', which would be fired at the sky, unblocking orgone energy in the atmosphere and causing it to rain. During a 1953 drought he was paid by farmers to make it rain, which he did, followed by several other successful 'weather modification' projects.[9]

---

[8] Sharaf 1994, 285–88.
[9] Sharaf 1994, 379–380.

In 1954 the US Food and Drug Administration began an elaborate persecution of Reich, obtaining an injunction against the distribution of orgone accumulators and any associated literature. For having violated this injunction, Reich was sentenced to two years' imprisonment; he died in prison halfway through his sentence. Reich was buried in the center he founded, Orgonon, Maine, which remains a base for Reichian research and the site of the Wilhelm Reich Museum. As if to prove that the US government was even crazier than Wilhelm Reich, the FDA managed to get six tons of his publications burned in Manhattan.

Reich influenced many notable people including Saul Bellow, William Burroughs, Sean Connery, Arthur Janov (*The Primal Scream*), Dwight Macdonald, Norman Mailer, Fritz Perls, and J.D. Salinger. Opinions vary on whether the 'orgasmatron' in the Woody Allen movie *Sleeper* is intended as a satire on the orgone accumulator.

Karen Horney

Karen Horney (pronounced 'horn-eye') was born near Hamburg in 1885. She qualified as a medical doctor and then as a psychoanalyst, and (a divorced woman with two daughters) moved to the US in 1930. She was prominent in the major psychoanalytic bodies, but because of increasing friction with orthodox Freudian psychoanalysts, she was forced out of the New York Psychoanalytic Institute, and founded her own breakaway organization, the American Institute for Psychoanalysis, in 1941. Among her romantic involvements was a famous one with the pop psychoanalyst and pop Marxist Erich Fromm.

Horney's contributions to psychoanalytic debates are too numerous to list here. She challenged the view—still obligatory among right-thinking psychoanalysts into the 1940s—that women suffer from penis envy, and argued that men experience 'womb envy'. Sadly, Horney was not joking, and both she and her psychoanalytic opponents took this kind of talk with deadly seriousness.

Horney came to challenge Freud on more and more issues. She is usually bracketed with Erik Erikson and Harry Stack Sullivan as part of the 'cultural' wave of psychoanalysts which modified Freud by giving greater weight to cultural influences on personality. This movement is important for the history of the doctrines of the psychoanalytic church but otherwise holds no lasting interest.

Horney was a capable and unpretentious writer and her books were widely read. Horney agreed with Freud that the historical origin of present emotional problems lies in childhood experiences, but she gradually came to reject the conclusion that unearthing those experiences explains or solves the problems. Instead, she reasoned, the childhood experiences have created a particular type of person, or 'character structure' (the influence of Reich), and it is this character structure, *now*, which generates the emotional problems. In this way, Horney could accept the mistaken Freudian theory that present emotional problems had their origin in childhood experiences while acknowledging the more important fact that recalling these early experiences was neither necessary nor sufficient for treating the present problems.

In her last major works, *Neurosis and Human Growth* and *Our Inner Conflicts*, Horney identified something she called "the pride system". People create ideal selves, different to their real selves, and make demands on both the world and themselves. Our ideal selves are unrealistic and impossible to live up to, so we tend to despise ourselves. "We waver between self-adoration and self-contempt" (Horney 1945, 112). Horney recommended that clients find their "real selves" rather than being limited by their ideal selves. In these writings Horney moves closer to a Cognitive-Behavioral approach, in which people's spontaneous thoughts, easily available to conscious inspection, create their emotional problems. She always remained too credulous about the decisive impact of early childhood and the reliability of free-association.

Ego Psychology

In the 1930s, as continental Europe came under the sway of National Socialist Germany, many psychoanalysts escaped to Britain or America. Freud became ill, and died in London in 1939. The official psychoanalytic movement began to loosen up somewhat. People were still denounced and excommunicated as heretics if they departed too much from Freudian orthodoxy, but the scope for acceptable revision or dissent was slightly widened. No doubt this process was helped along by the fact that one of the theoretical innovators was Freud's daughter Anna.

In 1923, Freud decided to divide the human mind into 'id', 'ego', and 'superego.' At first people tended to assume that the id replaced the unconscious, the superego was something like a conscience, and the ego was the conscious self. But as these ideas were developed by Freud and others, it became accepted that id, ego, and superego each have both conscious and unconscious aspects.

Instead of trying to get the ego to come to terms with the id, psychoanalysts began (as they believed) to unearth the unconscious parts of ego and superego, as well as id. In this shift in focus, psychoanalysts began to see themselves as achieving a balance between the three elements, id, ego, and superego.

This left the way open to develop a theory of the ego, looking at 'defense mechanisms'—ways in which the ego supposedly protects itself, unconsciously but with devilish ingenuity, from anxiety. Psychoanalysts listed a number of ways in which this could be done by the unconscious ego. For example,

- **Denial. Not acknowledging some uncomfortable reality.**

- **Reaction formation. Doing the opposite of what one feels (behaving very nicely if one is feeling hostile, for instance).**

- **Projection. Attributing one's own feelings or impulses to other people.**

- **Rationalization. Explaining away some disturbing phenomenon.**

To those who, like the authors of this book, don't place any credence in Freud's theory of the unconscious or in the id-ego-superego formula, this new development in psychoanalysis was a practical improvement. Instead of trying to convince clients of something that was utterly disconnected from real life—that their problems were rooted in forgotten phantasies from infancy—the new theory, ego psychology, might occasionally come close to the truth in specific applications.

For example, people often do assume that other people think and feel the way they do ('projection'). This was pointed out by, among others, Thomas Hobbes in the seventeenth century. An ego psychologist maintains that the unconscious part of the ego is motivating the person to 'project' his or her thoughts or feelings on to other people, because the person is afraid to confront the fact that he or she harbors such thoughts or feelings. But whether or not that is true, individuals may assume that others have the same impulses and subjective experiences that they do.

For instance, a woman who is always looking for ways to take unfair advantage of other people may just suppose that other people are constantly trying to take advantage of her, and may therefore be prone to attribute her failures to other people's scurrilous dishonesty. This may be 'unconscious' in the sense that she is adhering to a carelessly adopted theory about other people's behavior, a theory she has never critically examined.

There's no need to gild the lily by maintaining that this woman's ego has unconsciously devised this way of thinking because she is afraid of her own thoughts and feelings. A psychodynamic unconscious with a will of its own is unnecessary—and, in our view, does not exist.

Or consider the 'defense mechanism' called 'denial', which has become notorious in recent years. The current talk about 'denial' in pop psychotherapy owes its origin to the ego psy-

131

chologists, who were developing ideas stated earlier by Freud. It has come to be used to browbeat clients who have the temerity to 'deny' the therapist's explanations for the client's problems. There is no special state of mind called 'denial'. There is simply the fact that sometimes the client (rightly or wrongly) won't accept the therapists' opinions or the opinions of family members.

A young woman who's endangering her health by starving herself in pursuit of thinness may believe that she's grossly overweight. It may be helpful to assist her to see that she is not fat but thin. It may also be that she is very attached to the theory that she is fat, as we all often become attached to our pet theories and find it uncomfortable to give them up. A psychodynamic approach would maintain that the unconscious part of her ego feels threatened by the fact that she is thin, and therefore 'denies' this fact by distorting her perception of reality so that she perceives herself, incorrectly, as fat. There's no need for any such theory to explain her erroneous perception of her body, but a psychoanalyst who accepts some such theory may do roughly the right thing, in encouraging her to adjust her idea of reality to make it more accurate.

And so, ego psychologists like Anna Freud and her followers, still operating within the wrong-headed Freudian framework, actually and unwittingly introduced Cognitive-Behavioral elements into their theory and practice. Whereas earlier Freudian theory, preoccupied with the mythical 'id', was a theory that might have been specifically devised to be of no possible help to clients, ego psychology supplemented psychoanalysis in such a way that occasional help to clients might at least be possible.

Object-Relations Theory

Object-relations theory, once a major dissenting movement within psychoanalysis, has now become the mainstream. Like Freudian theory, it sees human beings as being decisively molded by their experiences through the age of six.

But instead of conceiving individuals as primarily formed by instinctual drives which crave pleasure, object-relations theory sees them as finding meaning in relationships with 'objects'. The most important objects are people, especially the child's mother and father, but also more limited objects like the mother's breast.

Freud had maintained that the infant craves satisfaction of its appetites for food and warmth and perceives bodily contact with its mother as a means to that end. As one object-relations theorist commented, to Freud all love is cupboard love. Object-relations theorists argued, correctly, that infants are programmed to seek bodily contact as an end in itself, independently of its instrumental role in yielding a payoff. Experiments with infant monkeys and humans show that they will sometimes go hungry for the sake of bodily contact.[10]

Object-relations theorists believe that individuals have an innate drive to form and maintain relationships, and that in childhood they 'internalize' the pattern of relationships they experience. Emotional problems later in life arise because individuals are unconsciously imposing the pattern they have internalized on other people.

In object-relations therapy, the relationship between the therapist and the client is all-important. The theory holds that the client will become attached to the therapist, and will seek to manipulate the therapist in accordance with the bad pattern of relationships acquired in infancy. The technique of therapy consists in making the client aware of this bad pattern of relationships, sometimes by a contrived situation of dramatic confrontation in which the therapist upsets the client's expectations.

If this works, the client will gain some insight into her bad pattern of relationships, and will be persuaded to reconstruct this pattern along more helpful lines, usually by reconstructing the client's relationship with the therapist, and then with close family members and other intimate associates.

---

[10] Eagle 1984, 10–16.

Object-relations theory thus retains some of the basic assumptions of Freudian psychoanalysis: that adult emotional problems are caused by experiences of early childhood, that these experiences leave a mark on the individual which is unconscious and cannot be discovered except with specialized help, and that it's necessary to find out what these experiences were before the problem can be mended.

From a Cognitive-Behavioral point of view, object-relations theory is an improvement over traditional Freudianism, especially because the kind of 'unconscious' it appeals to can often be interpreted as 'unexamined assumptions' rather than as a phantasy world with its own bizarre storyline, invisible to objective scrutiny. However, object relations theorists persist in the fundamental blunder of holding that our unhelpful ways of thinking and relating have their origins in early childhood. They suppose that we can shed light on adult relationships by going back to those early child-parent relationships (or rather, to our highly fallible conjectures about them). And they suppose that we have to know the childhood origins of our unhelpful ways of thinking and relating before we can change them.

Object-relations theory became influential from the 1950s through the 1980s, not only within psychotherapy but also among everyone concerned with child-rearing. The theory maintains that early childhood is a crucially important time for personal development, that a mother's love or some close substitute is essential for mental health, and that numerous emotional and behavioral problems are due to events in this early stage. The ideology of 'attachment' and later that of 'maternal bonding' became popular among social workers, therapists, and politicians. This belief-system was largely the creation of object-relations theorists, though it was adopted by a broader following who were not themselves committed to object-relations theory or even aware of it.

Empirical research has now demonstrated that these claims about child-rearing are mistaken. It's possible that exceptionally inhumane treatment, such as used to occur in some of the worst orphanages, may leave a permanent mark on the individual's personality. But within the more normal range of variation, no serious consequences for later adult life stem from the quality of parent-child relationships. No terrible permanent consequences automatically follow from lack of a good relationship with a mother or mother-figure. Infants benefit from being frequently held closely by older people, for instance, but it doesn't matter who does the holding. Children raised in communities which discourage exclusive attachment to one or two adults don't suffer any adverse consequences. Raising kids in one-parent families, or by same-sex couples, or putting them into daycare will not appreciably affect their adult personalities.

Even more dramatically mistaken is the theory, central to object-relations thinking, that individuals tend to model their relationships with other people after their early relationships with their parents. Children are naturally impelled to pursue other relationships, after infancy, usually with other children of the same or somewhat higher age, and to construct these new relationships on a fresh basis, *without* carrying over the patterns of their earlier relationships with their mothers. It appears that children are genetically programmed *not* to form their subsequent relationships on the model of relationships with their parents.

Teen and pre-teen relationships with peers leave a permanent mark on personality, whereas early relationships with parents do not. For example, the oldest child in the family often has a managerial role in relation to the younger siblings, and this role may persist throughout life for those same specific individuals, but this tendency to be managerial is lost in the school playground and in later life interactions with other people. Observation of children's relationships in the playground shows that they are completely random with respect to birth order. There is no way, by observing the behavior of children interacting with their peers, to perform better than chance at guessing who is an oldest child, who is a younger child, or who is an only child.[11]

Carl Rogers and Person-Centered Therapy

Within the profession of psychotherapy, Freudian psycho-analysis was challenged from three directions: by people who broke with the movement and went off to promote their own heretical form of psychoanalysis, by those (after about 1936) who remained within the 'official' psychoanalytic movement, while increasingly departing from Freud on important is-sues, and finally by those who set up as therapists but no longer accepted the name 'psychoanalyst'. This last category now comprises the vast majority of psychotherapists, but in the 1940s it was almost unheard of. The first major therapist to make this break was Carl Rogers, who has repeatedly been ranked by polls of therapists and psychologists as the most influential psychotherapist of all time.

Rogers began as a convinced psychoanalyst, though his training was in theology as preparation for church ministry. He came under the spell of Otto Rank, but when Rogers put forward his own distinctive approach to therapy, beginning in the late 1930s, he did not present it as a form of psycho-analysis. Rogers called it 'non-directive' or 'client-centered' therapy. Later it was called 'person-centered'; it is now usu-ally called 'Rogerian' therapy. Otto Rank's death in 1939 at the age of fifty-five may have ensured that Rogerian therapy would never be regarded as a branch of psychoanalysis.

Rogers believed that persons are inherently good and healthy. Humans and all life forms have an innate tendency to actualize themselves—to develop their potential. Rogers recommends that therapists have "unconditional positive re-gard" for clients. Because of Rogers, many people have up-held 'growth' as the ideal of what can be achieved by therapy, the assumption—a very American one—being that if hu-mans fulfill their innate potential, this must be good.

---

[11] Harris 2006, 98–100.

Is Rogerian therapy psychodynamic or cognitive? It's ambivalent. Rogers occasionally pays lip service to psychodynamic concepts, along with the usual blather about Freud the great discoverer, but in practice Rogers takes seriously what the client thinks, and doesn't insist on trying to uncover hidden forces that are unknown and almost unknowable to the client. On the other hand, he doesn't see it as the therapist's role to help improve the client's thoughts, but relies on some spontaneous inner force to bring about improvement.

Rogers inherited from psychoanalysis the format of rambling exchanges between therapist and patient, but Rogers began to call his patients 'clients' and to abandon the traditional couch in favor of direct person-to person conversation. The most conspicuous feature of Rogerian therapy is the technique of 'reflection', in which the therapist repeats back to the client what the client has said:

CLIENT: I'm worried that I won't pass the test I have to take tomorrow.
THERAPIST: You feel anxious that you'll fail tomorrow's test.

The technique is easy to make fun of:

CLIENT: Why the heck do you keep repeating back to me everything I say?
THERAPIST: You're concerned because you feel that I keep repeating back to you everything you say.

Reflection helps the client to express more precisely what she's feeling, and at the same time replaces the client's troubled emotion about feeling this way with calm acceptance.

Rogers's approach is based on the premise that the client does not need any advice, either as to the direction in which he wants to change or how to get there. Diagnosis and assessment have no part in the therapy—though they may be undertaken for research purposes, as Rogers held that therapy should be tested for its effectiveness. The therapist's role is to draw the client out, make unacknowledged thoughts and feelings more explicit, and thus assist in the client's self-actualization.

Limitations of Rogerian Therapy

Research shows that Rogerian therapy, like all major forms of psychotherapy does make a positive difference and does help clients, but for most emotional problems not as great a difference as Cognitive-Behavioral therapy. Rogerian therapy may be the closest thing in psychotherapy to a placebo.

If the client's own instincts for self-actualization are so reliable, why does she need the therapist at all? Surprisingly, it turns out upon close examination that Rogerian therapy, which seems to exalt the client above everything, rather exalts the therapist and his 'relationship' with the client. Many people can feel better from having a sympathetic ear, but if the client has not taken away any definite lessons from the therapist, then the client may not have been equipped with any new tools to deal with future problems.

If the therapist can see that the client is hurting herself because of faulty thinking, why wouldn't the therapist point this out to the client? There are two possible answers: that the therapist never has any such valuable insights or that it is somehow better for the client to discover these for herself. But both of these responses are mistaken: we can identify typical errors in thinking which lead to emotional problems, we do know of effective techniques for correcting these errors, and it is not necessary for clients to discover these for themselves.

Most of what we know we have learned from other people and just as we wouldn't wait for a child to invent the two-times table by itself, or independently come up with the rule to look both ways before crossing the street, so there is no reason not to teach people the best way to tackle their emotional and behavioral problems. The Rogerian theory that we ought to wait for the client to make progress in her own way is merely a remnant of the psychoanalytic theory that the client has to recall and relive the bad experiences of childhood without being directed to do so. It's part of the technique of effective teaching to sometimes prompt the student to think of the next step herself, but this occurs within a framework where the teacher knows more about the overall shape and direction of the material the student is learning.

The Rogerian emphasis on the therapist's empathy for the client also carries the risk that the client may become dependent on the therapist, or dependent on someone who can be counted on to display such empathy after the conclusion of therapy. There are some clients who single-mindedly concern themselves with solving their own problems, using whatever help the therapist can supply. These clients may just not care very much how the therapist feels about them, and such an attitude is entirely healthy.

Existential-Humanist Therapy

In the 1930s and 1940s, various ideas became popular with some therapists, leading to what are now called 'existential therapy', 'humanistic therapy', and 'existential-humanist therapy'. There's no single theory embraced by all therapists called by these names. There are various themes which are combined differently by different therapists.

One theme was the search for a 'third force' in psychology, something distinct from both psychoanalysis and behaviorism (or in some cases, hoping to combine the valuable elements in both psychoanalysis and behaviorism). A second theme was the view we find in Horney: that of self-actualization. A third theme was the influence of existentialism, at that time a conspicuous movement in French philosophy. (Then, as now, American literary intellectuals, mainly not philosophers, attentively followed the rise and fall of hemlines in Parisian philosophical fashion.)

The self-actualization idea was developed by Abraham Maslow, who advanced a 'hierarchy of human needs', purporting to show which human needs were most basic and which would come to the fore once the more basic ones were taken care of. Maslow reacted against psychology's preoccupation with pathology—what can go wrong—and tried to develop a theory of successful living. He considered that success might be indicated by 'peak experiences'—experiences of transcendent ecstasy. More recently, this idea has re-emerged in Mihaly Csikszentmihalyi's theory of 'flow'.

Existentialism holds that there is no pre-ordained purpose to human life and that humans must give their lives meaning by their own crucial choices. Several people began to import existentialist ideas into psychotherapy, beginning with Ludwig Binswanger who remained friendly with Freud, possibly because Freud could see no credible threat from that direction: Binswanger had little following at the time. The psychologist who put existential therapy on the map was the American Rollo May, an extremely popular therapist and writer in the 1940s and 1950s, though he did not add any new ideas of importance.

Two other influences on existential-humanist therapy were Paul Tillich's popular book, *The Courage to Be* (1952), and Victor Frankl's *Man's Search for Meaning* (1946). Tillich was a Protestant theologian who drew from existentialist ideas in a Christian framework, though he influenced many atheistic psychotherapists including Abraham Maslow and Albert Ellis. Frankl's moving work, an account of his experiences in the Auschwitz death camp, showing that those inmates who saw meaning in their lives were the ones who tended to endure, has had a wide and thoroughly deserved impact.

Existential-humanist therapy can mean a great many things, and the level of understanding of some of these ideas on the part of existential-humanist therapists is decidedly uneven. Hardly anyone seems to have noticed that 'self-actualization' and existentialism are flatly contradictory. Existentialism starts from the assumption that humans have no prior 'essence' whereas self-actualization implies that they do have such an essence: there is some way of life that is objectively best for each individual. Some existential-humanist therapists even speak of the client's 'destiny', even more blatantly contradicting the most fundamental principle of existentialist philosophy.

If we look at two popular writers today, Irvin Yalom is predominantly psychodynamic (with some Cognitive-Behavioral elements), while Stephen Diamond is predominantly Cognitive-Behavioral. Some of Diamond's cases might almost be models of pure Cognitive-Behavioral therapy. What these writers have in common is an emphasis on the 'existential themes', which they claim to be widespread preoccupations: death, the meaning of life, the individual's aloneness, and freedom of choice.

This leaves us with the factual question: are all or most therapy clients who appear with common emotional and behavioral problems really bothered by the great existential worries: fear of their ultimate death, dread of the meaninglessness of their life, anxiety at their aloneness, or terror at the realization that they're free to make choices? In our experience these kinds of concerns do occasionally arise, but are not typical, and it would not be helpful in most cases of depression, panic attacks, or phobias to attempt to lead clients into a confrontation with these wider issues. A general fear of death is most often encountered in young people and seems to fade as they get older. People know they're going to die, and the great majority seem to come to terms with this fact quite successfully, without special help.

Occasionally it can even work the other way. If you tell someone worried about their wife, their job, or their torture fantasies, 'A hundred years from now, you and everyone you know will be dead, and no one will give a rat's ass about your current epic problems', you may help them gain a sense of perspective and they may derive some comfort from it.

Gestalt Therapy

Frederick ('Fritz') Perls started as a psychoanalyst in Berlin in the 1920s. He rejected many aspects of Freudianism including the emphasis on transference and the primacy of sex.

He moved to South Africa and then to New York City. In 1942 he published his book *Ego, Hunger, and Aggression*, and was excommunicated from the psychoanalytic movement. He started small gestalt therapy groups in the 1950s, and these really began to make their presence felt in the 1960s.

Perls's style was provoking and confronting. More than once, Perls physically assaulted a client. Gestalt therapy was found to be particularly suited to group therapy and to 'weekend workshops': intense activity for two or three days rather than regular sessions of an hour or less over an extended period. These workshops were often highly emotional. There was much emphasis on living in the present, expressing who we truly are, learning to 'own' our projections of faults and virtues onto others.

A gestalt workshop would be a dramatic event. There would be several chairs on the stage, some of them empty, and the client would be asked to act out various roles, representing his various projections. Perls had early been impressed by *The Strange Case of Dr Jekyll and Mr Hyde*, and he would encourage clients to play out various parts of their own personality, especially the overdog and the underdog. Sometimes the client would be expected to 'play' the therapist. As Ellis remarked on such experiments, they always stopped short of having the therapist pay the client instead of the other way around.

Like several influential therapists, Perls was influenced by Jacob L. Moreno, who developed the theory of 'psychodrama' in Vienna and brought it to New York in 1925. Therapists of many persuasions have found Moreno's methods, especially the well-known technique of 'role reversal' useful.

Perls held that the human personality constantly seeks balance. He maintained that only the here-and-now exists, that therapy need not be concerned with uncovering the past. Though Perls rejected many psychoanalytic concepts, he was very keen on projection. When we project, we attribute to someone or something else what is in ourselves, what is a part of ourselves. Perls reacted against what he saw as over-intellectualism. The body is the equal of the mind.

Thought, feeling, and physical activity together form a natural whole.

Something of the gestalt therapy approach is captured in Perls's 'Gestalt Prayer':

I do my thing and you do your thing.
I am not in this world to live up to your expectations,
And you are not in this world to live up to mine.
You are you, and I am I,
and if by chance we find each other, it's beautiful.
If not, it can't be helped. (Perls 1969, 4)

The key idea of this statement is the focus on living in response to one's own needs, without projecting onto others or receiving their projections. By fulfilling their own needs, people can help others do the same and create space for genuine contact. There is a strong streak of egoism and even self-indulgence in gestalt therapy, making it well suited to the 1970s, the Me Decade.

Perls called his approach Gestalt Therapy, taking the name of an existing school of psychological research, concerned with perception, and based on the insight that when people perceive things, they organize what they perceive into unified patterns. *Gestalt* is the German word for shape or form, and in Gestalt psychology it conveys the sense of 'a meaningful whole'. But it would be a mistake to suppose that gestalt therapy is an application of Gestalt psychology or shares in its scientific seriousness. There is no reason why someone interested in Gestalt psychology would be drawn to gestalt therapy. Like most gestalt therapists, Perls was pretty ignorant of Gestalt psychology.[12]

George Kelly

In 1955, a truly remarkable book appeared by George Kelly, *The Psychology of Personal Constructs*. Kelly put forward a

---

[12] Henle 1986, Chapter 3.

new theory of personality, explaining all personality differences (and incidentally all psychiatric disorders) as due to different 'personal constructs', different individuals' ways of understanding the world. Kelly applied his theory to psychotherapy (he was impressed by Moreno's psychodrama), but it had little influence on the world of practical therapy for several decades (though it has significantly influenced psychological theories of personality). More recently, there has been a growth in adherence to Kelly's ideas (most noticeably in Britain, though Kelly was American) under the name 'Personal Construct Therapy'.

Typically, the therapist asks the client to compose a brief description of herself and then discusses this with the client. The therapist then makes a 'grid' which is a kind of detailed map of the client's personality. The therapist and the client explore ways of changing the client's personality in a direction which will be helpful to the client. One way of doing this is by psychodrama, having the client deliberately act the part of the different person who would exist if the grid were different. This is sometimes called Fixed Role Therapy. If the changes work, the new personality is permanently adopted by the client: the actor comes to live the part. In this type of therapy, we move away from specific problems to a whole-life makeover.

The 'grid' is very abstract, and when we look at case histories, as reported by Personal Construct therapists, we see that the gaps between the grid and anything of practical importance are usually filled in with scraps of therapy folklore, whatever notions happen to be rattling around in the poor therapist's head. These notions are often the pop Psychodynamic assumptions prevalent in the culture. There is the danger that a client's specific problem will be effectively minimized, as the therapy goes galloping off into every aspect of the client's life.

For example, one client is a schoolteacher who likes teaching but is shy and gets panicky in staff meetings. Instead of showing the client how to overcome this social anxiety, the therapist assumes that the client's personality was formed by early interactions with parents, and that her anxiety is somehow related to unacknowledged anger and hostility. These fallacious notions, the common coin of Psychodynamic therapy, are evidently taken for granted by the therapist and by the client. These and other lines of enquiry hold the attention of therapist and client for twenty-one months. The client's anxiety in staff meetings is stated to be dispelled by persuading the client to take a different view of her role in those meetings.[13]

People come to therapy for various motives, though the main motive is usually a troubling emotional or behavioral problem, and that is the orientation of this book. Some come to therapy for self-discovery or a total personal makeover for its own sake, and we can't say that they will be disappointed by existential therapy, humanist therapy, gestalt therapy, or personal construct therapy, though along the way they may pick up some erroneous beliefs about what has made them the way they are.

Behavior Therapy

Behavior therapy traces back to Russian scientists, the most famous being Ivan Pavlov. In 1901 Pavlov discovered the conditioned reflex: if a bell is rung whenever a dog is about to be fed, the dog will then salivate whenever it hears the bell. Exactly how animals and humans learn such habitual responses became a fruitful research program for psychologists, and gave rise to the theory of behaviorism. In the United States and other countries, most academic psychologists quickly rejected psychoanalysis and turned to the theory of conditioned learning.

One of the simplest forms of behavior therapy is aversion therapy. A person who has the problem of drinking too much alcohol is asked to drink a glass of whiskey, and every time

---

[13] Fransella and Dalton 1990, 106–130.

the glass touches his lips he is subjected to a distinctly unpleasant electric shock. A similar result can be achieved by skipping the electric shocks and just asking the client to imagine something unpleasant. Aversion therapy has not proved very effective and is now employed in only a tiny fraction of addiction treatments.

Joseph Wolpe was a medical officer in the South African army, involved in treating soldiers for what would now be called post-traumatic stress. The traditional treatment was to use a drug to get the soldiers relaxed and talkative, and then get them to talk through their experiences. Wolpe observed that this treatment rarely led to recovery. Widely read in philosophy and psychology, Wolpe became critical of psychoanalysis and impressed by behaviorism's focus on learned responses. In particular, Wolpe was struck by the possibility that emotional problems could be cured *without* reliving or even discovering the circumstances which had caused them.

Wolpe's approach is to begin by teaching the client techniques of relaxation, involving the conscious tension and relaxation of groups of muscles. Then, the client is asked to arrange the situations which arouse anxiety in a rank order, from most anxiety-generating to only slightly anxiety-generating. The client is then asked to imagine the slightly anxiety-generating situations while practicing the relaxation techniques. When the anxiety has been removed from these situations, we move on to the situations with somewhat more anxiety, and when this anxiety has been removed, we move further on up the scale. When a client has been completely 'desensitized' to all these imagined situations, we usually find that the anxiety has disappeared in the real-life situations too.

Wolpe's behavior therapy was demonstrably effective as a treatment for phobias. This success refuted the traditional view that phobias have deep roots in unconscious conflicts which need to be recalled and understood before they can be cured. The traditional, Psychodynamic response to any possibility of getting rid of something like a phobia without addressing deep unconscious conflicts, is that this will only be treating superficial symptoms. The buried conflicts will remain, and will come back to haunt the patient. But someone cured of a phobia by behavior therapy is no more liable to subsequent problems than someone who had never had a phobia. There are no deep unconscious roots of phobias, and a cure of a phobia is a complete cure: there's nothing left to cure.

Wolpe's therapy, even for something as straightforward and easily identifiable as a phobia, involved a big element of the cognitive, appealing to the patient's thoughts and imagination. For other emotional problems, such as depression, Wolpe's therapy did not get such convincing results, and attempting to apply it required even more detailed attention to the client's beliefs.

Ready for the Revolution

By 1950, people who thought seriously about psychotherapy were converging from several directions on the strategy of paying more attention to the client's thoughts (Beck 1979, 21–22).

We've seen that even psychoanalysts still considered orthodox had shifted their attention in a 'cognitive' direction, while the heretics—both the older heretics like the Adlerians and the newer heretics like Karen Horney—were likewise moving away from the assumption that remembrances of early childhood are crucially important. Applying behavior therapy to human clients turned out to be unfeasible without understanding how the client conceives of alarming or disturbing situations, and so behavior therapy tended to become more 'cognitive'. Those non-behavior-therapists who had broken with psychoanalysis, notably Rogers and Perls, were preoccupied with the way the client thinks and feels *right now*.

Therapy was ready for the big breakthrough.

7
The Conquistador with His Pants Down

I am not really a man of science, not an observer, not an experi-
menter, and not a thinker. I am nothing but by temperament a con-
quistador—an adventurer, if you want to translate the word—with
the curiosity, the boldness, and the tenacity that belongs to that
type of being.

—SIGMUND FREUD

For almost a century after Freud first announced his theories to the world, even harsh critics of Freud accepted that
he was honest, responsible, and at least fairly scrupulous by
the standards of his day. But since the 1970s, several scholars have closely scrutinized Freud's work and a very different picture has emerged.

We now know that Freud was habitually untruthful: his
accounts of his cases are routinely distorted and partially
fabricated, and so are his reports on how he developed his
theories. Where the accounts are not demonstrably false,
they are often cunningly worded to give a misleading impression. Freud also sometimes behaved in an ungentlemanly
manner and caused needless suffering to his clients in order
to further his own ambitions.

The Case of the Anguished Addict (1880–1882)

'Anna O.' was treated by Breuer, not Freud, and Freud broke with Breuer before inventing psychoanalysis. Yet Freud always referred to Anna O. as the key case which led to the founding of psychoanalysis. It supposedly showed that people with emotional problems are "suffering from reminiscences." Their suffering is due to buried memories of past events, and can be dispelled by recovering those memories and reliving them.

Why should we accept this theory? Because (says Freud) it works. And how do we know it works? Why, because of a whole string of cases where the 'patients' were speedily 'cured' by recovering those lost memories. And the first of these cases is the case of Anna O, whose symptoms, Breuer tells us, were quickly and completely eliminated once she had recalled and relived the traumatic event which started it all.

We now know that the story of Anna O., as originally reported by Breuer and as elaborated by Freud and later psychoanalysts, is a tissue of falsehoods. She had serious problems for years after the date of the supposed complete cure, and was committed to a sanatorium for treatment.

Anna O.'s problems were varied, bizarre, and complex. They included (on different occasions in the period 1880–82) being unable to speak her native tongue (German) and only able to communicate in a foreign language (English), being unable to drink water, even though tortured by thirst, having episodes of '*absence*' (pronounced the French way), as though unconscious. The evidence suggests that some of these symptoms were deliberate play-acting. But Anna O. did have real problems, including addiction to the morphine and side-effects of the chloral hydrate both prescribed by Dr. Breuer. This addiction, along with other relevant facts, was never mentioned in Breuer's and Freud's subsequent accounts of the case.

Some years later, Anna O., whose actual name was Bertha Pappenheim, became a prominent advocate for social work and feminism. She was hostile to psychoanalysis. Freud would be aware that he could count on the fact that she had no incentive to blow the whistle on the myth of Anna O., because this would expose intimate details of her private life to public scrutiny and probably destroy her career.[1]

The Case of the Bleeding Virgin (1892–1895)

The early case of Emma Eckstein is worth mentioning even though it predates the invention of psychoanalysis in its classical form. At this time, Freud (having fallen out with Breuer) was very much under the influence of his friend Wilhelm Fliess, who believed that abdominal diseases in women are related to the nose. Women's diseases could therefore be cured by treating the patient's nose, either by surgically removing part of it or by applying the miraculous new tonic, cocaine, to the inside of the nose.

Application of cocaine to the nasal passage will indeed ameliorate pains such as menstrual cramps and stomach aches, but this is now known to be due to the direct effect of cocaine upon the brain and can be achieved equally well by injecting cocaine into a vein in an arm or a leg. There is some connection between the nose and the genitals but Fliess misconceived and exaggerated it.

Emma Eckstein's symptoms included both menstrual and gastric pains. Under Fliess's influence, Freud viewed her as a case of "nasal reflex neurosis," and arranged for Fliess to operate on her nose. As a result of this operation, she suffered several severe bouts of bleeding, coming close to death on two occasions. In these emergencies, Freud had to call in consultants, one of whom found that the incompetent Fliess had left a half-meter of gauze in her nose. A second operation had to be performed to remedy the life-threatening effects of the first.

---

[1] Borch-Jacobsen 1996; Webster 1995, 105–135.

Following this fiasco, Freud continued to treat Fraülein Eckstein, in conformity with Fliess's theories, for another two years. He then wrote to his friend Fliess to communicate his remarkable discovery: Fliess had been right all along. Her symptoms were hysterical, and were caused by her love for Fliess. "She bled out of *longing*," Freud informed Fliess.[2] Subsequently Emma's love for Fliess became transferred to Freud, or so Freud believed. Her hemorrhages, Freud decided, were caused by her wishes, specifically the wish to be loved by her doctor.

Despite being left permanently disfigured and in continual ill-health by Fliess's surgeries, Eckstein became a convert to psychoanalysis and a practicing analyst herself.

This early case illustrates a number of Freudian themes. Freud was an enthusiastic proponent of the use of cocaine, the new wonder drug, for himself, his fiancée, and his patients. Some commentators have attributed his worsening delusions and dishonesty to the after-effects of this drug habit. Freud was already assuming that symptoms must have symbolic meanings, and that these meanings must nearly always be sexual. He saw symptoms as symbolic wishes, and he saw the wishes as unconscious sexual urges arising in infancy. Freud was already ignoring facts that appeared to go against his theories and manufacturing bogus 'clinical facts' which confirmed them. He was already exhibiting callousness and lack of compassion toward his patients, seeing them as mere fodder for his own theories and his own career. He was already convinced that all his female patients were unconsciously in love with him.

The Child Seduction Episodes (1896–1897)

In 1896, Freud announced to the world that he had made a great discovery. All 'neuroses' (emotional problems) are caused by sexual encounters in childhood. Freud referred to

---

[2] Masson 1985, 186.

these experiences as "seduction." He claimed that every one of his own neurotic patients had had such experiences. In 1897, Freud abandoned this theory and replaced it with the new theory that the supposed sexual experiences in childhood had not really happened, but represented the children's phantasies,[3] the fulfillment of their unconscious wishes. This change in Freud's theory led to the creation of psychoanalysis.

According to the once-standard historical narrative, relying on Freud's own later accounts, Freud listened to stories of childhood seduction, recalled by his adult patients, and at first believed them; later he came to see that these lurid and shocking tales had to be false.

> . . . almost all my women patients told me that they had been seduced by their father. I was driven to recognise in the end that these reports were untrue . . . (Freud 1953, Volume XXII, 10)

And so, Freud implied, he had developed the basic concepts of psychoanalysis in order to explain why his clients would unconsciously invent these stories and come to believe them.

Eighty-seven years later, in 1984, Jeffrey Masson gratified feminists and annoyed Freudians by publishing *The Assault on Truth*. Here Masson argued that the stories of seduction told to Freud by his clients were true, and that by originating the theory that these stories were wishful phantasies, Freud had taken part in suppression of the truth that there was and is widespread sexual molestation of children. Masson's interpretation was eagerly taken up by many feminists, and this helped to prepare the climate of opinion for the appalling 'recovered memories' witch-hunt of entirely innocent people in the 1980s and 1990s.

Close study of the records, however, demonstrates that Masson and his feminist followers are just as hopelessly wrong as the Freudians. The simple fact is that *there never were any stories of molestation in childhood, or of any other*

---

[3] The spelling 'phantasies' refers to unconscious processes. 'Fantasies' are conscious thought processes.

sexual experiences in childhood, reported to Freud by his patients. Freud himself made up these accounts. They were Freud's surmises as to what lay behind his patients' symptoms. Having informed his patients that these scenes had occurred, Freud then worked hard to convince them of this. Just how often he succeeded in convincing them is unclear. What is not unclear is that every one of them at first strongly and sincerely denied that anything like this had happened to them.

The Manufacture of Reminiscences

How do we know this? We can compare what Freud wrote about these patients at the time, or shortly afterwards, with what he wrote about the same patients later. In the earlier references, Freud repeatedly states that the 'primal scenes' of infant sex are inferred or constructed by the analyst and that the patient remembers nothing of them. The analyst then tries forcefully to convince the patient, who 'resists' this information because her unconscious knows that it's true. Even when the analyst succeeds in getting the patient to acknowledge that the sexual scene 'must' have occurred, the patient fails to recall it.

As the years passed, Freud gradually changed the words he used to refer to these cases, so that it appeared as though the patients had actually remembered these scenes and recounted them to the astonished doctor. A further twist is that in the earlier versions of these case histories, Freud states that other individuals involved in these early sexual experiences are siblings, playmates, teachers, strangers, governesses, or other servants. Parents are not mentioned, not once. It was only later, when Freud had come up with his theory of the universal Oedipus Complex, that these siblings, playmates, teachers, strangers, or servants were retrospectively transformed into fathers.[4]

---

[4] For details see Esterson 1993, 11–31.

Actually, any person of normal common sense, uninfluenced by the hoopla about Freud the 'great discoverer', would
wonder why at a certain stage in Freud's career, every single
one of his clients told him stories of infant sex with parents,
whereas subsequently in Freud's career, and in the clinical
experience of therapists ever since, such stories are not at
all common.[5] The story that Freud's patients had told him
they had been seduced by their fathers was useful for his
fable about the invention of psychoanalysis, but having performed this service, it was forgotten.

And there's something else, staring us in the face all the
time, like the blatant contradictions in the Bible and the
Quran. If Freud's patients had indeed spontaneously volun-
teered stories of molestation in infancy, as his later accounts
implied, then the patients could not have repressed these
memories, and so, according to Freud's own theory, these
memories could not possibly have had anything to do with
the patients' emotional problems as adults. For these patients' cases to have any relevance for Freud's theory, it just
has to be the case that the patients could not recall anything
of the experiences, and would sincerely protest that they had
never happened. And that is precisely what Freud reports in
his *earliest* accounts of these cases.

It does not necessarily follow that Freud was nothing
more than a cold-blooded liar. If we observe that twelve-year-
old Tommy always blushes when he meets Mary, we might
say that by his blushes, Tommy is 'telling us' that he is in
love with Mary. If we observe our opponent across the poker
table making a big raise before the flop, we might say he is

---

[5] We refer to spontaneous recollections of molestation in the first few
years of life. 'Recollections' conjured up after much coaching, or genuine
recollections of sexual encounters later in childhood, are not so rare. Freud
saw memories of seduction in later childhood as 'screen memories', created
by the unconscious to disguise the true source of disturbance, which must
always lie in the first six years. Masson would have had a point if he had
simply claimed that occasionally a real case of child abuse is neglected because of the Freudian prejudice that the child's recollection must be merely
a screen memory.

'telling us' he has a pair of aces. This usage of the verb 'tell' is metaphorical. To be strictly literal, neither Tommy nor the poker player are telling us anything. In the strictly literal sense, Freud's clients never told him they had been seduced in infancy by their parents or anyone else. Freud's inferences were characteristically far-fetched, and yet he had such confidence in them that he might have thought of them as information his patients were figuratively 'telling' him.

Similarly, when Freud at first reported that his patients had told him they had been seduced by siblings, playmates, teachers, strangers, and servants—but never fathers—and then later reported that the same patients had told him that these same seductions had all been perpetrated by their fathers, he was not necessarily engaging in willful fabrication. What the patients had 'told' Freud was never what they literally said, but the interpretation he had put on their 'symptoms'. First he had a theory that things said by patients that had nothing to do with early sexual experiences were unintentionally 'telling' him they had had sexual relations with persons other than parents, then later he had a theory that the very same things said by the same patients were unintentionally 'telling' him they had had sex with their parents.

But didn't Freud's patients actually relive the seductions? Didn't they recall them and re-experience them with much display of emotion? Actually, although this was the announced goal of Freud's treatment, it isn't clear how many of them did, or whether any of them did. We know that Freud not only reported cures where there was no cure, but also reported cases as completed when they were still going on. But those, if any, of Freud's early patients who did relive their infantile sexual experiences were 'reliving' what Freud had energetically persuaded them had occurred—and this was quite different from the phantasies he imputed to them years later.

So it's not simply that Freud thought that something had occurred and later thought that this same thing had been imagined to occur. The very essence of what had supposedly occurred or been imagined changed completely. Many of the supposed early experiences recalled in the seduction theory period were with other children. Freud's theory in 1896 is that most people do not experience premature sexual arousal, but in those few who do, it can cause neuroses in later life. Sexual arousal in infancy—nothing to do with the children's fathers—caused adult neuroses.

His later theory, developed over several years beginning in 1897, is that everyone without exception has early phantasies of sex with their mothers (which in girls switches to fathers around the age of five, when girls unconsciously realize that they have been castrated). Most people somehow work through these phantasies, but sometimes something goes wrong, and these people become neurotic. The culprit in causing adult emotional problems is no longer premature sexual arousal, but incest guilt, something Freud hadn't thought of at the time of the seduction theory.

Dishonesty or Delusion?

When Freud abandoned the seduction theory in 1897 (though he kept quiet about this change of mind for several years), he continued to maintain that sexual upsets in childhood were at the root of all neuroses, but now he thought that the seduction episodes *he had surmised* were not real events but products of his patient's wishful phantasies. The patients had not really been seduced, but had phantasized their seduction because of their own sexual desires. And since these episodes were constructed by Freud according to his theoretical convictions, he was free to change them retrospectively. Thus, what Freud thought in 1900 that his 1896 patients had 'told' him was quite different from what he thought in 1896 that they had 'told' him, and was somewhat different from what he thought in the 1920s they had 'told' him in 1896.

Freud's standard procedure in 1895–96 was that he would tell his patients they should recall a picture or an idea. When they told Freud of what they were thinking, Freud would tell them that this referred to their being seduced in infancy. Freud would watch their facial expressions, and any signs of alarm or disbelief would be greeted as proof that Freud's surmise (always the same surmise) was accurate. From the beginning, the stories of sexual experiences in childhood were composed by Freud, who then worked hard to convince the patients that these things had happened to them.

Instead of being simply a liar and con artist, Freud may have also been both seriously deluded and prone to a loose metaphorical way of talking.[6] At the same time, Freud must have known that some of his statements were factually misleading. His line of misrepresentation may be similar to that of the spirit medium who sincerely believes that she can channel spirits, but is also prepared to fake spirit manifestations in the good cause of convincing skeptics.

The fact that Freud's patients did not literally tell him that they had been seduced in childhood puts in a somewhat different light one of Freud's characteristic rhetorical tricks. Freud is a highly adroit persuasive writer. One of his effective ploys is to denigrate himself in a way that adds to his credibility and gains the reader's sympathy. In recounting the fable of the origin of psychoanalysis, Freud draws attention to his simple innocence in believing what his patients had 'told' him:

> If the reader feels inclined to shake his head at my credulity, I cannot altogether blame him.

This works upon the reader's mind quite skillfully: it suggests that Freud is a direct, straightforward sort of fellow, inclined to take people at their word. It also suggests that he is humble, in that he is ready to admit past faults and that he is open to changing his theory if the facts dictate it. These suggestions are the very opposite of the truth. However, more than anything else, this device diverts attention from the remarkable claim that all of Freud's early patients had told him they had

---

[6] On the issue of the extent to which Freud was consciously dishonest, see Cioffi 1998, 199–204. Cioffi attributes much of Freud's misrepresentations to his unusually fallible memory.

been seduced in infancy, causing the reader to overlook the possibility that these seductions had been made up by Freud, who then endeavored to browbeat his patients into accepting that these products of his own imagination were real.

Why did Freud abandon the seduction theory? As Cioffi shows, Freud gave several different reasons for its abandonment, reasons which both contradict each other and contradict the evidence.[7] When he abandoned the seduction theory, Freud also abandoned much else. During the period 1896–1899, Freud's theories were transformed, leading to psychoanalysis as we know it. The main aspects of this transformation were:

1. **From an approach of fiercely browbeating the patient to an approach of free association, apparently allowing the patient's thoughts to roam, though actually guiding them in a predetermined direction**

2. **From the belief that all adult neurotics have been prematurely sexually awakened in early childhood (but most people haven't) to the belief that everyone is always sexually awakened in early childhood**

3. **From the belief that decisive early sexual experiences are real to the belief that they are unconscious phantasies**

4. **From the belief that early sexual experiences have nothing necessarily to do with parents to the belief that the phantasized experiences are always about parents**

5. **From no mention of dreams to the reliance on dream interpretation, and the interpretation of everything else in the patient's life in terms of dream symbols**

---

[7] Cioffi 1998, 240–48.

What remains constant is Freud's unswerving determination to find the origin of all neuroses in early childhood sex. He's convinced that this is the great breakthrough which will bring him fame and fortune. He's casting around for a convincing story to present this finding, and for a theory which will be immune to any possible objection from the ranks of unbelievers.

The Case of the Deep-Throat Daughter (1901)

The case of 'Dora' is the first of the most famous landmark cases in Freud's career. We now know the patient's real name: Ida Bauer.

The 'Dora' case has been hashed over interminably in numerous works on psychoanalysis, and Freud's own account[8] is considered one of his masterworks. We do not need to give a complete account here. But some aspects of this case are useful to illustrate Freud's method.[9]

The eighteen-year-old Ida was sent to Freud by her father. She had physical symptoms, including shortness of breath and a persistent cough, all of which were assumed to be 'hysterical'. She was also found to be depressed and suffering from "hysterical unsociability."

Ida explained to Freud that she felt uncomfortable because her father was having an affair with "Frau K.," the wife of a close family friend, "Herr K." Herr K. had made sexual advances to Ida since she had been fourteen, and was now pressing his attentions on her again. Ida explained that she felt that her father, Herr Bauer, found this convenient, since it preoccupied Herr K., and left Herr Bauer a free hand to pursue his affair with Frau K. Ida had complained to her father about Herr K.'s attentions, so he sent her to Freud to be analyzed and thus disciplined.

---

[8] Freud 1953, Volume VII, 1–122.

[9] More detailed analyses of all the cases we describe in this chapter are given in Esterson 1993.

Freud brushed aside Ida's assertions about the motives of her father, who was, after all, paying Freud's fee. Freud saw Ida's rejection of Herr K. as a neurotic symptom, and throughout his exchanges with Ida, Freud tried to convince her that she was really in love with Herr K. and was duty-bound to yield him sexual favors. Any hesitation in so doing could only be a symptom of her 'illness'. Freud explained her symptoms in his usual facile and farfetched way. His explanation for Ida's cough, for example, was that she harbored the unconscious desire to give Herr K. oral sex.

By analyzing one of Ida's dreams, Freud inferred that she had wet the bed at an unusually late age, and that this was because she had masturbated in early childhood. Ida denied this, but Freud later observed that she was playing with a small purse[10] which she wore at her waist. This purse, says Freud

> was nothing but a representation of the genitals, and her playing with it, her opening it and putting her finger in it, was an entirely unembarrassed yet unmistakable pantomimic announcement of what she would like to do with them—namely to masturbate.[11]

He described this behavior of toying with her purse as Ida's "admission" of the masturbation and bed-wetting, an example of Freud's misleading use of language to suggest that his patients had literally asserted something when in fact they had done nothing of the kind. In any case, bed-wetting has nothing to do with masturbation. Freud knew less about sex than any farmer's wife. And fiddling with things has nothing to do with masturbation. Poker players, for example, often play with their chips. This does not represent masturbation.

Ida's sessions with Freud lasted eighteen months, after which she broke off the treatment. Freud regretted that he had not been able to persuade her to give in to Herr K.

---

[10] The word used for this purse is 'reticule', a word which is now somewhat obsolete and unfamiliar to many people.

[11] Freud 1953, Volume VII, 76–77.

Why could Freud never convince Ida of any of his theories and why did she break off the analysis? To account for this, Freud applied his theory of 'transference', by which psychoanalyzed patients would transfer their feelings onto the analyst, in this case Freud himself. The patient's irritation with the analyst could be explained as an expression of the patient's unconscious love for the analyst. If the patient developed a crush on the analyst, this too would prove that the patient loved the analyst. See?

Freud maintained that Ida was in love with Herr K., an emotion which stemmed from her repressed desire to have sex with her father. In Freud's judgment Ida's love for Herr K. eventually became transformed into a love for Freud. When Ida had a dream about smoke, Freud concluded that this proved that Ida was unconsciously hankering for a kiss from Freud himself, who habitually smoked cigars.

The Case of the Obsessive Officer (1907)

In this brief chapter we do not mention all of Freud's famous cases, though they all provide evidence of factual misrepresentation. The case of the Rat Man (1907) is particularly revealing. Freud nearly always destroyed his original case notes; factual discrepancies in his reports of his cases are usually found by comparing his first written-up account of a case with its later embellishments. In the case of the Rat Man, however, part of the original case notes somehow survived. Not surprisingly, in view of Freud's habitual flexibility with facts, there are distortions even in his first account of the case, when compared with the original notes.

The Rat Man, whose name was Ernst Lanzer,[12] came to Freud complaining of obsessive fears and compulsive influences. Lanzer had heard from a fellow army officer a vivid

---

[12] Some writers say it was Paul Lorenz. Anyway, it's the same case we're talking about.

story of a Chinese torture, in which a hungry rat was induced to eat its way into the rectum of the torture victim (the other torture victim, if you count the poor rat). Among Lanzer's obsessive thoughts was repeatedly imagining his father and his fiancée subjected to this form of torture (even though the father had been dead for some years).

Lanzer free-associated on the word *Ratten* (German for 'rats'), and came up with *Raten* ('installments'), and *Spielratte* ('gaming rat'), a slang term for a habitual or reckless gambler. Lanzer also talked of marrying (in German, *heiraten*) his girl-friend. Lanzer's father had indeed been a gambler. Freud also elicited that in his childhood Lanzer had once been punished for biting someone.

Putting this all together in his predictable way, and bringing in Freud's notion that children think of intercourse as occurring through the anus, Freud concluded that Lanzer unconsciously identified himself as a rat, having anal intercourse with his father and his girl-friend. This supposed phantasy of Lanzer's, dreamed up by Freud, stemmed from Lanzer's aggression against his father, which arose, as we have by now come to expect, from the father having threatened Lanzer with castration.

In his study of this case,[13] Patrick Mahony, himself a psychoanalyst and admirer of Freud, found numerous inaccuracies and misleading omissions. Freud claimed he had treated Lanzer for over eleven months, which Mahony shows to be impossible. Freud manipulated the order of events to make a better story. For instance, Lanzer reported to Freud that he would open the door of his apartment after midnight, apparently so that his father's ghost could enter, and then stare at Lanzer's penis. (Yes, there's no dispute that Lanzer was a tad eccentric.) When Freud wrote up the case, he stated that he had deduced from this information that Lanzer had once been punished by his father for masturbation. Freud's original notes show, however, that Freud came up with this the-

---

[13] Mahony 1986.

ory about punishment for masturbation before he had heard the report of Lanzer's unusual nocturnal habit. In another example, Freud reported that Lanzer had begun to masturbate compulsively, shortly after his father's death—cause and effect in Freud's opinion. The notes show that Lanzer reported his commencement of masturbation as occurring two years after the father's death, and did not say that there was anything compulsive about it.

In this case, Freud made his usual mendacious claim of the patient's total recovery, when in fact a letter to Jung penned after his written version of the case history described Lanzer as still having problems.[14]

The Case of the Bewildered Boy (1909)

After seeing a horse fall down in the street, a little boy named Hans developed a fear of horses, and a fear of going out into the street (at this time, horses were as common in city streets as cars are today). Hans was analyzed by his father, who corresponded with Freud. The father was a convert to Freud's ideas and eager to find them instantiated in his son's behavior.

The analysis of Hans showed Hans's father that the boy's fear of horses arose from his sexual desire for his mother and murderous feelings towards his father. When Hans said on one occasion that he was frightened at those times when his father was not there, both the father and Freud interpreted this as the sure sign of a repressed wish for the father's death.

After being taken to the zoo, Hans showed fear of the big animals, especially the giraffes. Later he had a dream about two giraffes, a big one and a crumpled one. The interpretation composed by Hans's father was that the big giraffe was

---

[14] Freud 1953, Volume IX, 155. See Mahony 1986 and the discussion in Esterson 1993, 62–67.

the father's penis and the crumpled giraffe was Hans's mother's vulva. Believe it or not, Freud applauded this interpretation as "penetrating"!

It's almost unnecessary to add that children may inherit a genetic predisposition to fear large animals, that Hans had witnessed a violent and disturbing accident involving a horse, and that any search for the origins of such a fear in his sexual desires is extraordinarily silly.

The Case of the Retentive Russian (1910–1914)

The case of the Wolf Man has often been hailed as one of the most brilliant, if not the most brilliant, of Freud's therapeutic achievements. It became Freud's most famous case, and was acclaimed by psychoanalysts as a showcase of the Freudian method. Unfortunately for psychoanalysis, the Wolf Man long outlived Freud, wrote his memoirs, and was later interviewed at length.

Sergei Pankeev[15] was treated by Freud for four and a half years, beginning in 1910. Central to Freud's analysis of Pankeev was his interpretation of a dream Pankeev recalled having had at the age of four. In the dream, Pankeev saw through the open window of his bedroom six or seven white dogs with big bushy tails, sitting on a large tree and facing the window. Pankeev screamed and woke up.

The following is Freud's interpretation. The dogs, which Freud chose to describe as wolves (why not?), represent Pankeev's parents: the number of the dogs being six or seven, instead of two, because Pankeev's unconscious is working hard to disguise the meaning of the dream. The fact that the dogs are perfectly still represents the opposite of stillness: violent motion, and therefore (wait for it . . .) sexual intercourse. The

---

[15] Pankeev was Russian. His name is pronounced 'Pan-kay-yeff'. In some discussions of the Wolf Man case, his name is spelled according to the German transliteration, 'Pankejeff'.

dogs' whiteness indicates bed linens. On the principle that objects often symbolize the opposite of what they seem to represent, the dogs' big tails refer to castration. That the dogs were staring at Pankeev indicates that Pankeev was staring at his parents.

From this, Freud deduced the following: at age one, Pankeev had watched his father and mother copulating doggy-style, three times in succession, while Pankeev was so horrified to see this that he soiled himself. The little boy was able to see from this that his mother lacked a penis, and therefore concluded that she had lost it due to castration.

Freud was never able to convince Pankeev that this episode had occurred, and the sleeping arrangements in Pankeev's fairly wealthy household would not have permitted it. For a small child watching a copulating couple to be able to make the discovery that the woman has no penis is an observational feat that "would defy the ingenious staging of any pornographic film producer."[16] Pankeev later called Freud's interpretation "terribly far-fetched."[17] However this 'primal scene' was the centerpiece of Freud's analysis. (Freud's own peculiar personal preoccupations recur in these cases: he had convinced himself late in life that he had seen his own parents copulating doggy-style, for example.)

When Freud planned to publish his account of the Wolf Man case (publication was delayed by the First World War), the psychoanalytic movement had to deal with criticisms from Alfred Adler and Carl Jung, both of whom had parted from Freud's movement and begun to recruit their own independent followings, and both of whom denied that sex was at the bottom[18] of all neuroses. It was essential to defend Freudism by 'demonstrating' that the cause of all neuroses lies in early childhood sex. The Wolf Man case was therefore seen as a fine propaganda weapon against these deviationists.

---

[16] Mahony 1982, 52.
[17] Obholtzer 1982, p. 35.
[18] Sorry.

Freud claimed in his 1918 case history that Sergei Pankeev had been completely cured. This was quite the opposite of the truth. Freud repeatedly claimed success in cases where it has been shown the facts were otherwise, and there is no proof that Freud ever had a real 'success'.

Pankeev outlived Freud by forty years, and remained prone to depression and obsessions for the rest of his life. His physical problems, which Freud pronounced to be hysterical and announced had been cured as the result of psychoanalysis, were actually genuine bodily ailments and were never cured. Owing to mistreatment by a village doctor early in life, Pankeev could not empty his bowels normally, and always had to use enemas. This condition was diagnosed by Freud as due to repressed homosexuality, and Freud declared it had been cured. In fact it persisted until the end of Pankeev's life.[19]

Pankeev was made the prize exhibit of psychoanalysis, but he became an embarrassment because of his continuing physical and emotional problems. The head of organized psychoanalysis, Kurt Eissler, through the Freud Archives, sent Pankeev regular sums of money to enable him to pay off a former lady friend who was blackmailing him. At the same time, Eissler dissuaded Pankeev from emigrating to America, with its amber waves of well-to-do neurotics, where he might spill the beans about his dealings with psychoanalysis and his continuing problems. Eissler also tried to dissuade Pankeev from talking to Karin Obholtzer, who eventually produced the book of interviews with him. She was able to secure Pankeev's agreement by promising him the interviews would not appear until after his death. In short, the facts about Pankeev were an embarrassment to psychoanalysis, so he was

---

[19] Pankeev wrote his memoirs (Gardiner 1971) and was interviewed at length (Obholtzer 1982). His recollections often contradict Freud's account, and in the few cases where it's possible to settle the matter, Pankeev is accurate and Freud inaccurate. There are also occasions where Freud gives different details at different times, the earlier ones being closer to Pankeev's account.

paid off to keep him quiet, but he rebelled somewhat against being silenced, and communicated his real feelings to Obholtzer for posterity. As Pankeev summarized it:

> In reality the whole thing looks like a catastrophe. I am in the same state as when I first came to Freud, and Freud is no more. (Obholzer 1982, 171–72)

The Case of the Uncured Analyst (1921–1924)

Horace Frink, a handsome man who looked a bit like Frank Sinatra, was a well-known figure in the American psychoanalytic movement, having published a popular book on psychoanalysis, *Morbid Fears and Compulsions*, in 1918. A practicing psychoanalyst, Frink had an affair for several years with one of his patients, the rich bank heiress and married woman Angelika Bijur. Freud became involved in February 1921, when Frink went to Vienna to undergo a training analysis with Freud. Frink idolized Freud and was eager to follow any of his suggestions.

Freud exhorted Frink to divorce his wife, and urged Bijur, who also became his patient, to divorce her husband. Freud even gave Bijur a signed photograph of himself with an inscription beginning "To Angie Frink," taking her future marriage to Frink for granted. Freud never met Bijur's husband or Frink's wife. It is clear from all the facts[20] that one of Freud's motives was to secure Angelika's financial fortune for the psychoanalytic movement.

Frink suffered from depression and hallucinations. Freud told Angelika Bijur that Frink was a latent homosexual who would turn into an outright homosexual and become seriously 'ill' if she ended the affair. Frink himself 'resisted' Freud's diagnosis of homosexuality, and expressed doubts about a long-term future with Angelika, who sometimes

---

[20] Edmunds 1988.

struck him as unattractive. Freud wrote to Frink in November 1921:

> May I still suggest to you that your idea Mrs. B had lost part of her beauty may be turned into her having lost part of her money. . . . Your complaint that you cannot grasp your homosexuality implies that you are not yet aware of your phantasy of making me a rich man. If matters turn out all right let us change this imaginary gift into a real contribution to the Psychoanalytic Funds.[21]

The divorces and the marriage did occur as recommend by Freud. Freud pronounced Frink cured. While on his honeymoon, Frink, known to be Freud's protégé, was elected president of the New York Psychoanalytic Society. Both Bijur's husband and Frink's former wife were devastated and both died shortly afterwards. Bijur's husband wrote an accusatory open letter to Freud which he planned to publish as an ad in the New York newspapers, but fortunately for Freud, he died before he could carry out this intention.

Frink's emotional disturbances grew worse, and his new marriage quickly turned sour. In May 1924, Frink committed himself to the Phipps Psychiatric Clinic under the care of his former teacher, Adolf Meyer, the most eminent American psychiatrist at the time, who found Freud's involvement in the case "nauseating." Meyer had had some sympathies for psychoanalysis, but from now on became more firmly committed to the 'biological' approach to psychiatry. (Nothing like Cognitive-Behavioral Therapy had yet come into existence.)

Angelika Bijur divorced Horace Frink, who became severely depressed and made repeated suicide attempts. He later expressed the view that he should never have left his first wife and that Freud had made serious mistakes. Frink resumed practicing as a psychoanalyst when his own mental problems had abated sufficiently.

---

[21] Edmunds 1988, 45. Reprinted Crews 1998, 270.

Individuals who do foolish things because they rely on a persuasive and charismatic advisor must retain some responsibility for their own choice of that advisor. Still, four people's lives were made more wretched by Freud's self-promoting and self-serving intervention. And because Freud was also invariably obtuse and inept about the most elementary human interactions, his intervention was a botched job, even from his own egoistical and mercenary point of view.

Looking on the bright side, Angelika Bijur's fees made up the bulk of Dr. Freud's income for a couple of years, and a scandal which might have discredited psychoanalysis and thus imperiled Freud's subsequent income was narrowly averted. The evidence of Freud's bad behavior in the Frink case was successfully tidied away for seventy years.

8
The Recovered Memory Craze

In the 1980s, a horrifying new craze began, spreading rapidly and eventually affecting many thousands of people in the United States and other countries. This malignant movement, comparable to the witch hunts of earlier times, reached a peak in the early 1990s. It was the phenomenon of recovered memories.

A person bothered by being overweight, or drinking too heavily, by anxiety attacks, or some other common problem of human existence, would go for help to a psychotherapist. The therapist would immediately identify the root of the trouble as sexual abuse in childhood. The client would deny any memory of such abuse. The psychotherapist would insist that this was entirely normal: the abuse was real, and the fact that it had been forgotten merely demonstrated how horrifying it had been. The cure of the client's problems lay in remembering. Therapists who took this approach applied it to all their clients without exception. The majority of these therapists and the overwhelming majority of the clients were women.

Client and therapist would then work together to recover the memory of the abuse. This would most often take several months, and then fragmentary images would begin to appear in the client's mind. The lack of clarity or convincingness in these 'memories' would make the client doubt that they were really memories of anything, but the psychotherapist, assumed to be an expert on the workings of the mind, would assure the client that this quality of the images was to be expected because of repression. With work, these images could be built upon, and they would eventually become vivid, compelling, and detailed. And with further persistence this would happen.

The client would thus, guided by the therapist, 'recover' memories of innumerable incidents of sexual abuse in childhood. This would be a highly emotional process. Parents and siblings would most often be among the perpetrators, who would also often include childcare workers, family friends, and outstanding members of the community. Often the incidents would involve torture, degradation, and satanic rituals.

The client would then be urged by the therapist to shun the 'perpetrators', and to press criminal charges. The therapist would declare that this would be curative and would also encourage the clients to fantasize about attacking, torturing, and dismembering the perpetrators.

The stories produced in this way often contained fantastic or manifestly improbable elements. According to the development of events, especially in legal proceedings, these would be edited out to make the stories more convincing. Therapists would explain that inaccuracies in the stories did not impeach their basic reliability. Some of these therapists believed in reincarnation, and in such cases, they found it just as easy to recover memories of sexual molestation in previous lives as in their client's current life.

Only a minority of therapists practiced or condoned 'recovered memory therapy' but this still had a huge impact on society. According to one estimate, out of about 255,000 licensed psychotherapists in the United States, over 50,000 became recovered memory practitioners, and they were joined by thousands more unlicensed practitioners offering to help with 'incest work'.

Recovered memory therapy was opposed by Cognitive-Behavioral therapists. It was also opposed by all orthodox Freudian therapists (now a tiny fraction of their number forty years earlier), who identified the 'recovered memories' as screen memories—possibly false, though to Freudians screen memories may be true or false but in any case are not the root of the problem. The recovered memory therapists reversed the move that Freud made in 1897, from surmised actual seductions to surmised seduction phantasies—though they did so in a culture saturated with broad Freudianism, and therefore accepting the reality of repressed memories.

The Recovered Memory Juggernaut

The recovered memory therapists believed, and often convinced courts, that memories can be completely forgotten for decades, and then recovered as fresh as the day they happened, that the mind has a sort of videotape which records everything that happens in accurate detail, even though it is not available to normal recall, that such forgotten events can cause neurotic disturbances like overeating or panic attacks, and that profound emotion at the time of recall helps to prove the truth of the memories.

Under the impact of the recovered memory movement, legal safeguards built up over centuries, in recognition of the fact that memories become distorted with the passage of time, were dismantled. Statutes of limitation and other laws were modified to permit and encourage suits for damages on the basis of decades-old incidents supposedly recalled in therapy. The state of Washington changed its laws in 1989 to permit recovery of damages for injuries resulting from child sexual abuse at any time within three years of *remembering* the abuse. Many other states made similar changes in their laws.

In at least one trial, prospective jurors who were skeptical about the possibility that memories could be repressed and then recovered, were excused from the jury, while it was known that at least one juror was a zealous proponent of this theory. This is exactly as if, in a trial for murder by casting evil spells, prospective jurors were interrogated about their

173

theological views, and only those committed to a belief in the efficacy of witchcraft were permitted to serve.

The Recovered Memory Bible

Numerous books appeared propagating the recovered memories craze. The biggest-selling was *The Courage to Heal* by Ellen Bass and Laura Davis, two psychotherapists who were radically anti-male feminists with no background of expertise in the psychology of memory. This book became the bible and the practical manual of the recovered memory movement. It probably gave rise to more human misery than any other twentieth-century book except Lenin's *State and Revolution* and Hitler's *Mein Kampf.*

Bass and Davis insist that "If you think you were abused and your life shows the symptoms, then [even though you have no recollection of the abuse] you were."[1] Bass and Davis boldly assert that "demands for proof are unreasonable." They strongly encourage the deliberate whipping up of hatred against the supposed abusers: "You may dream of murder or castration. . . . Let yourself imagine it to your heart's content" (128). Somewhat regretfully, they counsel against actual killing or maiming, and recommend clients to "get strong by suing," supplying a list of lawyers eager to take up such cases.

The Courage to Heal has a chapter entirely devoted to conjuring up lost memories and a chapter entirely devoted to convincing yourself that these conjured-up memories are true. In all this book's 528 pages, there is not a single word of caution that the 'memories' produced may be inaccurate.

Not just therapists and social workers, but many legislators, police, schoolteachers and others swallowed the theory that there are such things as 'repressed memories' which can 'come back' after years of being forgotten.

---

[1] Bass and Davis 1988, 22.

Could Any of the Stories Be True?

Is it possible that some of the people accused of sexual abuse by their now grown-up children, who recovered the memory after decades of not remembering, really are guilty? Yes, it's possible, just as you can stick a pin in the phone book and say that the person you have selected is a murderer. By chance you could be right, but only by chance.

Recovered memories of abuse were rarely corroborated by any other evidence. In fact, the customary pattern was that the therapy client's first coherent story would contradict ascertainable facts and would thus be disprovable. The story would then be creatively reshaped by the therapist, the client, and prosecutors, to make it consistent with the known evidence.

The recovered memories were usually the only evidence against the accused. In the overwhelming majority of cases, no physical or other corroborating evidence was ever found. We would never have suspected the abuse if it were not for the recovered memory. You might say that the client's current emotional or behavioral problems count as evidence, but that would be a mistake. Millions of people become anxious, or depressed, or eat or drink too heavily. Most of them were never sexually abused, and most people who were sexually abused don't develop such problems as adults. The widespread belief that children who were sexually abused inevitably grow up into adults with serious problems (even perhaps being more likely to themselves commit sexual abuse of children) is pure myth.[2]

But let's look at this from another angle. Suppose—just for comparison—that we start from well-documented cases of abuse. Do we find that the victims later forget that the abuse occurred? Most often, we do not. Victims of sexual abuse usually remember the abuse; they rarely forget it. The same applies to other nasty experiences. People interned in concentration camps, subjected to torture, forced to witness their loved ones killed in front of their eyes, escaping badly

---

[2] Lilienfeld, Lynn, Ruscio, and Beyerstein 2010, 166–171.

burned from a fire, or otherwise subjected to some extremely distressing experience, do not forget that this has happened to them. Every day the police call on victims of crime to interview them about recent rapes, muggings, or other violent attacks. A police officer may do this several times a week for years, without ever meeting someone who says 'What are you talking about? What crime? I don't remember being attacked.'

Some writers claim that there are recorded cases where survivors of trauma forget what happened to them. But on close inspection, nearly all such reported exceptions fall under one or more of the following:

1. Everyone forgets the great majority of what happened to them in the first two or three years of life. This has nothing to do with anything unpleasant in what happened, but applies equally to pleasant and unpleasant experiences. It's due to the incomplete development of the infant's brain, and is the same in all societies and cultures, irrespective of the quality of the child's experiences. Most 'lost memories' from this period never 'come back'.

   Virtually none of the recovered memory cases were confined to the first two or three years of life. Most of the claims involved repeated abuse over a period of several years.

2. There is also ordinary forgetting. We all forget much of what happens to us and children above the age of three often forget incidents of which they don't appreciate the full significance. A seven-year-old who is sexually abused may have forgotten this incident a few years later. Similarly, she may have forgotten having acute apendicitis and being rushed to hospital, or being in a car accident, or visiting Disneyland. One of the main influences on whether the seven-year-old will later remember any of these experiences is whether she is reminded of them by photographs or by people talking about the incidents.

3. A head injury or severe physical shock such as serious alcoholic poisoning can lead to loss of memory. The vast majority of recovered memory cases don't involve any such severe physical shock, and in any case, such a possibility does not make it any more likely that a memory recovered after many years could be reliable.

4. People who witness some event often get details wrong, even if they are asked about it immediately afterwards, and the liability to error increases if they are upset at the time (and of course increases the longer the delay between the incident and making a permanent record). The exact order of events may become jumbled up, or some minor details may be forgotten until the witness is reminded of them. But they don't forget that the incident occurred at all. For example, a mugging victim (much to the glee of the perpetrator's defense attorney) may mix up some of the details of exactly what occurred, such as things the mugger and the victim said at the time but the victim will not forget that he has been mugged.

5. If people recollect some event that happened years earlier, and are then asked whether they had ever forgotten that event, they will often say that they forgot it for a time, when all that they mean is that it never crossed their mind: they didn't have any occasion to think of it. Further questioning is necessary to pin down exactly what they mean, and such questioning will generally show that there was no period when they were *unable* to remember the event.

Last Year in Manhattan Beach

Coinciding with this mania for recovering adults' memories of childhood abuse, there was also an enormous proliferation of accusations and prosecutions for much more recent sexual molestation of children.

What happened in such cases was that once an accusation had been made, the alleged child victims would be handed over to social workers and psychotherapists, who would then interrogate the children for hours on end, day after day, week after week, and month after month. Often the browbeating would go on until the child was close to physical exhaustion. If the child denied anything occurred she was made to feel this was disappointing, if not shameful, whereas if she produced a juicy story she was showered with affection and other rewards, including the reward of being left alone for a while.

Subjected to such treatment, the children would often give the inquisitors what they wanted to hear. Once a story of abuse had been created, the therapists worked with prosecutors to massage this story into something as detailed as possible, eliminating elements which might arouse a jury's suspicions while adding more embellishments to nail down the case against the accused. It will not have escaped our sharp-witted readers that in such cases the real child abusers are the therapists, social workers, and prosecutors.

Children are sometimes sexually molested by adults. Molested children may deny that a recent act of molestation had occurred. They might do this for a number of motives, but not because they had forgotten the incident. It's also familiar to anyone who has worked with children that they typically adapt the stories they tell to fit whatever they think adults want to hear.

The case of an adult who has lived for twenty or thirty years with no recollection of being abused, and is then persuaded by a therapist that abuse occurred is very different from the case of a child who was allegedly abused a few weeks or months ago and now denies it happened. In the latter case, there is the possibility that the child was indeed abused and knows full well that it did happen, and for some reason, such as embarrassment or fearful uncertainty about what might ensue, decides to deny it.

Fibbing, either saying that something occurred when it did not, or denying something occurred when it did, is entirely normal and universal in childhood. The vast difference between lying and being unable to remember is perfectly clear to anyone, but is obscured by the treacherous phrase 'in denial', which is often applied in such cases.

However, pressuring children to *say* that something happened recently and pressuring adults to *remember* that something happened long ago are alike in this respect: either method may result in the creation of a belief, in the child's or the adult's mind, that something happened when in fact it did not.

The Myth of Satanic Cults

Many of these stories, both from children and adults, involved accounts of Satanic cults and Satanic ritual abuse. Belief in the existence of such cults had been spreading since the early 1970s, and the growth of this belief became more rapid in the 1980s, following publication of the wildly implausible 'survivor story' *Michelle Remembers*.

Such real or imaginary phenomena as ritual killing of animals and of blonde virgins, desecration of cemeteries, backward-masking of messages in heavy metal ditties, Goth make-up, Dungeons and Dragons, missing children, and the prominence of wizards and witches in children's literature all began to be linked by some writers to supposed Satanic cults.

There has been frequent and intensive investigation into the possible activities of Satanic cults. In many cases, reports of Satanic cult activity have been proven false, and in no case have they ever been corroborated.[3] There are rare, isolated murderers who avow that Satan is giving them instructions to kill people, just as there are similar murderers who get their orders from God, the CIA, or the Martians. There are groups of teenage daredevils, as ignorant of Satanism as of any doctrinal system, who may do things like daubing signs in public places. There are associations of violent criminals who use torture as a means of persuasion and who may also

---

[3] Victor 1993.

be superstitious. There are also avowedly Satan-worshipping congregations, totaling a few hundred members in the US, the best known being Anton Le Vey's Church of Satan; these churches are completely respectable and law-abiding, their membership unusually boring.

The Satanic cults which keep popping up in therapy are vast, well-connected networks of outwardly respectable people who secretly meet clad in black robes, and practice the ritual rape, torture, and sacrifice of animals, children, and virgin maidens. No such cult exists or has ever existed in the United States or anywhere else. But since the media were for a time filled with references to such imaginary cults, it's entirely possible that some day a group of people will form a cult along these lines.

Reincarnation Therapy

Lessons in Evil, Lessons from the Light by Gail Carr Feldman appeared at the height of the recovered memory craze. It was published by a reputable house, launched with a lavishly funded nationwide author tour, and came with rapturous blurbs from prominent writers and doctors. Like *Michelle Remembers*, it has been reprinted and still finds many eager believers. It is an account by a psychotherapist of one client, "Barbara".

When Barbara begins psychotherapy with Feldman, her problems are that she feels tense during sex with her husband and sometimes gets angry with her daughter. Dr. Feldman immediately grasps the fact that these symptoms must have arisen from sex abuse in Barbara's childhood. Barbara has vague feelings, which she may have picked up from previous therapists, that she might have been abused in childhood, but no actual memories of any such molestation.

Using hypnosis, Feldman takes Barbara back to the age of five, and the five-year-old Barbara reports the ritual killing of a cat by her grandfather, who makes her eat the cat's heart and drink its blood. Barbara is disinclined to accept that this is a real memory but Feldman knows better, and authoritatively informs Barbara that it must have happened.

After further encouragement from Feldman, Barbara produces many more macabre disclosures. It turns out that Barbara's childhood was crowded with incident. It was chop, chop, saw, saw, and scream, scream, with many corpses, both whole and in pieces, both freshly cropped and nicely matured, liberally bestrewn around the family hearth. Snakes in bodily orifices and the drinking of urine were among the more prosaic of the day-to-day occurrences of Barbara's overstimulated childhood.

Toward the end of the story, the patient is regressed to a prior existence and learns that her daughter is the reincarnation of her father in that previous life. Told this by Barbara, Dr. Feldman responds: "'Whew'. I gripped the sides of my chair. 'That is really something. . . .'" This finding neatly explains Barbara's anger towards her daughter, and the anger then goes away.

We also learn that Feldman herself has regressed to a previous life as an American Indian woman, and on one of these regressions is spotted by one of her current friends, also regressing to the same eighteenth-century Native American village. Informed of this by the friend (in the current life), Dr. Feldman reports "My mouth fell open"—but not with incredulity. In that previous life, Feldman died in childbirth, thus explaining her hostility to her (current) husband's sexual advances, which also evaporates immediately upon the discovery of its centuries-old cause.

Memories to Order

If a therapist is a believer in recovered memories, then a great many of her clients will produce memories of childhood rape. A substantial minority of these clients (it has been estimated at one in five) also produce memories of Satanic cult rituals, while a smaller number produce memories of previous lives.

What accounts for these differences in the memories? Recovered memories always conform to the views of the therapist. Many therapists believe in Satanic cults, and all *their* clients produce memories of Satanic cults. Comparatively few believe in reincarnation, but all *their* clients produce memories of past lives. As the recovered memories are produced, they are shaped by the expectations and beliefs of the therapists. If the therapist disbelieves some class of recovered memories, they are edited out. Bass and Davis, for instance, view any past-life recollections as symptoms of continuing 'denial', and keep their clients working on these memories to shift them into the current life.

There were always a few outspoken critics of the new craze, especially among research psychologists concerned with memory. The False Memory Syndrome Foundation (FMSF) was founded in February 1992, both to assist victims of unsubstantiated accusations arising from allegedly recovered memories and to promote research into the phenomenon of fabricated memories. The FMSF soon had thousands of cases on file.

The craze has now died down, leaving behind an immense waste land of devastated families. Judges and juries are now more likely to be made aware of the unreliability of 'recovered memories', and damages awarded against recovered memory therapists have choked off most of these cases at their source.

Fallacies of Memory

One of the reasons why the recovered memory craze was able to become so powerful so quickly was that it drew upon certain beliefs about the way memory works, beliefs which have been disproved by psychological research, but are still very popular.

One misconception is that, even if we seem to have forgotten something, it is really there, somewhere in the depths of our memory, and could possibly be recaptured in perfect detail if we only knew the right technique for finding it. It is true, of course, that we sometimes forget things and then later remember them again. However, all memories, whether interrupted by a period of forgetting or not, are imperfect and approximate. Remembering is an act of imaginative construction, and always prone to error.

Many experiences we have are completely forgotten, leaving no trace. You have now completely forgotten many of the things that have happened to you in the past twenty-four hours, but even if we confine ourselves to those things you could now remember if you tried, most will be completely gone a year in the future.

Memory is much more fallible than most people realize. For example, people who were around in November 1963 will usually tell you that they can remember exactly where they were and what they were doing when they heard the news of President Kennedy's assassination. More recent research suggests, however, that many of these recollections are false. A study was done of people's memories of the Space Shuttle Columbia Disaster in February 2003. Shortly after the disaster, subjects wrote down their recollections of how they had heard of this disaster and what their reactions were. These written accounts were then taken from them and filed, and they were again asked for their recollections years later. The later recollections were often wildly at variance with the earlier ones, with wholly new episodes and experiences occurring in the later ones. These people were firmly convinced of the accuracy of their later recollections, because of their vividness and precision.

Memory is a form of imagination. The memory of an event is the construction of a story from coded information in the brain that has to be shaped into something meaningful at the point of recollection. Of course, memory often is quite accurate, especially in broad outline. But memory always fades and breaks up into fragments. Vividness and precision of a memory are no guarantee that the memory is true. Quite the contrary, if the event happened years ago, and you feel like saying 'I can remember it as though it just happened', you are probably mistaken. If you remember the gist of a conversation you had with someone ten years ago, you might very well be right. But if you think you remember which side his hair was parted or if you have a very distinct conviction of the exact words he used, you're probably deluded—unless you made a written record of these things immediately after the conversation, and have been able to consult it.

An emotional quality to the memory is also unable to guarantee its accuracy, and may be grounds for suspicion. Suppose that you underwent an extremely unpleasant experience twenty years ago, for example, being badly injured in a car accident. You will, of course, remember that this occurred—you won't 'represss' the memory of it. But you will not feel terribly upset as you recall this episode. A memory of a horrifying experience is not itself usually horrifying, and never as horrifying as the original experience. If you do feel extremely upset today when you recollect something that happened years ago, this is probably because you enjoy the sensation of wallowing in your self-pity or resentment.

While we often forget things, and sometimes remember them again, this does not involve any repression. If we cannot remember something by the normal processes of casting our mind back, or by re-reading old letters, for example, then prolonged attempts to recall forgotten events will eventually lead to the production of apparent memories which are very likely new concoctions and seriously inaccurate.

9
Your Unconscious Has No Mind of Its Own

When a person thinks, talks, and acts, there's a lot going on in his body which he isn't aware of. We can call this his unconscious. For example, his pancreas is regulating the amount of glucose in his blood and his liver is secreting bile. Some unconscious bodily functions occur in his brain. Automatic brain functions control his breathing and heartbeat. They too belong to his unconscious.

When we're conscious, we're using our brains, but being conscious relies upon many things going on unconsciously in our brains, as well as in the rest of our bodies. We depend upon unconscious processes to stay alive all the time. And sometimes unconscious processes are directly involved in the exercise of consciousness. The most familiar example is what happens when we speak.

When people talk, they freely improvise sentences. As they're doing this, they usually don't give a thought to any rules of grammar, syntax, or logic, but nonetheless they comply with these rules. These rules are extremely complex: so complex that nobody knows all of them, or probably ever could. Scholars may spend their adult lives studying the rules governing ordinary speech in one dialect, say the American dialect of English, without ever discovering all the rules being applied or exhausting the subtlety and complexity of these rules.

The rules governing language are not like the rules of golf. They are generally transmitted without being stated or even known. Children or foreigners will be corrected if they depart from the rules, but even the individuals doing the correcting will normally not really understand the rule that is being applied. A two-year-old may actually be told: 'You don't say, "The dog bited me"; you say, "The dog bit me."' But in this example the two-year-old has picked up a rule that was never stated or explained, and has to be informed that in this case that rule is overridden by a different rule.

When someone speaks, they're doing something consciously. But a lot of what they're doing is unconscious, meaning that they're unaware of it. They are not only unaware of how they do it, they're usually unaware of what they're doing. We might say they are doing these things 'on automatic pilot' or 'without thinking'.

A person may speak English perfectly well without being aware of the rule that 'adjectives usually come before nouns' or even that there are such things as adjectives and nouns. People were using adjectives and nouns for many thousands of years before anyone discovered their existence. It's natural to say that such a person is following the rule that adjectives come before nouns, but it's less natural to say that a plant follows the rule to bend its shoots in the direction of the light. We're not tempted to say that the plant obeys its unconscious mind, because we know that a plant (unless it's a triffid) has no brain and no mind. But we may be tempted to say that a human speaker obeys her unconscious mind in complying with grammatical rules, because we know that this compliance is somehow controlled by the brain, and because each example of automatic compliance is something we can imagine being done deliberately.

Someone may follow a rule that then becomes 'second nature'. They then stop literally 'following the rule' and comply with the rule automatically. Someone learning to touch-type will follow the rule 'Always hit the letter S with the ring finger of the left hand', but someone who has learned to touch-type complies with this rule automatically, without thinking.

She may forget that she ever learned such a rule and may be stumped if asked, away from a keyboard, which finger she uses for the letter S.

Memories Are Made of This

We all know many thousands of facts we're not currently thinking about. If suddenly asked about any one of those thousands of facts, for instance in a quiz game, we instantly recall it. We all know that Paris is the capital of France, and we know this even if it hasn't crossed our mind for months. It seems that the fact that Paris is the capital of France is stored in our memory, and if our thoughts turn to that subject, we simply look up the fact which was there all the time, just as we might retrieve a photograph from a file folder. But although it seems that way, it isn't that way. That's an illusion, as we'll see.

Freud supposed that all our memories we're not currently aware of, simply because our attention is focused on something else, belong to our unconscious. Freud used this supposition to argue for his theory of the unconscious. Since we're unconscious, at any one time, of the vast majority of what we know, Freud concludes that there's far more material in the unconscious part of our mind than in the conscious part of our mind. Freud moves from this type of example, where we can quickly summon up a memory just by turning our attention in that direction, to his belief that there is a vast region of the unconscious mind, from which we cannot easily conjure anything up.

If we're currently not thinking of something we could easily recall, Freud calls this 'preconscious'. He makes a distinction between the preconscious and the unconscious, yet he sees the preconscious as a type of unconscious and he likes to use the existence of the preconscious (the accessible unconscious) as an argument for the existence of the inaccessible unconscious.

Sometimes we have a 'mental block' and can't remember something we believe we ought to be able to remember easily.

In such cases, says Freud, repression is the culprit. Such cases, where we can't recall something we feel we ought to be able to recall, are used by Freud to soften us up for the claim that there are many other things that we can't become conscious of, including things that we were never conscious of.

The item that we have forgotten due to a mental block will usually have nothing unpleasant about it that would make us want to forget it. But in such cases, says Freud, the fact is connected by association with something we do want to forget. For example if you can't recall the name of the villainous prosecutor in Season Three of *Dexter* (Miguel Prado), this lapse can be explained by the association with the Prado museum's most famous painting, *Las Meninas* (The Maids of Honor), recalling aspersions made against your mother's honor, which have caused you to be unconsciously anxious that you might be a bastard. (You can spend another three thousand hours of your time plus eighty thousand bucks of your savings, to uncover the deeper significance: your own wish at age five to 'dishonor' your mother.) One assumption behind stories like this is that memory ought naturally to be perfect, so that any failure requires some special explanation. Another assumption is that failure must be motivated: if we try to do something and can't do it, this must be because part of us wants us not to do it.

Do Objects of Consciousness Exist in the Unconscious?

How could Freud get himself into such a horrendous muddle?

It's an essential part of Freud's approach that entities in our unconscious minds are more or less the same as entities in our conscious minds, except that we're not aware of them. Freud always takes for granted that a conscious idea can be identified with 'the same' idea in the unconscious. We have a conscious idea of our mother, of the Moon, and of an apple. We also, claims Freud, have unconscious ideas, which include unconscious ideas of Mom, Moon, and apple, essentially the same as the conscious ideas.

According to Freud, ideas, concepts, emotions, and desires are pretty much the same whether conscious or unconscious. The big difference is that we can perceive them when they're conscious, whereas when they're unconscious we can't perceive them. It's as if they're in the dark, and therefore invisible, when they're unconscious, and when they become conscious it's because a light shines on them, leaving them otherwise unchanged. Consciousness is like an eye which sees some of the contents of the mind, but can't see most of them, because they're in darkness.

Freud was firmly committed to this theory, which he states explicitly,[1] and relies upon in all his analyses. Furthermore, he could not do otherwise, since the way Freud talks about the contents of the unconscious always presupposes that we know what he means when he employs nouns normally used to refer to objects of conscious experience. However, this theory is seriously mistaken. What's in the unconscious can't be the same as what's in consciousness. Whenever we say that something hitherto unconscious has become conscious, what has really happened is that something conscious has been created.

A Simple Analogy

Let's use a simple analogy to make this clear. Take a hand-held calculator which you can pick up anywhere for ten bucks. Now imagine that you were alive in the year 1860, and were able to get hold of such a calculator, miraculously delivered to you from more than a century in the future. What would you make of it?

You'd probably assume that this amazing gizmo contained a list of answers to all the questions that might be put to it. If you divide 847 by 63, to get 13.44, you might suppose that 13.44 was already stored inside the machine as the result of 847 / 63. Now if you were told that the machine con-

---

[1] For instance Freud 1953, Volume V, 615.

tained no list of answers but actually calculated the answer to each problem, and could just as easily calculate the answer to an arithmetic problem that none of its makers had ever thought of, you wouldn't at first believe this astounding claim, but if you did become convinced that the machine performed fresh calculations every time, you'd probably assume that these calculations were done using numerals of the kind you could see on the display panel, symbols like 8, 4, and 7. You might even suppose that it might be possible to open up the calculator and see these numerals being moved around.

Now we know perfectly well that, even when the calculator repeatedly gives the same result to the same repeated problem, it's making a new calculation every time. The calculator does not 'look up' the answer: it generates the answer by executing certain operations which look nothing like the answer. The answer is not there, inside the calculator. The answer doesn't exist until we key in the problem. And we also know that the calculator does not work with numerals like 8, 4, and 7, but with tiny on-off electrical impulses which no one can see, and which would be meaningless to us if we were able to see them.

What's really stored in your brain is not the fact that Paris is the capital of France, but something completely meaningless, totally unintelligible and inscrutable, to your conscious mind. When we say that you know that Paris is the capital of France, even while neither Paris nor France is in your thoughts, what we mean is that the moment your thoughts turn in that direction, but no sooner, you will become aware that Paris is the capital of France. Knowledge, like belief, is a disposition. We might say that there is something unconsciously encoded in the physiology of your brain, which ensures that in the right circumstances you will have the conscious experience of being aware that Paris is the capital of France. That conscious experience does not exist in any form when your thoughts are elsewhere. There is nothing of 'Paris' or 'France' anywhere 'in your mind' or in your brain when you're not thinking about Paris or France! Similarly, the answer to 847 / 63 does not exist unconsciously inside the calculator when no one has input that problem, and the flame of a candle does not exist unconsciously when the candle is out. It does not exist at all. All that exists is the disposition of the candle to have a flame when lit.

We're not saying that your mind is a calculator. We're simply drawing attention to the fact that being able to produce an appropriate answer at any time doesn't require that the answer exists when we're not producing it. There are many differences between your memory and a calculator. Aside from the most obvious facts—that you are conscious and the calculator isn't—your brain doesn't use a binary system of on-off electrical impulses, and your recall of a memory is always affected by the last time it was recalled (so it is never a simple repetition; part of what you're remembering when you remember a fact is due to the last time you remembered that fact).

What this analogy does help to bring out is that nowhere in the brain is there a list of stored facts or experiences which can be looked up, simply as one might look up and replay a video. Your memory is not a folder containing photographs or recordings. When you have a memory, or recollect something, you're constructing that memory from coded information which is meaningless to you until you've done the construction.[2] This work of construction we usually call 'imagination'. Remembering something is always an act of imagination, though not all imagination is memory.

Some people talk about 'retrieving' or 'dredging up' a memory. This way of talking implies that the memory exists while we haven't retrieved it. But the memory doesn't exist until we become conscious of it. We don't retrieve it from anywhere; we construct or create it. The memory is not standing there, like an actor offstage waiting for his cue. No object of consciousness—no idea, memory, image, thought, or mental representation—ever exists unconsciously.

---

[2] Like most things in this chapter, this point is not in the least original (see for instance Hobson 1994, 103), though we have tried to lay everything out with brutal clarity.

Some people use the term 'subconscious' instead of 'unconscious'. This is also a misleading way of talking. It suggests that what's in the 'subconscious' could be in the conscious, but just happens to lie 'beneath' the conscious. The misleading metaphor here is of an inky black pool (perhaps a black lagoon): things become conscious by emerging from the pool, breaking its surface, so that we can 'see' them.

A memory is constructed afresh every time it's remembered. But, of course, the memory is constructed afresh from some kind of stored material (otherwise memories would almost never be accurate, and they often are). The stored material is purely physical; it's part of the chemistry of your brain. We don't want to suggest that what's conscious isn't part of the chemistry of your brain. It's just that the way things appear to your mind when you're conscious of them is not the way any part or aspect of your brain would look to someone examining your brain, and in the case of 'stored memories', there is only the way things would look to someone examining your brain. There's nothing else there. Ideas do not exist somewhere in your mind when they're not in your thoughts. Even if there were unconscious ideas, it would not follow that they get up to the tricks the Freudians attribute to them, but in fact there are no unconscious ideas, any more than a candle that's out has an unconscious flame.

There is no idea that corresponds to the stored material except that the stored material is like a recipe that will make an idea. There's nothing you can do to dig the recipe out of your brain, any more than by pressing the buttons on your calculator you can get at a description of the calculator's electrical circuits. You can't possibly become conscious of this stored material 'from the inside' (any more than you can see on the display panel of your calculator the way in which the operations for finding 847 / 63 are stored) for that would be to transform it into something conscious. We can say that the fact that there's such a recipe in the physiology of your brain is a disposition to have a particular idea. The idea is conscious, never unconscious. The disposition is unconscious, never conscious. The idea and the disposition are not alike: they don't resemble each other in any way.

Generally speaking, in everyday life we assume that a 'stored memory' will not affect our intentions or behavior unless we transform it into an idea—something in our consciousness. We try to remember the combination of the lock we want to open, because we know that unless we can become aware of that number ('bring it to mind'), we won't be able to open the lock. However, the way that rules of language govern our speech without our being aware of those rules illustrates the fact that things we have experienced may affect our behavior even though we don't recall those experiences.

Subjects in experiments have been asked to memorize lists of words. It is found that, by 'salting' some of the lists with particular words, the subjects will later do better at remembering those words, even though they cannot recall that those words had been included at early stages of the experiment. In effect, it's possible to 'program' subjects to remember some words better than they could remember others, without the subjects being aware that this is happening. Notice that this is exactly what anyone would guess to be true, as long as they were uninfluenced by Freudian talk about 'repression' and 'resistance'.

So far, research has found that while some unconscious influences are extremely powerful (rules of language) others are rather limited. For example, legend has it that ads can affect our buying behavior by sending us messages we're not aware of, but in reality 'subliminal advertising' doesn't work.[3]

Dreams and Fantasies Are Conscious

The notion that we can somehow become aware of what's encoded in our unconscious (other than indirectly by transforming it into something quite different) usually goes along

---

[3] Pratkanis 1992.

with the belief that dreams or fantasies give us a view into our unconscious.

Dreams and fantasies are conscious events. The idea that dreaming is somehow unconscious is encouraged by the general view that someone who's asleep is said to be 'unconscious', which is short for 'unconscious of his physical surroundings'. The sleeper is indeed, for the most part, unaware of his physical surroundings, though he may get some awareness, as when a sound or a movement in the physical surroundings is converted into an element of a dream. But the dreamer is always conscious of what goes on in his dream. There can be no such thing as a dream we don't consciously experience while it's going on. The notion of an unconscious dream is like the notion of unfelt sensations of pain.

The state of dreaming is different from the state of wakefulness: they're different forms of consciousness, but they are both conscious states. The same goes for fantasies such as daydreams. Freud was well aware that fantasies are conscious, and therefore sometimes used the word 'phantasies' to signify the unconscious processes which he surmised were going on without the person knowing about them. Freud didn't always follow this verbal distinction strictly, but later followers of Freud, like Melanie Klein, did. In thinking about Freud's theory, it's best to keep the distinction in spelling between fantasies, which are conscious thought processes, and phantasies, which are unconscious processes, and which in our opinion don't exist at all. A patient's phantasy is merely her psychoanalyst's fantasy.

Dreams sometimes contain bizarre or fabulous events which couldn't possibly happen in waking life, but it would be a bit of a muddle to suppose that these events must give you some insight into what's going on in your unconscious. This would be like supposing that if a weird or whimsical picture appears on your computer screen, it must be telling you about the code in which the computer's operating system is written.

We don't have unconscious thoughts, memories, or experiences, things which are just like conscious thoughts, memories, and experiences except that we're not aware of them.

We do have unconscious dispositions to have thoughts, memories, and emotions. To say that sodium chloride has a disposition to dissolve in water doesn't mean that when not dissolved in water it's somehow dissolved in water in a ghostly sense. It just means that when conditions are right it will dissolve in water. We have unconscious dispositions to experience various thoughts, memories, and emotions, but these thoughts, memories, and emotions have no existence whatsoever when we're not experiencing them.

The prevailing confusion of the popular Psychodynamic worldview is illustrated in the movie *Inception* (2010). It's a very good story built on absurd and incoherent assumptions. When we dream, according to the movie, we're in our 'subconscious'. But there we observe people who we're told are 'projections of our subconscious'. But they can't be projections of our subconscious if we're *in* our subconscious! We should be able to see our subconscious projecting them, but instead we just see them. The movie has to tacitly assume that when we're in our subconscious, there's another subconscious we can't observe, which is feeding things into the subconscious we do observe. In other words, the movie can't help tacitly acknowledging that the 'subconscious' we observe in the dream is really something we're conscious of and can't be conceived of except as something we're conscious of. The movie introduces us to different 'levels' of the subconscious, even down to the absolutely deepest level, but we never see a level where the 'projections' are being manufactured. It's as though we keep expecting to see a sausage machine but all we ever see are sausages. This paradox is removed once we recognize that 1. when we're dreaming we're not in any kind of subconscious at all, but conscious, and 2. our ideas and images of persons, stories, and situations, in dreams or in waking life. simply don't exist in any sense at all when they're not in our consciousness.

Dreams and Primary Process

Freud believed that the unconscious mind strings ideas together in a way different from the conscious mind—although he supposes that the ideas themselves are pretty much the same. The way the unconscious mind does it he called "primary process" and the way the conscious mind does it he called "secondary process." Just what processes go on in the brain, causing thoughts to be possible, is something we don't know much about. Yet we can still criticize Freud's idea of primary process, because he lets us know that primary process is the kind of thinking that goes on in dreams and in the minds of newborn babies. This is why he believes that dreams can tell us about the unconscious mind.[4]

We might wonder why, in that case, newborn babies dream. However, the serious problem with Freud's view is that any dream we think about and talk about can only be inside the realm of what Freud calls secondary process.

An idea that occurs to some people is that the dream as it happens when sleeping is much less coherent and well-ordered than it seems to be when remembered upon waking up. According to this view, the 'story' is put into the dream at the point when it is remembered immediately after waking. Possibly then, the 'real' dream, before it has been given shape by consciousness, would tell us something about our unconscious. Research on dreams doesn't seem to bear out this theory. Dreams, it appears, do happen as they seem to happen, in real time, as intelligible sequences of events, much as they are remembered when awake (though the remembered dream may often have deleted much of the content of the real-time dream).

Anyway, this possibility doesn't affect the question of primary process. If the dream story is constructed upon waking, that would be secondary process, and anything intelligible in the dream would still be something in consciousness. It would still be just as true that the dream tells us nothing about the unconscious (nothing that other conscious experiences can't tell us). The only difference would

---

[4] Most of what Freud had to say about primary process is in the last-but-one section of the last chapter of *The Interpretation of Dreams*. Freud 1953, Volume V, 588–609.

be that the dream that is available for our inspection would have been created upon waking and not while asleep. There would then be no way to get at 'the real dream' which happened when we were sleeping. But if the intelligibility is put into the dream in real time, during sleep, there's still no way.

Some people say that dreams are illogical, but this is a mistake. Nothing *illogical* can be witnessed or imagined as actually happening. Logic alone doesn't give us any information about what may or may not happen. For example, a person you observe in your dream may abruptly change into a different person. That can't happen in the world of waking life and to suppose that it did happen in this world would be to suppose something contrary to laws of nature. But it does not conflict with *logic*. Awake or dreaming, you may 'think illogically' (make unsound inferences) and no doubt you're more prone to logical errors when dreaming. But any describable sequence of events can never be inherently illogical. Nor can it even be a-logical, for some logic is required to make sense of any story.

Is There Such a Thing as Primary Process?

Freud has the idea that primary process is a primitive way of thinking which does not involve what we normally consider rationality. According to Freud's theory, the infant who cannot get what she wants hallucinates what she wants. Images of gratification in the infant's mind are related in ways other than logic, and this form of thinking survives into adulthood, appearing in dreams. As applied to dreams, this theory confuses physical law with logic. What happens in dreams never contravenes logic and it is impossible to follow the narrative of a dream (or any story) without relying on logic.

Very little is known about the pre-thought processes which give rise to thought, but the theory that rational thought is preceded by anything like primary process looks unpromising. It's inherently unlikely, because logic is implicit in any assertion or judgment as to fact, just as arithmetic is implicit in any sense of number.

What we find in the intellectual processes of babies is that they start with definite theories about the world which they abandon or modify in the light of experience, replacing these theories with progressively better theories.[5] We also find that intuitive (unconscious computational) devices are in place before there are extended chains of reasoning. For instance, babies have an innate statistical sense: if they see mostly white balls and a few red balls put into a container, they show surprise if only red balls are then taken out, and no surprise if only white balls are taken out.[6]

What Freud has done is to take the thought processes which occur when an educated person chooses to engage in loose, associative thinking, consciously relaxing some of his habitual critical faculties, and suppose that this style of thinking is pre-logical. The result is similar to what often occurs in poetry.

Freud has the newborn baby thinking the way Mallarmé writes verse, or rather the way Mallarmé would write if he had the preoccupations of Rabelais, De Sade, or Genet. In fact the newborn baby thinks like Galileo with Popper at his elbow. A baby has to learn about the world, and does so in the only way we know of: wildly guessing at hypotheses and then replacing these hypotheses with successively better ones as the earlier ones are refuted by experience.

No Such Thing as Repression

According to Freud, the key to understanding our emotional and behavioral problems is repressed memories. Past events (which may be past thoughts, feelings, or wishes of the patient) are forgotten. Although forgotten, they continue to exist as memories in the unconscious mind. The person pushes these memories into the unconscious, and thereby

---

[5] Gopnik, Meltzoff, and Kuhl 1999.
[6] Gopnik 2009, 81–84

forgets them. But they are still there, and they strive to enter consciousness. There is therefore a struggle, in which the person is trying (unconsciously) to keep these ideas buried, unrecognized in the unconscious (forgotten), but these ideas are striving to return to consciousness (to be remembered). They have been repressed because they are too dreadful to contemplate, and they continue to be repressed for this reason. Therefore, devilishly clever and highly motivated that they are, they come back in disguise to torment us.

Let's summarize, point by point, Freud's view of repression and the unconscious. The first five points are 'broadly Freudian' and would be accepted by most psychodynamic therapists. The last two points are 'narrowly Freudian' and would not now be accepted by most psychodynamic therapists.

1. **The act of initiating repression is unconscious (not deliberate).**

2. **Material (memories, thoughts, or emotions) is repressed because it is painful to allow into consciousness (and not, for example, because some other thought is more interesting or enjoyable to contemplate or is judged to be more important).**

3. **Repressed material, because it has never become conscious, is not observable (until the repression is ended).**

4. **Repressed material cannot be recovered by normal processes of recollection or introspection (If it's easy to recover, this shows it was never repressed.)**

5. **There is always 'resistance' to uncovering whatever has been repressed.**

6. **All the most important repressed material involves sexual desires.**

7. All the most important repressed memories are of events in the first six years of life. Later repressions are of no consequence except in covering up or pointing to these early repressions.

Comments on some of these:

1. *The act of initiating repression is unconscious.*

Freud sometimes spoke as if repression could be a conscious act. Some discussions of Freud (like the critique of Freud in Sartre's *Being and Nothingness*), assume that the initial act of repression is conscious. However, the balance of psychoanalytic opinion after Freud is that repression occurs unconsciously, and we should remember that a key ploy in Freud's persuasive patter is to blur the distinction between familiar real-life phenomena and his own peculiar theoretical fancies.

We're all familiar with the act of 'putting something out of our mind' (which doesn't mean that we can't recollect it later if we decide to), whereas we all know perfectly well that deliberate repression (I will now forget this painful matter, and then I won't be able to remember it no matter how hard I try) is something we have no idea of how to do. In stories where this kind of thing is called for, a magic spell or potion is indispensable. We can't forget some particular thing at will (Some people will exclaim: 'If only we could!'). We tend to forget most readily what we deem unimportant. What is *distinctly unpleasant* will always stand a better chance of being remembered than what is *uninteresting*.

People can sometimes turn their attention deliberately away from something they don't wish to dwell upon. Someone worrying about tomorrow's interview may switch on their favorite TV show, with the intention of taking their mind off the interview and stopping the worry. This deliberate or intentional decision not to think about some topic does not fit the distinctively Freudian theory of repression.

Because the distinctively Freudian concept of repression is so different from everyday 'putting out of our minds', some psychoanalysts have used the term 'suppression' for deliberate putting out of mind, reserving 'repression' for unconscious repression only.

2. *Material (memories or emotions) is repressed because it is painful to allow into consciousness.*

We may stop thinking about one thing because some other thought happens to be more interesting or enjoyable to contemplate. A man stops thinking about what he will have for dinner when a shapely woman walks by. There is nothing unpleasant or shameful about the topic of what he will have for dinner, but it is less interesting than the woman's body. It may additionally be that there is something unpleasant about the first thought: instead of thinking about his dinner, the man may have been thinking about tomorrow's prostate exam. This makes no difference to the basic process of being distracted from one thought by another thought.

7. *All the most important repressed memories are of events in the first six years of life.*

Later repressions, says Freud, are of no consequence except in covering up or pointing to these early repressions. The movie *Spellbound* (1945) is pure propaganda for psychoanalysis, yet in the end it coyly cops out, as it has to for the sake of public decency. The protagonist recovers the childhood memory that he was involved in the death of his brother. If the movie were going to unpack the Freudian package, it would have gone on to explain that this memory (true or false, it scarcely matters) is a screen memory diverting attention from the real underlying trauma: the child protagonist's guilty urge to enjoy juicy pulsations with Mom.

So the key aspects are these: 1. These memories are repressed because they are painful to contemplate; 2. The memories *cannot possibly* be recovered by making a deliberate effort to remember, either by casting one's mind back, or by attempting to 'refresh one's memory' by examining old records or thinking about associated matters. This feature is most important: any forgotten matter that can be recalled by these familiar approaches is *definitely not* an example of Freudian repression. 3. The act of repression itself is unconscious. The person does not know that they are repressing. 4. The memory can be recovered, but only by a painful process of 'analysis', which typically takes years, and consists in the patient coming to agree with the analyst's guesses about the patient's buried memories of childhood. To the Freudian and to many other psychodynamic therapists, the mere fact that something can be remembered readily without a prolonged struggle shows that it is of no great importance, while any reluctance to 'remember' something or to fall in with the hunches of the analyst, and especially any display of annoyance or indignation, is good evidence that the matter in question is genuine and vital.

The following, then, are *not* examples of repression:

1. A person forgets something.

2. A person doesn't bring something to mind for a long time (because he has no occasion to) and then later brings it to mind.

3. A person doesn't bring something to mind for a long time and then becomes actually unable to remember it, and then it 'all comes back to him' (often prompted by some clue, such as an old photograph).

3. A person suffers a physical trauma, such as a severe head injury or extreme alcoholic poisoning, and forgets things, usually for a temporary period but sometimes permanently.

4. Over time, a person's recollection of some event tends to become less accurate, as it is shaped to fit the person's views. (This process of 'confabulation' may not involve the removal of anything unpleasant; it may just as easily involve the exaggeration or creation of something unpleasant.)

In the strict Freudian sense of repression, it would be reckless to claim that anyone in the history of humankind has ever repressed anything.

A possible succession of events which comes closest to the events of Freudian repression is as follows: A person is upset by some item, decides to put it out of his mind, succeeds in putting it out of his mind, then fails to think of it for many a long year, then 'forgets' it in the sense that if he tries to recall it he can't, then something happens to 'refresh his memory' and the item 'comes back to him'. We have to admit that this is possible (though rare), but it lacks some of the attributes of Freudian repression. For example, the Freudian would hold that the difficulty of recalling the forgotten item (just before it is successfully recalled) arises because some part of the mind is 'unconsciously aware' that the item is painful to contemplate. However, if we consider this succession of events and instead of having the item put out of mind because it was upsetting, have it put out of mind because, while unequivocally attractive, it was a distraction from some urgent task requiring a lot of application, then the whole story works just as well.

Other Kinds of Memory

To keep it simple, the only kind of memory we have considered here is declarative long-term memory, since this is the sort of memory generally appealed to in arguments for an unconscious mind. This doesn't mean we doubt the existence of other kinds of memory.

Let's suppose that due to some experience in childhood, a person, without being aware of the fact, experiences a slight increase in his bodily 'alarm' response whenever he sees anything that resembles a pair of wide staring eyes—for example, the front of a car with its headlights looking a bit like eyes. We can suppose either that he doesn't notice the slight alarm (but it could be detected by measuring his heartbeat, sweating, and so forth) or that he does notice it but mistakenly attributes it to something else ('I always feel slightly on edge in traffic; I guess it's because my Uncle Fred was killed by being hit by a truck'.)

This kind of thing is sometimes called a type of 'memory' and it is entirely unconscious. It does not involve any thoughts or ideas, though just like other bodily processes, it might prompt them. We mention this example only to make clear that we accept that 'unconscious memories' may affect both thinking and behavior.

The Unconscious Is Aimless and Fragmented

Freud thought of the unconscious as the hangout of instincts or 'drives'. The motives that cause us to act are rooted in our unconscious. He saw the 'unconscious mind' as like a hydraulic system of pipes filled with liquids under pressure.

A better view of the unconscious (that part of it that is directly connected with mental operations, as well as that part which is not) is to think of it as a lot of little gadgets that we use to take care of tasks we can't or won't think about.

It may sometimes seem as if a gadget has a will of its own. If a car tends to drift to the left, we might say that the car wants to go the left. If our laptop crashes whenever we try to install a particular search engine, we might say that the computer really hates that search engine. If the thermostat is set to seventy Fahrenheit, we might say the thermostat knows when the room is below seventy and then decides to switch the heating on. But these are jokey metaphors. Anyone taking them literally is liable to be diagnosed as psychotic, precisely because gadgets have no consciousness.

Since the unconscious is a lot of separate gadgets, it has no will of its own, and no opinions or desires. Gadgets, however, can sometimes do things we find inconvenient and frustrate the purpose they were designed for. The idea that our unconscious is *trying* to frustrate our plans is like the idea that the weather is trying to make us late for an appointment. No part of the unconscious has any opinions about the state of the universe, but even if some parts did, the unconscious is a motley crew of many different components which cannot get together and conspire against the mind. Consciousness is unitary, whereas the unconscious is a collective term for sundry specialized devices.

The Unconscious Has No Mind

People who have denied the existence of an unconscious mind have never denied the existence of the unconscious. What they have denied is that the unconscious includes a mind, that the unconscious has a mind of its own. Three examples of such people are William James, Franz Brentano, and Jean-Paul Sartre. Not James nor Brentano nor Sartre disputed that there are all sorts of things going on in the human brain that we're not aware of, and that mental operations depend on these physiological processes.

That the mind is defined by being conscious is a natural assumption embedded in our language. We talk about 'keeping something in mind' or 'bringing something to mind'. Something 'crosses our mind' or 'springs to mind'. If we feel an inclination to do something but have not determined to do it, we say we have 'half a mind' to do it. In ordinary English, as in any natural language, the mind is the kingdom of consciousness.

The meanings of words sometimes change. At one time it would have been considered absurd to talk about 'invisible light' or 'inaudible sound', but now everyone knows that dogs can hear whistles pitched too high for humans to hear, while insects can see ultra-violet light, invisible to humans. Scientific instruments can detect sound and light that even dogs and insects can't perceive. At one time, 'information' was something conveyed from one conscious being to another, while today no one objects if we talk about the information contained in DNA. So perhaps the word 'mind' could be expanded to take in things which we're not aware of. So far this has not happened in ordinary English, and we can see no reason why we should encourage it to happen.

Recent pop psychology books often claim that there is an unconscious mind, though most of them mean only that there are unconscious computational processes in the brain that the mind makes use of. Most of these authors do grasp the fact that the psychodynamic view of the unconscious is seriously wrong.[7] While it's unfortunate that these writers talk about an unconscious mind, this is purely a terminological matter, as long as we don't lose sight of the fact that this 'unconscious mind' contains no thoughts or intentions. If we call unconscious processes which are useful to the mind 'mental', this is like calling the general's valet a soldier. It's a harmless way of talking as long as we make sure that we never take it seriously.

Unconscious Thoughts?

In his generally excellent book *Strangers to Ourselves*, Timothy Wilson claims that part of the unconscious is mental, and even that there is such a thing as 'unconscious thinking'. He doesn't say right out what he's counting as unconscious thinking, but he discusses some examples of unconscious bodily processes, and we can assume that he means to imply that these are examples of unconscious thinking.

One is the human sense of balance, done by the inner ear, technically called 'proprioception'. This doesn't look to us like thinking. It's a physiological response, like shivering in the cold, which no one would say involved thought. Another example is ordinary perception, such as the ability to see objects. Wilson's reasoning here seems to be that perception involves drawing conclusions. For instance, if something vanishes in one position and quickly appears in a nearby position, we see it as having moved. When we see something, we're doing something conscious, which like all conscious operations depends upon unconscious brain processes. But why should we say that the unconscious part of seeing something is thinking? It seems to be thoughtless.

---

[7] For instance, Mlodinow 2012.

Wilson has not actually given us any example of a process that could reasonably be called unconscious thought. He has merely given us examples of processes which happen without thought, but which we could imagine might be done differently, by means of thought. The motions of a swallow's wing could be modeled by mathematical equations, but it would be misleading to say that a flying swallow solves equations. It's just this kind of muddle that leads Wilson to suppose that he has identified something called unconscious thinking.

Even if there were such a thing as unconscious thinking, this would not be enough to give us an unconscious mind that looked anything like the psychodynamic description of the mind, and *this* is something Wilson clearly understands, in fact much of his book is devoted to showing just that.

A Popular but Faulty Argument

What might make us think we should expand the meaning of the word 'thinking' to include unconscious processes, along the lines that led physicists to acknowledge invisible light or inaudible sound? There is one popular argument for such a conclusion, that we ought to mention, since a lot of people find it convincing.

Sometimes a person is thinking about a problem without appearing to make much progress. Then she's interrupted, and stops thinking about it for a while. Then she comes back to it and—lo and behold!—she quickly has a huge insight that gets her on the track of solving the problem. The conclusion many people draw from this is that her mind must have been working hard on the problem while she wasn't consciously thinking about it, and that that unconscious mental activity has borne fruit with the great new insight that gives her the key to the solution. If this were true, lawyers could get away with billing the hours when they're asleep.

But how do we know that the person wouldn't have had that great insight within the next few seconds if she had *not* been interrupted? Or (more modestly) how do we know that the probability of her having that insight wouldn't be the same without the interruption as with it? After all, the great majority of occasions where we worry at a problem and then get interrupted *don't* lead to a leap in comprehension when we resume thinking about it later.

Sometimes the opposite happens. A person is thinking about some problem and feels they're making progress. Then they're interrupted, and when they get back to thinking about it, they don't recover that felt power to make progress. The most famous example is Coleridge writing the first fifty-four lines of 'Kubla Khan', then being interrupted by "a person on business from Porlock," and never being able to finish the poem because unable to recover the frame of mind preceding the interruption. In the vast majority of cases, though, we just start again from where we left off.

But suppose that it were true (though not yet demonstrated) that an interruption, followed by a delay, increases the probability of having an insight; it wouldn't follow that this increased probability was due to the mind working away at it during the interval. It could be (to take only the most obvious possibility) that when we get back into thinking about the problem after a delay, all the relevant aspects don't come back to us perfectly simultaneously. So for an instant we're looking at the problem with some aspects missing, and this enables us to see it in a different light, so that (in the handful of cases where we do get an insight, out of the thousands where we don't) that breakthrough insight springs to mind. It's also possible that something as simple as a lower level of fatigue, when we come back to the problem, might help. Any enhanced likelihood of a breakthrough insight after an interruption might be due to a fresh look rather than to any work done by the brain during the intermission.

Does It Matter that There Is No Unconscious Mind?

In the death throes of any belief-system, there eventually arises the point where defenders of the dying doctrine declare: 'You critics are so pathetically naive! You insist on taking these ideas *literally*. But that was never intended!'

In the case of psychoanalysis, a latter-day defender might say: 'Granted, there are no unconscious ideas or motives which are similar to conscious ideas and motives except that we're not conscious of them. How simple-minded of you to suppose that we psychoanalysts ever maintained anything so manifestly silly! Do you take us for fools? What we really meant all along, of course, is that something goes on in the brain which affects conscious behavior very much *as if* there were unconscious thoughts and unconscious urges. It's merely a helpful metaphor which enables us to quickly make sense of the way in which unconscious brain processes affect thinking and behavior. And what you have conceded allows plenty of room for psychoanalytic interpretations. For example, a person may have an unconscious disposition to react with love and sexual arousal when the image of their mother springs to mind, and with fear and guilt when the image of the father springs to mind. And so, there could be an Oedipus Complex, without it being *literally* true that the person ever phantasized that they might kill their father in order to have sex with their mother.'

Our response to this must be, first, that the metaphorical story of unconscious adventures may become too elaborate to be considered feasible. It's one thing to have an unconscious disposition to feel fear and resentment at anything which reminds you of your father and quite another thing to have an unconscious disposition to link this fear and resentment with unremembered threats of castration conditional upon your wanting sex with your mother. That's too intricate a story to be embodied in anything like a conditioned response or 'bodily memory'. And, second, such unconscious dispositions can be modified or removed (if they can be modified or removed at all) by simple conditioning. There's no need to conjure up a narrative of imaginary events and then embark upon a complicated game of pretending that these events somehow happened. If someone has a response of 'fear and resentment' to images of 'father', this disposition can be changed simply by elementary behavioral methods: repeated exposure to images of 'father' associated with pleasant and relaxing stimuli. And, third, it still remains true that the specific responses claimed by psychodynamic theorists should be capable of being tested empirically. If there is Oedipal anxiety, it ought to be possible to demonstrate its existence by experiment. Few psychodynamic theorists now accept the reality of the Oedipus Complex, but the same goes for any other supposed intricate concatenation of unconscious beliefs and motives.

The Psychodynamic Unconscious and the Actual Unconscious

We can sum up our view of the unconscious in a table:

The Psychodynamic Unconscious	The Actual Unconscious
Content is similar to Conscious Mind.	Content is unintelligible to Conscious Mind.
Unified	Fragmented, 'modular'
Content has been repressed	There is no repression.
Associative, symbolic	Intuitive, computational
Content can be retrieved, but resists	Content is never retrieved but may sometimes be transformed into something conscious. Most unconscious content can never be so transformed; some content can be easily transformed; some content can be transformed if we're attentive; there is no resistance.
Purposive, willful	Aimless
Revealed in dreams	No more revealed in dreams than in any other conscious activity

10
Heroes of the Revolution

Albert Ellis was born in Pittsburgh in 1913. Ellis's father was an adventurous small businessman: sometimes the family would have plenty of money; other times conditions were comparatively hard. The family moved to New York City when he was four, and he lived there for the rest of his life.

Albert loved school and was an outstanding student, always first in the class, though he felt acutely nervous when expected to talk in front of the class. Poor health was his faithful lifelong companion. From the age of five, when tonsillitis developed into a serious infection culminating in nephritis, Albert experienced fairly serious illnesses. He was hospitalized at least nine times in childhood, he had insomnia and violent headaches, and his eyes were oversensitive to bright light. Later he was diagnosed with diabetes, and had to carefully monitor his diet.

He was almost six when he was caught in a situation of sexual exploration with a girl, both of them largely ignorant about sex, but interested in finding out more. The girl's parents were outraged and furious, but Ellis formed the impression his own parents "covertly admired his audacity."[1]

---

[1] Wiener 1988, 21.

The Ellises were not a close family. Albert's father was often away from home for long stretches on business, and his mother would often leave the children to their own devices, effectively putting little Albert in charge of his two younger siblings. During Albert's many months in the hospital, his parents would rarely visit. When Albert was twelve, someone who knew his parents witnessed his father sharing a railroad sleeper with Mrs. Ellis's best friend, an indiscretion which prompted a divorce. The whole event made so little difference to the family that Albert did not hear there had been a divorce until six months later. Albert's father married his railroad sleeper companion and remained friendly with Albert's mother, though he was around the household less than before.

Albert, his brother Paul, and a neighboring child, Manny Birnbaum, became close friends, and remained close as long as they all lived. All three of them entered Baruch College of the City University of New York, to study accountancy. Paul and Manny remained accountants. Albert had decided he would one day become a famous novelist, and planned to support his fiction writing by business activities, for which a knowledge of accountancy would be useful.

Meanwhile, he was turning out numerous manuscripts: mostly works on politics, philosophy, and sex, but also including novels, plays, song lyrics, and poems. None of these juvenile works was ever accepted for publication. Among them was a self-help guide entitled *The Art of Never Being Unhappy*, subsequently lost.

Ellis became a paid organizer for a leftwing group, and wrote a never-published simple explanation of Marx's *Capital*, concluding that Marx's theory of surplus-value was mistaken, and a distraction from the real job of making a revolution.

After graduating from Baruch aged twenty, with a degree in business administration, Albert went in for a succession of entrepreneurial ventures, one with his brother and several with his father. According to one account, he was turned down for a job writing for the *New York Times Magazine*, when the interviewer decided Albert looked too frail, and wouldn't have sufficient stamina for the job.

Eager for a date yet finding himself shy around girls, Ellis set himself the task of talking to one hundred girls, at the Bronx Botanical Gardens, within a month. He got one date (she didn't show up), but just as he had suspected, this exercise had caused his nervousness with girls to greatly diminish.

Active in fringe leftwing politics, he also found himself distressingly anxious about public speaking, as he had been at school, and applied the same technique of exposing himself to that which he feared: he set himself to speak frequently in front of groups. This too proved effective in diminishing his anxiety, and he eventually came to relish public speaking. Looking back on these events much later, Ellis said: "I invented rational emotive behavior therapy naturally, beginning even back then, because it was my tendency."[2] He even claimed to have made a list of rules for himself at the age of four, including "Making a fuss about problems makes them worse" and "Wait before you panic."[3]

Ellis the Psychoanalyst

At twenty-four, still a virgin, Albert had a complicated relationship with a beautiful aspiring actress. Almost immediately after their marriage, he sought and obtained an annulment, but he continued to counsel her on her personal problems, and she remained a fan of his, eventually becoming a supporter of REBT. Ellis has since had a few long-term romantic relationships and several shorter-term liaisons. As far as can be ascertained, all his former partners continued to admire him as a man and a genius.

In his early twenties, Ellis found that people often sought him out for advice on their personal problems—and that he greatly enjoyed helping these people by discussing their

---

[2] Wiener 1988, 22.
[3] Wiener 1988, 18.

problems with them. This led him, in 1941, to study for a master's degree in clinical psychology at Columbia University. He got his master's in one year and then embarked upon a five-year PhD program. Ellis wanted to write a dissertation on the sexual emotions of college women. Approval was at first given, then withdrawn. He instead wrote an innocuous study of personality tests, for which he was awarded his doctorate.

While working on his doctorate he also held down a job (contrary to university rules), as assistant to the president of a small gift and novelty distributor, and saw a number of psychotherapy clients. He hung a sign in the window of his mother's apartment: "Albert Ellis, M.A., Psychologist."

New York was the world capital of psychoanalysis, and Ellis accepted the psychoanalytic approach as fundamentally sound, though he accepted some of the departures of Adler and Horney. An essential preparation for any aspiring psychoanalyst is to be analyzed himself, and Ellis spent two years being analyzed and supervised in his own analytic sessions by Richard Hulbeck. This was the name then being used by Karl Wilhelm Richard Huelsenbeck, formerly Dadaist poet-provocateur in Zurich and Berlin, and later author of *Memoirs of a Dada Drummer*. Hulbeck was a Horneyite and more actively 'interventionist' than most psychoanalysts. He was also an existentialist and taught Ellis the principles of existentialist philosophy.

Ellis later claimed that his own psychoanalysis under Hulbeck had helped him. He became more aware of his tendencies to compulsiveness and to becoming easily irritated, and learned how to keep these tendencies under control. Ellis attributes this success partly to the psychoanalysis and partly to his own independent work on these problems.

Ellis also made attempts to apply ideas from Carl Rogers's recently published *Counseling and Psychotherapy*. However, Rogers's nondirective approach went against the direction in which Ellis was moving, toward more, not less directiveness.[4]

---

[4] Wiener 1988, 57.

In the late 1940s, Ellis taught at Rutgers University and New York University, and in 1948 was appointed clinical psychologist at the Northern New Jersey Mental Hygiene Clinic. This was the period in Ellis's life where he had considerable contact with psychotics, rather than with the middle-class neurotics who tended to constitute most therapy clients. By 1950 he had risen to become chief psychologist for the New Jersey State Department of Institutions and Agencies.

His third book was co-authored with another psychologist, Ralph Brancale, and a dispute arose as to whose name would appear first. This dispute was mixed up with Ellis's disagreements with the New Jersey administration: he was blamed for publishing so much and so frankly about sex, for having private patients as well as his state job, and for living outside the state. At the same time he was involved in a much gossiped-about sexual affair, which may have added to the friction with his employers.

Ellis resolved the acrimonious problem of co-authorship by abjectly and insincerely apologizing to his co-author. The book was eventually published as *The Psychology of Sex Offenders*, with Ellis's name first. In 1952 Ellis quit his New Jersey job to concentrate on his private practice in midtown Manhattan.

Goodbye to Psychoanalysis

Ellis went along with the psychoanalytic view that people's emotional problems are due to forgotten experiences in early childhood. He applied all the usual psychodynamic techniques of free association, dream analysis, and resolution of transference difficulties through interpretation. Where he failed to make headway, like any good Freudian, he blamed the patient's resistance or lack of insight. Yet Ellis agreed with Horney and Adler, as against the Freudians, that, if you knew what was troubling the client and where the client's discoveries should end up, there was no good reason not to explicitly point this out.

Ellis published a series of articles, beginning in 1949, calling for reform of psychoanalysis to make it more scientific, less dogmatic, and more actively concerned with effective results. At first these ideas were presented as reforms within the psychoanalytic movement, but by 1953 he had broken away, and no longer called himself a psychoanalyst. He had already, by 1950, begun to use occasional foul language as a way of getting through to his clients and grabbing attention in the profession. He acquired the reputation of using words like 'fuck' and 'horseshit' rather frequently, though it is not a required component of the REBT system, and many REBT therapists do not emulate Ellis in this respect. Ellis has taught the principles of REBT to thousands of therapists; their personal styles vary considerably. When asked about his use of language, Ellis responded that he spoke to clients in just the same style as he conversed with his friends.

Ellis became increasingly dissatisfied with psychoanalysis because he observed that although clients sometimes felt better after psychoanalysis, they rarely improved in a way that would help them get rid of their symptoms and be more in control of their lives. Such inferences from clinical experience, without statistical controls, are notoriously treacherous, and precisely this kind of inference from personal impressions has led countless psychoanalysts to become ever more certain of the truth of the Freudian paradigm. But Ellis's conclusions turned out to be sound.

From an early age Ellis took an interest in philosophy. He was impressed by the Stoics and by Bertrand Russell's popular work, *The Conquest of Happiness*. At first influenced by the then-popular school of logical positivism, Ellis discovered Karl Popper and came to see that scientific theories can never be finally established but always remain provisional. He was also heavily influenced by Alfred Korzybski's General Semantics, and continued to quote from Korzybski all his life. Another influence was Paul Tillich's best-selling work of pop theology, *The Courage to Be*.

Ellis read widely, though not deeply or systematically, in both philosophy and psychology, but Ellis never became a 'grand theorist' in the style of leading psychoanalysts. His focus was always on what worked, what helped people, and

REBT still awaits a serious theoretical elaboration. Ellis has authored or co-authored over eighty-five books, many pages of which, however, reiterate the same few fundamental and practical points, with very little fresh thinking and even little in the way of fresh verbal formulation. "As ever, I am a proselytizer and a propagandist," he wrote later.[5]

> Gaunt and angular, always in motion, he sounded like a (very effective) vacuum-cleaner salesman. With patients, he pushed and pulled until he had persuaded them to give up the irrational beliefs that had sustained their depression. "What do you mean you can't live without love?" he would cry. "Utter nonsense. Love comes rarely in life, and if you waste your time mooning over its all too ordinary absence, you are bringing on your own depression. You are living under a tyranny of *should*'s. Stop 'should-ing' on yourself!" (Seligman 1998, 72)

No doubt Ellis said something more earthy than "Utter Nonsense." As early as 1950, Ellis abandoned the couch, in which the analyst sits behind the 'patient', in favor of a face-to-face interview. He also began to employ behavioral techniques, speculating that if harmful ways of thinking arose from early experiences, they could possibly be changed by new practical experiences. This was the period when behavior therapy was beginning to show convincing results, especially in the cure of phobias.

Ellis moved further away from psychoanalysis when he concluded that people cling to 'irrational' ways of thinking by repeatedly telling themselves irrational things about themselves and their circumstances. Thus, even if some harmful way of thinking arose in a childhood trauma, it persists years later because the person keeps on telling himself this wrongheaded message. But if this is true, it may be possible to change the message by a deliberate effort and by working at it.

---

[5] Ellis and Ellis 2010, 310.

Ellis was impressed by the famous assertion of the ancient Stoic philosopher, Epictetus, that "What upsets people is not things themselves but their judgments about the things." This observation harmonized with Ellis's own experience with clients: he concluded that they frequently reacted disproportionately to events, because of their deeply-rooted beliefs.

The Tom Paine of Sex

Ellis became known as a bold and shockingly liberal advocate of sexual freedom and was one of the chief drivers of the 'sexual revolution' of the 1960s. His early popular books included *Sex Without Guilt* (1958), *The Encyclopedia of Sexual Behavior* (1961), *The Art and Science of Love* (1960), *Sex and the Single Man* (1963), and *The Intelligent Woman's Guide to Manhunting* (1963). As well as being welcomed by many thousands of ordinary readers, these books were found useful by marriage and family therapists and helped to gain a following for Ellis's ideas and his psychotherapeutic techniques. One of Ellis's clients, Saul Bellow, called him "the Thomas Paine of the sexual revolution."

Alfred Kinsey's controversial work was becoming familiar to the widest public. Ellis advised Kinsey and they were about to collaborate on a new project when Kinsey suddenly died. There were major censorship cases involving Henry Miller's *Tropic of Cancer*, Joyce's *Ulysses*, Cleland's *Fanny Hill*, and *Playboy* magazine. Sexually explicit material was beginning to appear which could not have appeared legally a few years earlier, though it would now be considered quite tame.

Ellis's first book, *The Folklore of Sex* (1951) documents what the media were saying, on January 1st, 1950, about sex, and his rejoinders to them. Doubleday had a contract to publish the book, but asked for removal of some passages Ellis had quoted, and Ellis partly acceded to this. Doubleday published it, but under an obscure imprint, and the book was not widely reviewed.

Ellis's views on homosexuality were at first welcomed by homosexual rights advocates, but as these activists became more militant, they began to criticize Ellis. Ellis considered that homosexuality should be entirely legalized and socially tolerated, but also that homosexuality could be "treated" and "cured" in those cases where clients were not happy being homosexual. He also held that homosexuals are "disturbed" and that their disturbance is the source of their homosexuality. Ellis's book *Homosexuality: Its Causes and Cure* (1965) became a target for the gay rights movement. In time, Ellis soft-pedaled this aspect of his views, and the book went out of print and was never revived. His autobiography confirms that he definitely abandoned the theory that gayness is always a symptom of disturbance.[6]

The Development of REBT

In the mid-1950s, a small group of colleagues were invited to Ellis's seminar to discuss his new approach to therapy. One was therapist Penelope Russianoff, who became a longtime friend of Ellis and proponent of REBT. She played a therapist much like herself, and wrote some of her own lines for the part, in the movie *An Unmarried Woman*.

Between 1953 and 1955, Ellis formulated Cognitive-Behavioral psychotherapy, which he presented to the American Psychological Association in 1956 under the name, 'Rational Therapy' and put into print that same year. Although this name accurately identified its appeal to the clients' conscious beliefs and goals, Ellis found that it led to the misunderstanding that emotions were to be minimized or made totally subordinate to reason. Ellis's approach to psychotherapy has twice been renamed, each time to correct misunderstandings, not to reflect any change in content. In 1961 he renamed it 'Rational Emotive Therapy' (RET). He subsequently found, however, that his therapeutic approach was being commonly misunderstood in another way: as consisting entirely of conversations between therapist and client, in which the client

---

[6] Ellis and Ellis 2010, 454–55, 492–93.

was merely urged to adopt different ideas. In fact, Ellis's method had always emphasized practical assignments for clients, getting them to change their behavior along with their thinking. In 1993 he again lengthened the name by calling it 'Rational Emotive Behavior Therapy' (REBT).

Skepticism about Childhood Influences

Like many other psychoanalysts, including Adler, Rank, and Horney, Albert Ellis believed that emotional problems arise because of what happens in childhood, but that these problems then acquire a life of their own, so that it is not necessary, as Freud had thought, to revisit childhood.

At some point, however, Ellis began to doubt that these problems had originated in childhood at all. In *How to Live with a Neurotic* (1957) Ellis firmly reiterated the traditional view that problems begin in childhood, and he did not change these strong assertions in the revised edition of that book, published in 1975.

But then he gradually came to the opinion that people's tendency to cause emotional problems for themselves is to a considerable extent innate and has little or nothing to do with what happens to them as young children.[7]

Many later Cognitive-Behavioral therapists differed with Ellis on this point, and maintained that childhood experiences do cause emotional problems in later life. Some of them, like Jeffery Young, founder of Schema Therapy, placed renewed emphasis on the desirability of retracing the supposed childhood origins of present problems. Young and some other Cognitive-Behavioral therapists collaborated with clients in 'recalling' how childhood interactions with parents 'caused' the clients to develop irrational or negative thoughts. The best that can be said for this exercise in delusion is that it may do little harm—as long as the therapist never loses sight of the two important Cognitive-Behavioral insights:

---

[7] Ellis 1976.

1. **Recalling, reliving, or 'gaining insight' into those early experiences will not cure a person's current problems.**

2. **Changing the way the client thinks now can cure the problem, with or without any recall of its (in fact non-existent) origin in childhood.**

In 1976 Ellis argued that a person's genetic tendency to irrational thinking was more important than any early experiences. REBT lost interest in how the irrational beliefs were acquired and focused entirely on how they were perpetuated. Yet in the 1970s and 1980s, the Freudian idea had an iron grip on the American intellectual and journalistic classes. Divorce, single parents, mothers with careers, and daycare all came under suspicion as possibly harmful to the personal development of children. It's not surprising that some therapists attracted by Ellis's method were reluctant to follow him in defying this hardened orthodoxy. But Ellis lived to see the orthodoxy challenged and then discredited, beginning with the work of behavioral geneticists, and then with the writings of David Rowe and Judith Harris in the 1990s.

In boldly discounting early childhood influence, Ellis was twenty years ahead of his time. Psychotherapy has produced some crazy and harmful ideas, so it is worth entering this achievement of Cognitive-Behavioral therapy on the credit side. At a time when the ideologies of 'attachment' and 'bonding' possessed the minds of social scientists, social workers, journalists, politicians, and experts on child raising, a growing number of psychotherapists, led by Ellis, arrived at the clear understanding that people's emotional problems are *not* rooted in the events of their early childhood.

Ellis's ABC Method

The core of the REBT approach is the famous ABC method:

A. **Activating Event**
B. **Belief**
C. **Consequence**

D. **Disputing the Belief**
E. **Effective new philosophies**
F. **New Feeling (or behavior)**

A client visits a therapist because of C., the emotional or behavioral consequence of A and B. So, a person may become extremely nervous (C) when called upon to speak in public (A). (Fear of speaking in public is Americans' number one fear, ranked higher than fear of death.)

The therapist questions the client and the client responds by voicing the belief (B) which generates the nervousness. The belief might be: 'I *must* not make a complete fool of myself'. Why *must* you not make a complete fool of yourself? 'That would be just terrible, and I wouldn't be able to stand it'. The therapist then encourages the client to challenge this belief. What does it mean to make a complete fool of yourself? 'It means I would appear ridiculous to others'. What's the worst that could happen to a public speaker? People sometimes do appear ridiculous to others—is that the end of the world? Would you really not be able to stand it? (D)

The therapist convinces the client that the demand for a one hundred percent guarantee that she will not screw up while public speaking is unreasonable. The client is convinced that her beliefs are not realistic. The objective then is to get the client to adopt a new set of beliefs that will spring to mind when the activating Event (A) happens. These beliefs will be along the lines: 'I would *prefer* not to look ridiculous because I screw up while public speaking, but I recognize that there can be no God-given guarantee that I won't. If I do, that's too bad, but of course I can stand it' (E).

This new belief leads to a new feeling—being less fearful of public speaking, and if the new belief completely replaces the old, being not fearful at all. (F)

Thinking and Beliefs

Ellis attributed emotional and behavioral problems to 'irrational beliefs', and his method aims to change them to 'rational beliefs'. All such terms should be viewed as special, technical words within the system of therapy, chosen partly because they are easy to explain to clients. 'Faulty unexamined assumptions' might be slightly more accurate than 'irrational beliefs' but is more of a mouthful. Some later Cognitive-Behavioral therapists have replaced Ellis's straightforward terminology with horrendous pseudo-medical and behavioral science jargon, with terms like 'dysfunctional mentation'. Building a wall of jargon between professionals and the public is a familiar trade union stratagem which should always be resisted in favor of plain speaking.

One question is whether Ellis's 'beliefs', embodied in what he called 'self-statements' (Beck's 'automatic thoughts') are conscious, unconscious, or preconscious. There have even been claims that these thoughts are 'illogical' or perhaps 'a-logical', and belong to Freud's 'primary process'.

Freud distinguished between the 'preconscious' (things we're often not thinking about, but can bring to mind at any moment without any trouble) and 'unconscious' (things which we can't easily bring to mind, and which have been repressed). Freud paid no attention to another category: things which we may overlook due to sheer inattention.

Joe is a talkative, outgoing person who has a habit he is unaware of, though it occasionally irritates people who listen to him. He interpolates the phrase 'you know' into his speech, an average of once every three sentences. One day, Joe hears a tape recording of his own conversation and is surprised and upset. For the first time, he recognizes he has this annoying verbal habit. Self-statements or automatic thoughts are a bit like that. They are recoverable by ordinary conscious processes, they are not hidden, but you do have to pay attention in a particular way. Part of the skill of being a psychotherapist is to be able to help clients identify the thoughts and beliefs which prompt their emotional upsets.

The relevant thoughts are quick and normally unexamined. They are not 'primary process' nor are they without logic. They may embody logical mistakes, as any reasoning may, however they cannot be bereft of all logic. If there were no logic, no conclusion would follow from any premise, so the two statements 'I always screw up' and 'I screwed up this time' would have no connection with each other. Without logic, the client wouldn't be able to draw any conclusions from 'I always screw up' and this could therefore have no effect on her feelings or behavior.

Against Positive Thinking

An easy but serious misunderstanding of REBT is to think that it consists of accepting a more upbeat philosophy of life, spraying yourself with happy thoughts. In the 1920s the French psychologist Emile Coué popularized what he called auto-suggestion, recommending repeating to yourself the statement "Every day, in every way, I am getting better and better." Somewhat similar ideas have been promoted in the US by the 'success' writers Napoleon Hill and W. Clement Stone, and by the Christian preachers Norman Vincent Peale and H. Robert Schuller.

It's doubtful whether this kind of blanket optimism can do much good. Coué was right to see that people upset themselves by telling themselves upsetting things, but the things they tell themselves are quite precise responses to specific circumstances. The thought that 'everything's fine' is not a convincing or workable reaction to some occurrence that is not fine. Often what's required is not some all-purpose positive thought but a more precise and reasonable negative thought (where 'negative' means recognizing the reality that things are not as we would like them to be). If someone's anxious about a job interview, they may be thinking 'This interview is sure to go badly, as everything I try to do goes badly'. It is helpful for the person to think instead: 'Some things I do are successful and others are unsuccessful. I may not get the job, for any number of reasons, and if that happens, it's not the end of the world. I'm tough enough to handle it and move on.' It is not helpful for the person to think 'I just can't fail because I succeed at everything I try', because this does nothing to equip the person for possible disappointment.

Beliefs and Causation

In doing Cognitive-Behavioral therapy, the focus is on changing both thinking and behavior, expecting that emotional changes will follow. In order to explain the system to clients, we often need to make statements like 'Your feelings flow from your thinking'. This may sometimes be misunderstood as a general theory of mental causation. However, Cognitive-Behavioral therapy does not rely on any theory that thoughts are always primary. It might be, for instance, that thoughts and emotions mutually influence each other, or that there is something else (such as attitudes which can't be put into words) that influences both thoughts and emotions. Cognitive-Behavioral therapy does not have to commit itself on such broader questions: all that's necessary is to accept that, as a practical matter, a person's emotional response to some event is modified by that person's thinking, and can therefore be changed by changing the thinking.

Against Self-Esteem

In the 1970s there was an explosion of interest in self-esteem. Many people assumed that self-esteem is a good thing and you can't have too much of it. All kinds of problems such as poor educational performance and delinquency were blamed on low self-esteem. Some government agencies started spending millions of the taxpayers' dollars on campaigns to raise self-esteem.

Ellis always opposed the self-esteem movement. The self-esteem movement starts from the correct observation that some people make themselves unhappy by rating themselves harshly, but then makes the mistake of concluding that the way to help them is to encourage them to rate themselves more generously: to boost their self-esteem. In contrast, Ellis maintained that it would be better if people did not rate themselves at all.

A common American assumption, both inside the self-esteem movement and outside it, is that people can accomplish anything if only they have enough confidence in themselves. But this assumption is mistaken. Having boundless self-confidence does not confer ability. There are 'deluded dunces', untalented people who wrongly suppose that they are highly talented. Often, circumstances will arise that demonstrate to them their lack of talent, and then, if they have been deriving reassurance from the belief that they have talent, they may become depressed.

Concerns about educational performance are often highlighted by showing that US students perform poorly on various tests of academic knowledge, compared with students of other countries. Yet if the students' rating of themselves is measured, we find that US students rate themselves highly. US students, on average, rate themselves more highly at (for example) math than students in other countries rate themselves, while objective tests of performance show that those students are better at math than US students. Many American students are dunces who extract comfort from the delusion that they are aces. This delusion does nothing to raise their test scores; they remain dunces.

Self-esteem is rating yourself highly as a total person. A person with high self-esteem feels good because he feels good about him*self*. But since everyone experiences failures and disappointments, high self-esteem, conditional on performance, will be fragile.

Instead of promoting high self-esteem, Ellis argued that it would be better to promote unconditional self-acceptance. A person can accept themselves as they really are, good at some things, bad at other things, without rating themselves as a total person. If they then want to improve their performance at some endeavor, they can take steps to do so, not because they will then feel better about themselves, but because they will feel gratified at having made progress in attaining their goals.

Not only can high self-esteem set people up for a crash, when reality demonstrates to them that their performance is not always outstanding, but high self-esteem can be a source of anti-social or criminal behavior. In all of Nathaniel

Branden's books, all concerned with 'authentic self-esteem', there is never any mention of the possibility that someone may have too much authentic self-esteem.

As research has now shown, one problem with violent criminals is that they have high self-esteem. Because they have a high opinion of themselves, they are impatient when other people don't behave in accordance with this high opinion. The common Psychodynamic response to learning of this fact is to suggest that while these thugs display high self-esteem on the surface, deep down they have very low self-esteem. This is the way many people tend to think, after a hundred years of Psychodynamic thinking. But researchers have specifically tried to test for this hidden low self-esteem, and have found no trace of it. This is one more unfalsifiable and therefore untestable claim of Psychodynamic theory. The truth is that either violent criminals have excessively high self-esteem, all the way down, or they have deeply hidden low self-esteem which nobody has any idea how to detect, demonstrate, or treat. As far as anything which is detectable or observable goes, violent criminals have high self-esteem and are violent criminals in part *because* they have high self-esteem.

Ellis Plagiarized

Numerous successors to Ellis have been influenced by his ideas without attribution, and generally Ellis was tolerant of such unacknowledged emulation. A few cases irked him, most conspicuously the case of Wayne Dyer whose 1976 best seller, *Your Erroneous Zones*, sold tens of millions of copies and made Dyer very rich. Dyer had attended Ellis's workshops and *Your Erroneous Zones* is wall-to-wall REBT but makes no mention of Ellis or of REBT (or for that matter, of the entire Cognitive-Behavioral movement in psychotherapy). Having become a best-selling author and media celebrity with *Your Erroneous Zones*, Dyer later moved on to a series of books of a mystical nature, which depart from the Cognitive-Behavioral approach.

A Strange Ending

At the end of Albert Ellis's life, when he was in his nineties, he became embroiled in a bizarre confrontation with people he had formerly trusted.

For over forty years, Ellis lived in an apartment in what became the Albert Ellis Institute in Manhattan. Beyond everyday living expenses, he donated all the considerable income from his books, lectures, and therapy sessions, to the Institute which bore his name. By the turn of the century it had become a large and profitable enterprise.

Ellis enjoyed a close friendship followed by a long-term romantic relationship with an Australian therapist, Debbie Joffe, who became a staff therapist at the Institute and Ellis's personal assistant. In 2004 the board of the Institute fired Joffe, on the grounds that she had allowed an outsider, a public relations consultant, into a group therapy session Ellis was conducting. As expected, Ellis argued strenuously against the dismissal of Joffe, whom he now married. Relations between Ellis and the board became more strained, in a series of escalating conflicts, though when the conflict reached a certain point, two board members came out firmly and openly for Ellis and against the board majority.

The board began to subject Ellis to petty indignities, for example sending back medical supplies which had arrrived for Ellis by mail, instead of delivering them to him, and refusing to repair the leaky roof of his apartment. The board also removed Ellis himself from the board, though following a legal action, the board's action was judged unlawful and Ellis was reinstated.

The board's general view was that Ellis had become incompetent due to old age, and he certainly was in worsening health and hard of hearing. For years Ellis had given public Friday night workshops at the Institute but the board now barred him from doing this, claiming that at one session he had hit someone with a cane (an allegation denied by Ellis and other witnesses). Ellis continued with the workshops by renting a room in a building next door to the Institute, still attracting a crowd of admirers and psychotherapy students every Friday night. Videos of these events show Ellis sharp, lively, and in full command. The Institute was a busy hive of activity, with numerous people coming in and out every day, for courses and therapy sessions, most of them quite unaware that the great man whose name was celebrated in the organization's name had become something between a prisoner and a squatter in this very building. It was as though Jesus Christ had moved into the Vatican, been excommunicated for heresy, was denounced and harassed by the Pope and Cardinals, and had to commute to the Coliseum to deliver his weekly sermons to the faithful.

It's difficult for an outsider to form a satisfactory account of the dispute between Ellis and the Institute board. Statements by both sides are easily available online, but they do not readily yield a plausible story. The grounds given for the dismissal of Joffe don't appear anywhere near strong enough for the board to fire her outright and thus deliberately pick a fight with Ellis. The dispute does not seem to have originated in any ideological or theoretical disagreement, though Ellis did claim that the Institute's commitment to REBT, as opposed to a more vague and general form of Cognitive-Behavioral therapy, was becoming diluted. However, all the leaders of the other schools of Cognitive-Behavioral therapy—Aaron Beck, Martin Seligman, William Glasser, David Burns, and others—spoke out in support of Ellis and against the board.

Ellis's health continued to worsen and he died on July 24th, 2007.

Aaron Beck

Like Ellis, Beck began as a psychoanalyst and like Ellis he at first thought of his innovations as occurring within psychoanalysis. Unlike Ellis, Beck's approach had a more academic dimension. For the most part, Beck followed in Ellis's footsteps, but with one major difference, as we shall see.

As a convinced psychoanalyst especially interested in depression, Beck conducted research which he fully expected would corroborate the psychoanalytic theory of depression. He looked at the dreams of depressed people and non-depressed people. Since psychoanalysis holds that depression is anger turned against the self, Beck expected that the dreams of depressed people would have more elements of anger than those of non-depressed people. In fact, what Beck found was that there is not a huge difference, but that the dreams of depressed people show *fewer* signs of anger. They do, however, show more signs of hopelessness. While this unexpected finding did not immediately cause Beck to abandon psychoanalysis, it did shake his confidence in it.

In recounting how he came to Cognitive-Behavioral therapy, Beck recalls that, while treating a woman who felt anxious and related stories of her many sexual exploits, he drew the conclusion, a natural one for someone of a psychoanalytic background, that the woman was anxious because of her possibly uncontrollable sexual urges.

"It's very clear why you are feeling anxious. . . . Since your sexual impulses are unacceptable, they cue off anxiety." I said, "Does that sound right?" She said, "Oh, yes. You're right on target." I said, "Do you feel better now that you know this?" She responded, "No, I feel worse." I replied, "Thank you for being so frank, but can you tell me a little bit more about this?" She responded, "Well, actually, I thought that maybe I was boring you, and now that you said that, I think I really was boring you." I asked, "What made you think that you were boring me?" She replied, "I was thinking that all during the session." I said, "You had a thought, 'I am boring Dr. Beck,' and you didn't say it?" She replied, "No, I never thought to say that." I said, "You had that thought just this one time, right?" She responded, "Oh, no, I always have that thought." I said, "Oh? That's really strange. How come you never reported this before?" She responded, "It just never occurred to me that this would be the sort of thing that you'd be interested in." I asked, "Did you have any feeling when you had this thought?" She replied, "Well, this is what has really made me anxious." I asked, "Do you ever get this thought when you're not in the session?" She said, "Oh, I get it with everybody. I'm always very anxious because I think that I'm boring people." (Beck 1997, 276–77)

The therapist starts from the usual kind of psychoanalytic cliché: this client is anxious because of her uncontrollable sexual impulses. The truth is almost the opposite: the
reality is that she's anxious because she feels she needs to
impress everyone she meets, and this partly motivates her
sexual escapades. The thought that she's anxious because
she may bore people is not repressed, it's easily available, but
it goes unmentioned and overlooked because such thoughts
are usually not voiced and because it's not what the client
believes the therapist is looking for. But Beck was alert and
open enough to follow it up.

A more orthodox psychoanalyst would have classified the
client's anxiety that she might be boring the therapist as
part of the 'transference', the client's crush on the therapist,
and would therefore have failed to grasp its implications. So
the client would have been correct in assuming that this was
not what the therapist was looking for.

Beck called this client's thought that she might be boring
everyone she met an 'automatic thought', and he quickly realized that these automatic thoughts are universal: we all
bombard ourselves with automatic thoughts all the time.
Ellis had called these thoughts 'self-statements'. They are
just the kind of thoughts psychoanalysis tends to overlook
or view as irrelevant, but they give rise to emotions such as
anxiety.

Now Beck was looking for his clients' automatic
thoughts and paying attention to his own. He found that
automatic thoughts often have to do with a person's self-
evaluation. They are usually not mentioned to other people.
Because these thoughts are quick, unpremeditated, and un-
voiced, they are often accepted as self-evidently true by the
person having them, and not criticized. So someone who
thinks 'I always screw up' does not give this propositions
the same critical attention he would give if he heard someone say: 'Space aliens have captured the White House',
though the former thought is actually just as questionable
as the latter.

Beck noticed that the claims made by automatic thoughts are often not well reasoned from the available evidence, and that when some event happens in a person's life, the way she reacts to it emotionally is mainly determined by her automatic thoughts. Just as Epictetus said, it's not events that upset us but the way we interpret those events. And, so, just as Ellis had done some years earlier, Beck concluded that it was possible to attack people's bad feelings, their anxiety, depression, or paranoia, by getting them to question these thoughts.

An automatic thought is not isolated. A person tends to have similar automatic thoughts over time. These thoughts flow from beliefs—not elaborately-formulated, publicly discussed beliefs like Jesus is the son of God or Beijing is the capital of China, but gut beliefs, unexamined assumptions.

As he was developing these ideas and communicating them, Beck still thought of himself as a psychoanalyst and contended that he was making advances in psychoanalytic theory. But whenever he spoke with psychoanalysts, they told him that this was not psychoanalysis, and he should stop calling himself a psychoanalyst.

Cognitive Schemas

Beck concluded that people have typical ways of understanding the world, which he called Cognitive Schemas. Cognitive schemas may involved cognitive distortions, mistakes in reasoning which lead to unfortunate conclusions.

Among the cognitive distortions:

- All or nothing thinking:
  If events don't turn out exactly as I want, then that's a total disaster.

- Mind reading:
  Assuming we know what people must be thinking: if Joe doesn't call, it proves he doesn't like me.

- Negative prediction:
  Always expecting a bad outcome, regardless of the evidence.

- Labeling:
  Applying a term which then comes to define the whole of life. If something turns out worse for me, I'm a 'loser'.

Ellis and Beck

At first glance, the differences between Beck's and Ellis's Cognitive-Behavioral therapies appear fairly slight, especially as therapists in each tradition borrow freely from the other. Both hold that people make problems for themselves by their faulty thinking, and both see the role of psychotherapy in changing faulty thinking into more helpful thinking. Many of the methods they use to change the client's thinking are similar.

Yet there is one huge difference in their approaches. Ellis finds virtually all the malign effects of faulty thinking to stem from 'musts', 'shoulds', or 'demands' whereas the Beckian school only rarely addresses the 'musty' or 'demanding' aspect of faulty thinking. We have been through all of the hundreds of examples of faulty automatic thinking in the exhaustive (and exhausting) standard work, *Cognitive Behavior Therapy* (Beck 2011) and not one of them is a demand or a 'must'. In many of Ellis's books every single example cited is a 'must'.

Ellis may occasionally challenge the client's thinking on a matter that is not a 'must', but generally he is interested in locating the 'must'. For example, if a client says 'No one likes me', both a Beckian and an REBT therapist might encourage the client to question this, but the REBT therapist will quickly move on to elicit such thoughts as 'No one likes me—and I just can't stand that' or 'People *should* like me'. The Beckian assumption is that any inaccuracy in the client's view of reality may be the source of the client's problems, while the REBT therapist will maintain that merely believing a factual inaccuracy will not in itself generate emotional problems: only 'musts' are liable to do that.

This fundamental difference leads to other differences. Making an inventory of the client's whole belief system is a more time-consuming process than identifying the client's faulty demands, and so an REBT therapist will usually get to the point of challenging the client's faulty thinking sooner. Having located a 'must', the REBT therapist will often begin to challenge the person's beliefs in the first session, whereas this would be unusual for a Beckian.

Because of its closer connection with academic work and therefore with research, Beck's therapy has prompted new findings in such areas as personality types and their relation to beliefs. For instance, Beckian therapists often use the Sociotropic-Autonomy scale to identify a client's personality type, whereas this would be unusual for an REBT therapist.

Adlerian Therapy Comes Full Circle

Adler's theory of the unconscious was more realistic than that of Freud or Jung. He was less inclined to conceive of the unconscious as a vast realm inhabited by mysterious beings, and more inclined to conceive of it as merely consisting of elements of people's motivations of which they were not fully aware or would not recognize.

Adler was the original pioneer of 'brief therapy', deliberately setting tight deadlines, and usually expecting to provide definitive help within eight to ten weeks. He categorized people's 'styles of life' according to very practical criteria, classifying individuals as the socially useful type, the ruling type, the getting type, and the avoiding type.

Finally, Adler was very ready to challenge clients' conscious assumptions, by explicit argument, in order to improve their functioning. The Adlerian therapist Harold Mosak has proposed five 'basic mistakes' which it is the task of therapy to challenge:

1. **Overgeneralization, or the excessive use of terms like 'all', 'never', 'everyone', as in 'Everyone should like me' or 'I never do anything right'.**

2. Seeking false or impossible assurances of security.

3. Misperceptions of life's demands: 'Life's too hard'.

4. Minimization or denial of one's own worth.

5. Faulty values ('You'd better take advantage of others before they take advantage of you'.)

This is clearly a form of Cognitive-Behavioral therapy. So Adlerian psychotherapy, officially termed 'Individual Psychology', has come full circle. After helping to inspire Albert Ellis to originate Cognitive-Behavioral therapy, Adlerian therapy has now become predominantly Cognitive-Behavioral, with its psychoanalytic baggage considerably downplayed or in some cases abandoned.

What remains unhelpful in Adlerian thinking is all connected with the now discredited theory that family dynamics in early childhood form the adult personality. Most Adlerians continue to believe in the power of 'birth order', though this has been empirically refuted, and they continue to believe in 'life-styles' fixed in early life.

Martin Seligman and Learned Helplessness

Ellis and Beck were the great pioneers of Cognitive-Behavioral Therapy. Since the 1960s they have had numerous admirers and developers, both avowed and unacknowledged. But one name stands out as pre-eminent: Martin E.P. Seligman.

Seligman came into the world of psychotherapy from academic theory and research. After World War II, academic psychology in the United States was completely dominated by behaviorism, the theory that psychology could best advance by ignoring subjective mental states and focusing on observable behavior, especially as it could be modified by rewards and punishments.

Most behaviorists were only 'methodological behaviorists'— they believed that humans do have conscious, subjective states, but that these could be ignored as irrelevant for scientific purposes. A few behaviorists, notably B.F. Skinner, came close to 'metaphysical behaviorism', denying that people have conscious, subjective states at all (or that if they do, these states have any effect on their behavior), a position still maintained by a few philosophers like Daniel Dennett.

In the early twentieth century there were three separate areas: academic psychology, psychiatry, and psychotherapy. Psychotherapy was overwhelmingly psychoanalysis, whereas academic psychology was overwhelmingly behaviorism. The domination of academic psychology by behaviorism coincided with the domination of psychotherapy by psychoanalysis. And so there was very little contact between academic psychology and psychotherapy.

Psychiatry, the branch of medicine concerned with supposed mental diseases, was dominated by traditional 'biological' treatments, such as drugs, lobotomies, and electroshock, all then very primitive. But psychiatry was somewhat open to influences from both psychoanalysis and behaviorism. The question facing many psychiatrists was: Are you more appalled by the ludicrously unscientific procedure that is psychoanalysis or by the cruel, dangerous, and untested procedures which go by the name of 'biological psychiatry'? Neither psychoanalysis nor biological psychiatry could reasonably claim to have any good evidence that they had made a net contribution to the relief of human misery. Behavior therapy, derived from behaviorism, offered hope of another way, but behavior therapy did not work well for all mental problems.

In one sense psychoanalysis and behaviorism were poles apart, but in another sense they were in complete agreement: the patient's conscious thoughts were of trifling importance except insofar as they afforded clues to what really mattered: the patient's unconscious or the patient's learned responses, both alternatives being things over which the patient himself had little conscious control.

Both academic psychology and psychotherapy have undergone a "cognitive" revolution, but at first there was little contact between these two revolutions and little similarity. 'Cognitive' means to do with thought. The revolutionaries in academic psychology were revolting against behaviorism, which denied the importance of thought, saying that what mattered was observable behavior and its reinforcement. The revolutionaries in psychotherapy were revolting against psychoanalysis, which downplayed the importance of the patient's conscious thoughts, saying that what mattered was desires and motives unknown to the patient, going on in her unconscious mind.

Despite the different origins of cognitive psychology and cognitive psychotherapy, both types of revolutionaries now find that they have a lot in common, and Cognitive-Behavioral psychotherapists are eager to learn from new research conducted by cognitive psychologists. Martin Seligman is unusual in playing a major part in both the cognitive revolt against behaviorist psychology and the cognitive revolt against Psychodynamic therapy.

In 1965, the young Seligman was involved in research on dogs, when he began to pay attention to something that other researchers didn't consider significant. In an experiment trying to see whether dogs would learn from the association of a mild but unpleasant electric shock with a sounded tone, researchers were disappointed to find that the experiment had to be stopped because most of the dogs would become completely listless and passive. Unlike traditional behaviorists who viewed this behavior as an annoying glitch, Seligman began to take seriously the notion that the dogs had learned to give up. This may not sound like a big deal, but it was a firm principle of behaviorism that animals could learn only by rewards and punishments for specific behaviors. Instead of learning by conditioned association, these dogs had 'drawn a conclusion' from their experiences: the conclusion that it was not worth trying.

From this insight arose the whole theory of 'learned helplessness' which was demonstrated to occur in both animals and humans. Many people, after repeated unpleasant experiences which they cannot escape, won't try to escape from unpleasant experiences even when they easily can. Some people, however, won't give up, but will always try to escape the unpleasant experiences. Through studies performed on groups of humans (who were not given electric shocks but subjected to such annoying experiences as irritating noises), it was found that a substantial minority would 'never give up', and these individuals would do better in the long run because they would act to improve their circumstances when it became possible to do so. A much smaller minority were predisposed to give up from the getgo: they would not need a protracted period of uncontrollable unpleasant sensations to become passive.

Further, it was found, in both human and animal studies, that individuals who had learned the helpless response could be taught to change to the more pro-active response, and that individuals who had never learned the helpless response could be trained in advance so that when they had to endure a series of experiences which they could not change, they would still not adopt the helpless response.

Seligman and other psychologists found that how people react to bad experiences is governed by what Seligman called their explanatory style, which could be optimistic or pessimistic. Seligman was rediscovering from the findings of laboratory research what Ellis called 'beliefs' and what Beck called 'cognitive schemas'.

Whether or not you're vulnerable to helplessness depends on the way you explain things to yourself. Pessimists tend to assume that bad events are due to something permanent, whereas optimists think that bad events are temporary hitches. Pessimists attribute bad events to general, pervasive causes, whereas optimists attribute them to narrow and specific causes. So after being chewed out by the boss, the pessimist will say 'My boss is a prick' whereas the optimist will say 'My boss is in a bad mood'. Pessimists tend to suppose that bad things are due to something within themselves, whereas optimists will attribute the bad things to something external.

When he began this research in 1965, Seligman was already aware of the new styles of psychotherapy practiced by

Albert Ellis and Aaron Beck. And when he began to apply his own findings to psychotherapy, he relied heavily on Ellis's ABC method (Seligman 1998, 207–234)

Later Seligman took psychology and psychotherapy in a new direction when he developed 'positive psychology' and 'positive psychotherapy'. These disciplines were born of his conviction that psychology and psychotherapy had become too much focused on what goes wrong. Instead, he proposed to bring new happiness and fulfillment to people who were not diagnosed with emotional or behavioral problems.

Postscript

As we've shown in this book, there has been a revolution in psychotherapy, the New therapy replacing the Old. But, as we explained in Chapter 1, most movies, TV dramas, and novels don't recognize the revolution. They present psychotherapy as though it's all pretty much the same, and as though it's all still preoccupied with your dreams and your childhood.

There are hundreds of different types or schools of psychotherapy. The differences among them are not minor. We listed some of these different schools of psychotherapy in Chapter 2. Most of them can be classified as predominantly *New* (Cognitive-Behavioral) or *Old* (Psychodynamic).

Contrary to some popular views, research shows that psychotherapy works and that some types of psychotherapy work a whole lot better than others. The evidence is clear that Cognitive-Behavioral therapy works better than Psychodynamic therapy.

Sixty or seventy years ago, the great majority of psychotherapy was of one basic type: it was called psychoanalysis and followed the ideas of Sigmund Freud. Today only a small minority of psychotherapists consider themselves psychoanalysts or followers of Freud. Those therapists who have rejected psychoanalysis but held onto some its most fundamental assumptions are the people we classify as Old therapists—the Psychodynamic therapists.

Those therapists who have rejected the basic assumptions of psychoanalysis, especially the notions of repressed memories, the decisive importance of early childhood, the use of free association, and the vital relevance of dream interpretation—these are the New therapists, the Cognitive-Behavioral therapists. In Chapter 3 we showed what actually goes on in therapy, contrasting the Old and the New therapists in specific examples.

Although more and more therapists are leaving the Old ideas behind, the lingering smell of these ideas still permeates American culture. In Chapter 4 we showed how these ideas originated in old Vienna, and in Chapter 5 we explained why these ideas have to be rejected. In Chapter 6 we traced the history of American psychotherapy, through its major innovators up to the early 1950s. At first, these innovators were dissidents and heretics within psychoanalysis, then they were people who deliberately stepped outside psychoanalysis. Both kinds of innovators were moving in a 'cognitive' direction—they were giving more attention to people's *thinking*.

In Chapter 7 we summarized some of the shocking revelations that have come out about the founder of the Old therapy, Sigmund Freud. In Chapter 8 we outlined the disgraceful 'recovered memory' witch-hunt of the 1980s and 1990s, a disastrous application of unsound Psychodynamic theories about the mind, childhood, and memory. In Chapter 9 we explained why the Psychodynamic picture of the so-called unconscious mind is so seriously wrong.

Finally, in Chapter 10 we explained some of the key ideas of Cognitive-Behavioral therapy by outlining the achievements of three 'heroes of the revolution', Albert Ellis, who originated Cognitive-Behavioral therapy, and Aaron Beck and Martin Seligman, who both developed Ellis's insights and took them in different directions. These great therapists and theorists of therapy have changed the course of psychotherapy, entirely for the better in our opinion.

Replies to Some Criticisms

At the end of *Three Minute Therapy*, we listed and replied to some common criticisms of Rational Emotive Behavior Therapy, our preferred type of Cognitive-Behavioral Therapy. In *Therapy Breakthrough*, we have in effect already answered some other common criticisms by the arguments we have given.

Here we'll reply to criticisms made by Robert Fancher in his book *Cultures of Healing*.[1] Although this dates from 1995, similar criticisms are often voiced by others, and we don't know of any published reply to Fancher from a Cognitive-Behavioral standpoint.

Fancher addresses just one school of Cognitive-Behavioral therapy, that of Aaron Beck, though most of what he says applies to all schools including ours. Many of the narrow points made in Fancher's arguments are correct up to a point, but we don't accept that they succeed in overthrowing the essential principles of cognitive therapy. Let's remind ourselves of what these are:

a. **Emotional and behavioral problems are at least partly caused by the way people think**

b. **It's therefore possible to help people by showing them how to change their thinking**

c. **Cognitive therapists have identified some of the typical ways in which people cause problems for themselves by the ways they think.**

So, in evaluating arguments against Cognitive-Behavioral therapy, we have to consider whether they really touch these basic principles. Many of Fancher's arguments just fail to make contact with these essential principles of cognitive therapy. And so we believe we can accept a lot of what Fancher says without abandoning these essential elements.

---

[1] Some other critics are discussed in Still and Dryden 2012.

Fancher offers numerous criticisms and believes he has disposed of Cognitive-Behavioral therapy. He refers to the claims of Cognitive-Behavioral therapy as "myths," and claims to have demonstrated that "its ideas do not bear scrutiny" (242). In the rest of his book, Fancher offers equally negative arguments against psychoanalysis, pure behavior therapy, and "biological psychiatry." He himself practices psychotherapy, so he can't be arguing against all psychotherapy, yet he refuses to tell us anything about the psychotherapy he practices. So, we can't test the arguments he offers against Cognitive-Behavioral therapy by observing how parallel arguments might apply to his own type of therapy. We can't determine how he conceives that his own form of therapy escapes the kind of complaints he lodges against Cognitive-Behavioral therapy.

Here, then, are some of Fancher's major arguments against Cognitive-Behavioral therapy:

1. There are many ways to interpret reality, and none of them is the right way. Therefore Cognitive-Behavioral therapists must be wrong when they say that they can identify faulty thinking and begin to correct it in a short space of time (208–09).

This argument 'proves too much', in that it (or a closely parallel argument) could be used to show that any set of logical techniques for bringing about improvement in any area of life must be misconceived.

Cognitive-Behavioral therapists don't try to totally transform our clients' religious, political, or metaphysical views, in fact we disagree among ourselves about these and other matters. In this respect, Cognitive-Behavioral therapy is like remedial math or a weight-loss program: it identifies some typical errors and trains the client to get rid of those errors.

Fancher might suggest that Cognitive-Behavioral therapists could expand their range of types of faulty thinking, or perhaps reduce it. But this is an open question for research and debate. Any change of this sort would modify the techniques of cognitive therapy without abandoning it. The currently accepted list of types of common 'distortions' in thinking or 'irrational beliefs' has evolved and is perpetually under review. It is discussed among therapists in journals and other printed or online venues, and is continually debated.

2. Normal, ordinary thinking is irrational. It does not proceed by evidence and logic, but by other techniques such as "the construction of imagistic models and intuitive comparisons between models and events." Therefore reliance on evidence and logic can't be equated with mental health (213).

We should put claims about the irrationality of normal thinking in perspective. Every adult human who is not severely brain-damaged performs a continual stream of logical inferences, for the most part flawlessly.

For example, knowing that the train leaves the station every day at 6:00 p.m., we infer that it will leave the station at 6:00 p.m. today. Knowing that the candidate with the most votes wins the election, we infer that candidate Smith wins if he gets twice as many votes as candidate Jones. Inferences like this are of course blindingly obvious—because the average human is a virtuoso logician, compared to any other known life form. No one could practice as a car mechanic or a lawyer, play a videogame like *World of Warcraft*, or follow the plot of a TV show like *Breaking Bad*, without continually employing logic, and nearly always getting it right. No human, outside of intensive care, could survive for a day without using logic and adapting to observable evidence.

In that broad context, we do find 'man bites dog' examples where people often make errors in reasoning. Some folks love to write and read books proclaiming that humans are 'irrational', citing these common errors, though the mere fact that millions of people read books giving examples of irrational reasoning, and pointing out the mistakes in such reasoning, is itself difficult to reconcile with general irrationality. The popular theory that people are generally irrational has been criticized effectively by Ray Scott Percival.[2]

The fact that people sometimes make intuitive leaps, instead of computing everything minutely, can be a great aid to rational thought. People often reach conclusions based on "imagistic models and intuitive comparisons." There's nothing irrational about that, such conclusions are not necessarily unsound, and the models and images people habitually turn to can be modified in therapy, as part of the modification of thinking.

Fancher says we're wrong to suppose "that health [he means freedom from emotional and behavioral problems] has any correlation with sound logic and sound evidence" (213). No correlation at all? This looks like an empirically testable claim. We could do research to see if there's any correlation between illogical thinking and emotional and behavioral problems. We would expect to see a positive correlation.

But now let's assume (with Fancher) that normal thinking is predominantly irrational. This would not rule out the possibility that focused application of a bit more logic and evidence in specific areas could be helpful, and this is all that cognitive therapy needs. Fancher says:

Normal thinking is not rational thinking. Thus, irrational thinking cannot be the source of psychopathology. (213)

Compare this with:

Healthy life is not free of bacteria. Thus, bacteria cannot be a source of ill-health.

3. Cognitive therapy holds that all disturbed thinking arises from factual and logical errors. But some of the errors made are not factual and logical and some are not errors at all. Cognitive therapy is mistaken in supposing that it is

---

[2] Percival 2012.

merely 'correcting' clients' thinking; it is also recommending values which are neither correct nor incorrect. Furthermore Cognitive-Behavioral therapy claims to promote 'rational values', but there are no rational or irrational values since reason is instrumental (224–25).

These assertions don't contradict the claim that Cognitive-Behavioral therapists *sometimes do* identify factual and logical errors which lead to emotional problems and *sometimes can* succeed in helping clients correct those errors, resulting in relief from those problems. Actually, Fancher never faces these claims head-on and denies them, though that is what he would have to do to begin to refute Cognitive-Behavioral therapy.

If we accept these assertions by Fancher, they don't refute Cognitive-Behavioral therapy. Cognitive-Behavioral therapists often treat value judgments as though they were factual claims. If a client says 'Life wouldn't be worth living if my spouse left me', and the therapist says 'What's the evidence that life wouldn't be worth living?', this may, strictly speaking, be an inappropriate appeal for factual evidence in the face of a value judgment.

Such inaccuracies arise because the terminology of cognitive therapy is largely derived from the language that works with clients. The client (unless she's a philosophy sophomore) will probably not respond 'You can't ask for factual evidence of a value judgment!' but will probably take the question in the spirit in which it's offered, and begin to question whether she really needs to stick with the view that life wouldn't be worth living.

Therapists sometimes assume that certain value judgments are acceptable, but Fancher somewhat exaggerates this tendency. The client usually comes to the therapist with a definite problem which she hopes can be fixed. The client has purposes which are frustrated by her emotional and behavioral problems. The therapist does not need to endorse those purposes, but simply offers the service of helping the client to pursue her own purposes more effectively by curing or alleviating her emotional and behavioral problems. The only value-judgment made here by the therapist is that it is part of his job to offer this service to the client.

4. Sweeping negative beliefs about oneself, one's world, and one's future may be arrived at rationally (213–16).

Cognitive-Behavioral therapy doesn't try to eliminate sweeping negative beliefs. 'I will never win a major award for my contributions to astrophysics' is a sweeping negative belief that may be arrived at rationally. 'The fact that I will never win a major award means that my life is meaningless and I ought to jump off the Golden Gate Bridge' is a sweeping negative judgment that cannot be arrived at entirely by evidence and logic. There has to be something else going on. Fancher thinks—or at least, he thinks at times—that our emotions are (or ought to be) directly caused by things that happen to us, so that it is 'rational' to be depressed following a series of setbacks.

Other times Fancher seems to take a view contradictory to this (231–33). No doubt influenced by the undeniable fact that Cognitive-Behavioral therapy does work for many clients, he supposes that Cognitive-Behavioral therapy works, not in the way it says it does, by enabling clients to stop thinking in the ways that are causing their emotional and behavioral problems, but by giving them an acceptable yet false theory which then reassures them and makes them feel better.

So Fancher leaves us with two possibilities:

a. We can't change our emotions or behavior by changing our thinking.

b. We can change our emotions or behavior by changing our thinking, but only by coming to believe in something false.

a. and b. are contradictory. They can't both be right. a. also contradicts the success of Cognitive-Behavioral therapy. a. further contradicts some psychological research, which indicates that thinking does play a part in determining emotion.

5. Statements are not always reports of what a person is thinking or inferring (210–11).

This is perfectly true, but Fancher is mistaken to think that Cognitive-Behavioral therapists don't know it. One client may say 'I'm such a klutz' and this may indicate continual self-downing leading to depression. Another person may say 'I'm such a klutz' and it may be a form of politeness. Cognitive-Behavioral therapists are trained to get a sense of the client as a whole person and understand her attitude to life. They don't take isolated statements out of context.

6. Cognitive-Behavioral therapy favors the social and political status quo, seeing it as benign (222–23, 229–233).

This is a strange one. Fancher asserts this and appears to be arguing for it, but when we look closely at what he says, he doesn't actually give any argument.

He does point out that Aaron Beck sometimes calls the thinking of disturbed people "idiosyncratic," the implication being that we're tying to make them think more like everyone else. Now, first, Beck could be mistaken, and we could correct that mistake. Many other Cognitive-Behavioral therapists never use this label.

But let's suppose that Beck is right and that some faulty thinking can be improved by making it more typical—making the individual client more like the majority of people in this one respect. How is this any different from a dentist curing your toothache and making you more like the majority of people who have no toothache?

An idea which we've heard before (it's nowhere stated or implied by Fancher, but he may have it at the back of his mind) is that if you're too happy with things in general, you're going to be less inclined to work to change unjust or inhumane social conditions. If that *were* Fancher's position, we might reasonably ask whether the psychotherapy he administers is designed to make his clients more miserable.

However, we don't accept that being unhappy improves your chances of making a difference. The depressed or phobic person is not a more effective agent for social reform than the undepressed or unphobic person. If instead the argument is that, being less miserable, he will be less motivated to change the social order, then if we look at social reforms and revolutions throughout history we observe that they are not driven primarily by individual discomfort, but by a commitment to some abstract vision of a good and just society.

7. People can arrive at false conclusions using correct logic and true conclusions using faulty logic (212).

It's a trivial and uncontroversial fact, which Fancher as a professor of philosophy ought to know, that a sound argument can lead only to true conclusions. This fact implies the even more important and useful fact that if an argument has led to false conclusions, then the argument is not sound, which means that either the premises of the argument are false or the logic of the argument is faulty.

8. Sometimes, errors can lead to less distress and more rational thinking to more distress (213–14).

Aside from merely random effects, where one error cancels out another, the stock example here is the 'optimism bias', the much talked-about fact that optimists (who see the world as selectively rosier than it really is) are happier than pessimists or than people who are perfect 'realists'. It's often said that depressed people have a more accurate grasp of facts than normal people.

In general, illogical and non-evidence-sensitive thinking will lead to more distress than logical and evidence-sensitive thinking. The fact that within this broad picture there may be some exceptions is an interesting curiosity which is still under investigation. On the 'optimism bias', we offer two comments:

a. It's only *slightly* depressed people who have been shown, in some studies, to be more 'realistic' than undepressed people. Severely depressed people are, on average, not realistic at all, but interpret facts with strong selective pessimism.

b. Recent research shows that optimistic people, when educated about their optimistic bias, and aware of the fact that they are under-rating the likelihood of bad events (for example, of themselves getting cancer), remain just as happy as before. In other words, what's decisive may not strictly be their erroneous belief, but their tendency to focus on the favorable outcomes rather than dwelling on the unfavorable ones. And that tendency is entirely reasonable.

9. Cognitive-Behavioral therapy confines itself to factual and logical errors (209).

This is the one point where we think Fancher's criticisms are justified as applied to Beckian therapy, but not to other types of Cognitive-Behavioral therapy. REBT therapists have long criticized Beckian therapists for being so preoccupied with the realism and accuracy of clients' thinking.

From our own REBT standpoint, merely unrealistic or inaccurate beliefs about facts are not crucial to emotional and behavioral disturbance, and it's not always worth correcting them. What is crucial is the 'musts' or demanding thoughts that clients bring to their thinking.[3]

10. Understanding reality is such a complicated business that any "simple set of rules" can't be right (208–09). Cognitive

---

[3] Edelstein and Steele 1997.

therapy has a constricted view of thought and emotion, and cannot account for creativity (217).

Psychotherapy isn't trying to explain everything. It leaves some room for biochemistry, literary criticism, and jurisprudence.

The Future of Psychotherapy

Cognitive-Behavioral therapy will continue to out-compete Psychodynamic therapy, for at least three reasons:

1. **Many therapists pay attention to the findings of research into what works best.**

2. **Increasing numbers of people looking for a therapist are insisting on Cognitive-Behavioral therapy.**

3. **Cognitive-Behavioral therapy is more in line with the findings of scientific psychology, as researched and taught in university departments of psychology.**

We therefore expect present trends to continue. Psychodynamic therapy will continue to shrink and Cognitive-Behavioral therapy will continue to expand.

The eventual culmination will be that there will be a single profession of psychotherapy, all its members trained in a common body of theory and practice. We don't recommend that such an outcome be legislated into existence, or otherwise artificially imposed, which would mean that certain aspects of psychotherapy would be outlawed or decertified, but we can predict that it will evolve naturally.

When Freud and his friends set up the institutions of psychoanalysis, they were striving to protect their own theories from dilution or rejection, and that meant protecting them from criticism by forming an embattled cult. Most leading dissenters from psychoanalysis set up their own rival institutes and associations. At some point it will be necessary for many of these competing organizations to form a common professional body. We expect that certain doctrines which today have some popular following, like repressed memories, mother-child attachment, or free association, will become so tiny in their number of adherents that these ideas will no longer be viewed as belonging to standard psychotherapy.

This doesn't mean that Psychodynamic therapists will not be free to disseminate their views or to practice professionally. Today, for example, there are doctors who believe in homeopathy, and offer homeopathic medicine to patients. But to be accredited as physicians, they have to be fully qualified in conventional medicine, even the parts they disbelieve in. A similar situation will probably come to prevail, with all psychotherapists being educated in Cognitive-Behavioral therapy, but with some actually offering other kinds of therapy. Eventually we can expect to see even the remnants of Psychodynamic therapy forgotten, as animal magnetism and phrenology are now forgotten.

As long as there are therapists who put the client first, listen to the client, and help the client achieve her own chosen goals, and as long as therapists pay attention to all the relevant scientific research in psychology, we can expect that psychotherapy will continue to improve, as it has improved in recent decades. Psychotherapy adds to the amount of happiness in the world, and we can expect it to get better and better at doing just that.

Appendix
Is Psychoanalysis
Falsifiable?

Some readers of this book may react to our Chapter 5 by saying 'First you claim that psychoanalysis is unfalsifiable, then you argue that it's false. Isn't that a contradiction?'

Other readers may have picked up the idea that Popper's view of falsification has been discredited or does not apply to Freud. In particular, they may know that Adolf Grünbaum, in his *The Foundations of Psychoanalysis* (1984) was critical of Freud and yet concluded that Popper was mistaken to allege that psychoanalysis is unfalsifiable.

To get a clear picture of the issues here, we need to bear in mind the following elementary points about Popper's criticism of Freud:

1. Popper has a high opinion of Freud, whom he thinks has discovered important truths.

2. Popper's criterion of falsification is intended to distinguish science from non-science. Popper does not think that non-science is necessarily worthless, meaningless, or unimportant, or that we cannot seriously try to determine its truth or falsity.

3. Popper claims that the basic theory of psychoanalysis is unfalsifiable by observation (empirically unfalsifiable) and therefore psychoanalysis is not a science.

Popper readily accepts that many of the theoretically less central assertions of psychoanalysts might be falsifiable.

4. For Popper, the same literal statement may be falsifiable or unfalsifiable, depending on the attitude toward that statement of its proponents, its place within the theory, and how the theory is applied. The proponents of a theory show (especially by their response to objections in the form of apparent counter-examples) whether the theory is falsifiable or non-falsifiable.

Popper's most extended discussion of Freud is in his *Realism and the Aim of Science*, written in 1958 but not published until 1983. Popper indicates that this discussion is similar to the thoughts he had back in 1919, when he "became suspicious" of Freudianism, Adlerianism, and Marx's historical materialism, all of which seemed to their adherents to be confirmed by an endless stream of observational evidence. Popper's view, in 1919, in 1958, and in 1983, is that the theories of Freud, Adler, and Marx are impressive intellectual achievements which are, at the very least, on the track of important truths, but that they cannot claim to be scientific in the sense that the theories of physics, chemistry, or biology are scientific. The crucial difference between these non-sciences and the sciences is that the theories of the sciences are submitted to empirical testing.

Empirical testing means trying to falsify theories by observing what happens. The scientist searches for observations which would contradict the theory if the theory were false. He tries to make things happen which the theory does not allow to happen, thereby refuting the theory. The scientist may believe that his theory is true and may be hoping that it is confirmed by the tests—that it survives attempted falsification—but still, the scientist recognizes what would count as the theory failing the test. The tests carry weight because we can say what possible results of the tests would show the theory to be false. If *anything* that might happen can be taken as not falsifying the theory, then the theory does not rule out any possible observable occurrence and thus says nothing of a scientific nature.

In *Realism and the Aim of Science*, Popper examines Freud's assertion in *The Interpretation of Dreams* that all dreams are to be explained as the fulfillment of wishes. *The Interpretation of Dreams*, the foundational work of psychoanalysis, is one of just two of Freud's books which were carefully updated, rewritten, and amplified in successive editions over a period of decades, and Freud never gives up his commitment to his crucial claim about all dreams being wish fulfillments. Popper's detailed criticism of Freud's arguments[1] is quite devastating and no one has yet attempted to defend Freud against this criticism.

What Popper is most concerned to show here is that the way Freud approaches his material is such that no possible dream that anyone might ever be imagined to have could count as an exception to his law that all dreams fulfill wishes. This is what makes Freud's theory unscientific. The theory is immunized in advance against all possibility of refutation.

While it's pretty clear that Popper thinks that Freud's claim about dreams is false, and that Freud's arguments are sometimes disingenuously evasive, neither of these is his main point. A scientific theory might be false (Newton's theory of gravity) and a non-scientific theory might be true (some of the ancient Greek theories about atoms). Popper's main point is that Freud's theory is non-falsifiable and therefore non-scientific. Psychoanalysis could be improved and made scientific if psychoanalysts would view its main theories as hypotheses which could be refuted by specified observed events—and would then actively look for such refutations.

Freud's unfalsifiable and therefore unscientific claim about dreams is one fundamental theory of psychoanalysis.

---

[1] Popper 1983, 163–174.

Also fundamental is the theory of the universal Oedipus Complex. To avoid possible quibbles about the word 'complex' and about people in a coma, we can phrase this as: 'Every competent adult human went through an Oedipal phase in childhood, in which they unconsciously wanted to have sex with their mothers and kill their fathers, and this phase has been a major influence on the formation of their personalities'.

As we mentioned in Chapter 5, the question of how we could tell that some individuals did not have an Oedipus Complex—what we would expect to observe if that were true—was repeatedly put to many psychoanalysts over several decades, and their replies (or refusals to reply) made it clear that no imaginable observation would ever be judged by psychoanalysts as a falsification of the theory of the universal Oedipus Complex.

One psychoanalyst gave a reply which at first glance looks like an exception. He said that someone who did not have an Oedipus Complex would be an idiot.[2] But this is not very helpful. The claim that everyone has an Oedipus Complex is replaced by the claim that every non-idiot has an Oedipus Complex. We wanted to specify how we could decide that a person had no Oedipus Complex; now we want to specify how we could decide that a non-idiot had no Oedipus Complex. One non-falsifiable claim has been replaced by another non-falsifiable claim. And, since the great majority of cases of idiocy already have an explanation which is other than absence of an Oedipal phase (a congenital condition of the brain or a brain injury), the two non-falsifiable claims are very nearly identical.

Still another central component of Freud's theory is his instinct theory (first the theory of libido, and later the dual instinct theory of a life instinct and a death instinct, both the earlier and the later theories including the claim that all pleasure is sexual). Close examination of this theory would

---

[2] Hook 1959, 214–19.

again show that the way psychoanalysts apply it, they do not view it as a claim that could be proved wrong by any imaginable example of human behavior or physiology.

To keep our perspective on these matters, we should remember that, at least up until the 1930s, no article seeking to disprove the theory of dreams as wish-fulfillments or the theory of the universal Oedipus Complex, or the instinct theory (libido theory), could have appeared in any orthodox psychoanalytic journal, and any individual publicly arguing against any of these theories could never have been accredited as a psychoanalyst (or remained within the psychoanalytic fold if already accredited).

Grünbaum's book came out before it became clear to everyone that Freud was dishonest in reporting his cases, that he routinely claimed a cure where there was no cure, and that much of his case reporting is inaccurate. These facts about Freud's methods were just beginning to reach a wider reading public in the early 1980s. They had been prefigured earlier in writings of Frank Cioffi, such as his 1974 article, 'Was Freud a Liar?',[3] but these were largely ignored at the time. Grünbaum, like Popper, follows the consensus which prevailed until the 1980s, in accepting that Freud's accounts of his cases are fundamentally trustworthy. The fact that Freud manufactured or adapted case material to suit his rhetorical and ideological demands of the moment— that he was not just a mountebank but also a crook—makes a lot of Grünbaum's arguments somewhat immaterial or moot. But any theory may be judged on its merits, independently of the dishonest methods which may have been used to promote it, and the question remains whether Popper was right to say that the main theories of psychoanalysis are immune to potential falsification and therefore do not belong to science.

Grünbaum's strictures against Popper take one of three forms. He quotes Freud himself as saying that he is open

---

[3] Cioffi 1998, 199–204.

to refutation. He cites examples where Freud allegedly changed his view because of a refutation, and Cioffi shows that in every one of these examples, Freud did not do this[4] (though since some of these are, for example, specific conclusions about specific patients, they would have been irrelevant to Popper's argument in any case). And Grünbaum gives examples of instances where Freud *has* been refuted (and therefore must be falsifiable)—completely missing Popper's key point that falsifiability refers to the willingness of the theory's proponents to accept falsification under specified conditions. What Grünbaum needed to do was to find an instance where an empirical finding would prompt the orthodox psychoanalytic community to acknowledge an error in their theory, causing them to abandon the theory and replace it with a better one. Even Cioffi slips at one point, asserting that, for instance, astrology is both falsifiable and falsified (218). But this would only be relevant if astrologers themselves were to announce potential falsifiers (refuting observations) of astrology, and actively search for these falsifiers.

According to Popper, we can't determine the falsifiability of a statement just by looking at it. The same statement ('e = mc^2' or 'All pleasure is sexual', or 'All dreams are wish-fulfillments') can be falsifiable or unfalsifiable, depending on whether they are viewed by their adherents as empirically testable.[5] It was a commonplace of early discussions of psychoanalysis that there were any number of observations which seemed, to those outside psychoanalysis, to refute psychoanalysis. Psychoanalytic theory had ways of dealing with such seeming refutations, immunizing itself against them. This was the starting point for Popper's suspicion that psychoanalysis was not a science. It's therefore beside the point to come up with new ways in which psychoanalysis might be refuted empirically, if these ways would not be acceptable to psychoanalysts. There has never been any shortage of such refutations.

---

[4] Cioffi 1998, 225-235, 240-251.
[5] Popper 1968, 82.

Cioffi shows in some detail how Grünbaum misrepresents both Freud and Popper.[6] Cioffi observes that Grünbaum sleepwalks his way through Freud.[7] Cioffi might have added that Grünbaum also sleepwalks his way through Popper.

Grünbaum's main example of Freud's scientific approach is what he calls "the Tally Argument." The term is taken from a passage where Freud asserts that the psychoanalytic patient's

> conflicts will only be successfully solved and his resistances over-come if the anticipatory ideas he is given tally with what is real in him. (Freud 1953, Volume XVI, 452)

Freud is here responding to the common criticism that psychoanalysts talk their patients into accepting such theories as the claim that they must have had certain sexual feelings, now forgotten, when they were children. He's conceding that psychoanalysts "anticipate" these theories and "suggest" them to the patients, but he's saying that this doesn't matter.

Exactly what Freud means here is a bit ambiguous: it presumably doesn't mean that you can never talk someone into accepting something false. What Freud seems to be getting at is that only the ideas that "tally with what is real" in the patient will resolve her conflicts and effect a cure. It's still not clear why, if the patient accepts a bunch of ideas and is then cured, we can't say that only some of the ideas, not others, effected the cure, so Freud seems to think that we can observe what is real in the patient independently of what effects a cure, perhaps by the patient's emotional response to different suggestions. This interpretation is borne out by Freud's assertion, immediately following the above quotation, that erroneous ideas suggested to the patient by the analyst will "drop out." But in that case there would be nothing empirical about the Tally Argument: it would just refer to the analyst's evaluation of his own guesses.

---

[6] Cioffi 1998, especially 210-239, 240-264.
[7] Cioffi 1998, 252, 262.

The Tally Argument only has a shot at making psychoanalysis falsifiable if it instead refers to the efficacy of psychoanalysis in effecting cures. If psychoanalysis had a higher cure rate than other therapies, then this might form part of an argument for the truth of psychoanalysis. Yet critics and defenders of psychoanalysis in 1917 would all be familiar with the fact that no one could produce any information about the comparative cure rates of different types of therapy. Freud, to say the least, was not interested in any such information. Adlerian therapy had been going its own way for six years, and Jungian therapy for four, and there were the surviving pre-Freudian types of therapy such as that of Pierre Janet. Freud did not welcome comparative studies of the outcomes of different forms of therapy or any statistical studies of the outcomes of psychoanalysis.

From the very earliest days of psychoanalysis, critics made the point that its claims of therapeutic success (or of the clinical confirmation of its analyses) could just as easily be made by other forms of therapy. As examples of this line of criticism, Cioffi cites Aschaffenburg (in 1906), Lyman Wells (in 1913), and Woodworth (in 1917).[8] In this respect, Freud is exactly on a par with any other 'alternative' healer, such as a homeopathic physician or a chiropractor: the healer is convinced by details of some of his patients' experiences, including the usual quota of remarkable recoveries which follow any treatment, however worthless, that his ideas are on the right track. This is not to say that any one of these therapies is necessarily wrong—only that this typical belief in their efficacy on the part of the dedicated practitioner does not count for much. Of course Freud's clinical experience confirmed his theories—what else would we expect?

William Warren Bartley III drew Popper's attention to one example of a seemingly refutable Freudian claim.[9] Freud holds that paranoia, in both women and men, arises from re-

---

[8] Cioffi 1998, 17–18
[9] Popper 1958, 169.

pressed homosexuality. So it follows that a paranoiac could not also be overtly homosexual. If we found an overt homosexual with the symptoms of paranoia, this would refute Freud's theory about the origin of paranoia. Popper immediately accepted this, pointing out that this theory was not fundamental to psychoanalysis; it could be abandoned without any abandonment of the central claims of psychoanalysis. Even so, Popper added that "Freud could say of any paranoid active homosexual that he is not *really* paranoid or not *fully* active" (169).

Neither Bartley nor Popper mentions the actual case where Freud discusses a possible refutation on a related matter. As an example of Freud's openness to possible falsification, Grünbaum cites Freud's 1915 article 'A Case of Paranoia Running Counter to the Psychoanalytic Theory of the Disease'.[10] Here, according to Freud's account, he was called upon by a lawyer to determine whether a young woman, who apparently showed signs of paranoia, was actually paranoid. Freud found signs of paranoia, but was concerned by the fact that the woman exhibited "no trace of a struggle against homosexual attachment." On his second interview with the woman, it emerged that she had a difficult relationship, with homosexual aspects, with an elderly female work colleague. And so the theory was saved.

Freud purports to be concerned about a possible refutation, and then purports to find a fact which shows that this example is no refutation. Grünbaum cites this case as evidence that Freud was open to refutations of his theories.

This case has several suspicious features. In Freud's account the woman consults a lawyer about a man's unwanted attentions, and the lawyer decides that he will believe her or not according to whether a psychiatrist says she is paranoid (not by an investigation of the truth of her allegations, for after all, she might be both paranoid and a victim of unlawful harassment). Freud decides after one session with her that

---

[10] Freud 1958, Volume XIV, 263–272; Grünbaum 1983, 108–09.

either he must give up his homosexual theory of paranoia, or declare her not paranoid (with the assumption that her complaint against the man is warranted). But it had never been clear that Freud's theory required that there be a currently observable "struggle against a homosexual attachment." This enrichment of the theory seems to have been cooked up just for this occasion.

This case is not like the hypothetical one mentioned in the exchange between Bartley and Popper. The woman is not knowingly a lesbian, which would require that she not be paranoid. For this reason, she could not have directly informed Freud in the second session that she had a homosexual attachment to the work colleague, for this would have contradicted Freud's theory, assuming that she was paranoid. If she was aware of her homosexuality, it could not have been repressed, and it could not then be the cause of her paranoia.

And so what must have happened in the second session (assuming that any part of this tall tale is true) is that the woman mentioned some kind of difficulties with a female colleague, unconnected with homosexuality, which Freud, and not the woman herself, decided to interpret as signs of unconscious homosexuality. So why didn't Freud simply assert the woman's unconscious homosexuality from the start? Because this whole story is an exercise in persuasive rhetoric; Freud is following his script as the fearless yet conscientious seeker after truth. He affects to be puzzled: here is a paranoiac who isn't a repressed homosexual—oh, woops, yes she is! Our hero has had a narrow and exciting escape!

Freud's initial finding that she showed no signs of homosexuality and his later finding that she did are both equally inferences from behavior which to another observer might appear to be irrelevant to her possible repressed homosexuality, or might indicate the opposite. Given five minutes of conversation with any heterosexual, Freud would have no difficulty deducing that this person was, or equally conclusively was not, a repressed homosexual. This is the same

Freud who wrote on a different occasion that he had "never yet come through a single psychoanalysis of a man or a woman without having to take into account a very considerable current of homosexuality."[11] Freud could always find what he was looking for.

The case has the usual Freudian drolleries. The woman's statement that she heard a noise (which she took as a clue that she might be being watched) is interpreted by Freud to mean that she felt a throb in her clitoris. And the woman's alleged homosexual infatuation with the older colleague is supported by Freud's claim that the colleague represented the woman's mother (for all women without exception, remember, around the age of four, had a homosexual lust for their mothers).

It follows from Popper's approach that a non-scientific theory may be transformed into a scientific theory if its adherents decide to treat its claims as falsifiable. We might be tempted to see such episodes as the object-relations theorists rejecting Freud's instinct theory, in part because of research into primate behavior, or Beck's discovery that the dreams of depressed people do not have a high anger content, as being movements in the direction of science within psychoanalysis. The actual history of psychoanalysis is a bit different. Most adherents who became influenced by considerations of empirical testability quit 'official' psychoanalysis altogether, while, insofar as we can still distinguish a mainstream of psychoanalysis, it has shrunk to become one of numerous rival sects. Going a little beyond Popper we might surmise that empirical refutations play a part in the rise and fall of belief-systems which do not themselves recognize the refutations.

According to Popper, a non-scientific theoretical system may be true or false, though this cannot be decided by observation. As an example, Popper holds that determinism and indeterminism are non-scientific because they are both empirically irrefutable, though one must be true and the

---

[11] Freud 1958, Volume 7, 60.

other false. Popper presents arguments that determinism is false and indeterminism is true.

Non-scientific theories may be criticized in a number of ways (most of which also apply to scientific theories), such as consistency, economy, or compatibility with other parts of our knowledge. A non-scientific theory which purports to be a science may also be criticized by showing (as Popper did with Freud) that it is not a science. Someone may be attracted to a non-scientific theory believing it to be a science, and may become disenchanted when he realizes that it has no falsifiable implications. Thousands of people have turned against psychoanalysis for just this reason, some of them after reading Popper.

The main fault in Popper's analysis of psychoanalysis is that he had far too much respect for it. He thought that Freud had discovered important new truths which were unfortunately embedded in an unscientific doctrine. If this were true, it might be possible, as Popper hoped, to make the doctrine more scientific while preserving some continuity of identity with its earlier unscientific form. In fact Freud discovered no important new truths, any more than Franz Anton Mesmer or Franz Joseph Gall did, and merely perpetrated one grotesque muddle after another. Injecting scientific thinking into psychoanalysis is not therapeutic but lethal.

Popper's demarcation between science and non-science remains. And according to this principle, there is no contradiction in saying both that psychoanalysis is unscientific because it is empirically unfalsifiable and that psychoanalysis is false.

Select Bibliography

Adler, Alfred. 1964 [1956]. *The Individual Psychology of Alfred Adler*. Edited by Heinz L. Ansbacher and Rowena R. Ansbacher. New York: HarperPerennial.

———. 1979 [1964]. *Superiority and Social Interest: A Collection of Later Writings*. Edited by Heinz L. Ansbacher and Rowena R. Ansbacher. New York: Norton.

Amman, Ruth. 1991. *Healing and Transformation in Sandplay: Creative Processes Become Visible*. Chicago: Open Court.

Badcock, Christopher. 1992 [1988]. *Essential Freud*. Oxford: Blackwell.

Bandura, Albert. 1997. *Self-Efficacy: The Exercise of Control*. New York: Freeman.

Bass, Ellen, and Laura Davis. 1988. *The Courage to Heal: A Guide for Women Survivors of Child Sexual Abuse*. New York: Harper and Row.

Baumeister, Roy F., J.D. Campbell, J.I. Krueger, and K.D. Vohs. 2003. Does High Self-Esteem Cause Better Performance, Interpersonal Success, Happiness, or Healthier Lifestyles? *Psychological Science in the Public Interest* 4.

Baumeister, Roy F., and John Tierney. 2011. *Willpower: Rediscovering the Greatest Human Strength*. New York: Penguin.

Beck, Aaron T. 1979 [1976]. *Cognitive Therapy and the Emotional Disorders*. New York: Penguin.

————. 1997. The Past and Future of Cognitive Therapy. *Journal of Psychotherapy Practice and Research* 6:4 (Fall).

Beck, Aaron T., and Gary Emery. 2005 [1985]. *Anxiety Disorders and Phobias: A Cognitive Perspective*. New York: Basic Books.

Beck, Aaron T., A. John Rush, Brian F. Shaw, and Gary Emery. 1979. *Cognitive Therapy of Depression*. New York: Guilford.

Beck, Aaron T., Fred D. Wright, Cory F. Newman, and Bruce S. Liese. 1993. *Cognitive Therapy of Substance Abuse*. New York: Guilford.

Beck, Judith. 2005. *Cognitive Therapy for Challenging Problems: What to Do when the Basics Don't Work*. New York: Guilford.

————. 2011 [1995]. *Cognitive Behavior Therapy: Basics and Beyond*. New York: Guilford.

Becker, Ernest. 1997 [1973]. *The Denial of Death*. New York: Simon and Schuster.

Binswanger, Ludwig. 1975 [1963]. *Being-in-the-World: Selected Papers of Ludwig Binswanger*. London: Souvenir.

Bisson, J.I., P.L. Jenkins, J. Alexander, and C. Bannister. 1997. Randomised Controlled Trial of Psychological Debriefing for Victims of Acute Burn Trauma. *British Journal of Psychiatry* 171.

Bly, Robert. 2004 [1990]. *Iron John: A Book about Men*. Cambridge: Da Capo.

Borch-Jacobsen, Mikkel. 1996. *Remembering Anna O.: A Century of Mystification*. New York: Routledge.

Bouveresse, Jacques. 1993 [1991]. *Wittgenstein Reads Freud: The Myth of the Unconscious*. Princeton: Princeton University Press.

Bowlby, John. 1982 [1969]. *Attachment*. New York: Basic Books.

Branden, Nathaniel. 1971 [1969]. *The Psychology of Self-Esteem*. New York: Bantam.

————. 1970. *Breaking Free*. Los Angeles: Nash.

Breger, Louis. 2000. *Freud: Darkness in the Midst of Vision*. New York: Wiley.

Bruer, John. 2002 [1999]. *The Myth of the First Three Years: A New Understanding of Early Brain Development and Lifelong Learning*. New York: Simon and Schuster.

Burns, David D. 1981 [1980]. *Feeling Good: The New Mood Therapy*. New York: Signet.

————. 1999 [1990]. *The Feeling Good Handbook*. New York: Penguin.

Campbell, Joseph. 2008 [1949]. *The Hero with a Thousand Faces*. Novato: New World Library.

Campbell, Terence W. 1994. *Beware the Talking Cure: Psychotherapy May Be Hazardous to Your Health*. Boca Raton: Upton.

Chambless, D.L., and T.H. Ollendick. 2001. Empirically Supported Psychological Interventions: Controversies and Evidence. *Annual Review of Psychology* 52.

Cioffi, Frank. 1998. *Freud and the Question of Pseudoscience*. Chicago: Open Court.

Corsini, Raymond. 1973. *Current Psychotherapies*. Itasca: Peacock.

Crews, Frederick. 1986. *Skeptical Engagements*. New York: Oxford University Press.

————. 1975. *Out of My System: Psychoanalysis, Ideology, and Critical Method*. New York: Oxford University Press.

————, ed. 1995. *The Memory Wars: Freud's Legacy in Dispute*. New York: New York Review of Books.

————, ed. 1998. *Unauthorized Freud: Doubters Confront a Legend*. New York: Penguin.

————. 2006. *Follies of the Wise: Dissenting Essays*. Emeryville: Avalon.

Csikszentmihalyi, Mihaly. 2008 [1990]. *Flow: The Psychology of Optimal Experience*. New York: HarperCollins.

Diamond, Stephen A. 1996. *Anger, Madness, and the Daimonic: The Psychological Genesis of Violence, Evil, and Creativity*. Albany: SUNY Press.

Dobson, Deborah, and Keith S. Dobson. 2009. *Evidence-Based Practice of Cognitive-Behavioral Therapy*. New York: Guilford.

Dobson, Keith S. 2010. *Handbook of Cognitive-Behavioral Therapies*. Third edition. New York: Guilford.

Dryden, Windy, ed. 1996. *Developments in Psychotherapy: Historical Perspectives*. London: Sage.

———. 2000. *Rational Emotive Behaviour Counselling in Action*. London: Sage.

———. 2003. *Rational Emotive Behaviour Therapy: Theoretical Developments*. Hove: Brunner-Routledge.

Dryden, Windy, and Jill Mytton. 1999. *Four Approaches to Counselling and Psychotherapy*. London: Routledge.

Dryden, Windy, and Peter Trower, eds. 1986. *Rational-Emotive Therapy: Recent Developments in Theory and Practice*. Bristol: Institute for RET (UK).

Dufresne, Todd. 2007. *Against Freud: Critics Talk Back*. Stanford: Stanford University Press,

Dyer, Wayne W. 1976. *Your Erroneous Zones*. New York: Funk and Wagnalls.

Eagle, Morris N. 1984. *Recent Developments in Psychoanalysis: A Critical Evaluation*. Cambridge: Harvard University Press.

Edelstein, Michael R., and Mick Berry. 2009. *Stage Fright: 40 Stars Tell You How They Beat America's #1 Fear*. Tucson: See Sharp Press.

Edelstein, Michael R., and Will Ross. 2013. *Rational Drinking: How to Live Happily With or Without Alcohol*. Amazon digital (ebook only).

Edelstein, Michael R., and David Ramsay Steele. 1997. *Three Minute Therapy: Change Your Thinking, Change Your Life*. Lakewood: Glenbridge.

Edmunds, Lavinia. 1988. His Master's Choice. *The Johns Hopkins Magazine* (April).

Ellenberger, Henri F. 1970. *The Discovery of the Unconscious*. New York: Basic Books.

Ellis, Albert. 1951. *The Folklore of Sex*. New York: Doubleday.

———. 1962. *Reason and Emotion in Psychotherapy*. New York: Lyle Stuart.

———. 1965. *Homosexuality: Its Causes and Cure*. New York: Lyle Stuart.

———. 1975 [1957]. *How to Live with a Neurotic: At Home and at Work*. North Hollywood: Wilshire.

———. 1976. The Biological Basis of Human Irrationality. *Journal of Individual Psychology* 32.

———. 1990 [1977]. *Anger: How to Live with and Without It*. New York: Carol.

———. 1998. *How to Control Your Anxiety Before It Controls You*. New York: Carol.

———. 1999. *How to Make Yourself Happy and Remarkably Less Disturbable*. Atascadero: Impact.

———. 2000. Rational Emotive Behavior Therapy as an Internal Control Psychology. *Journal of Rational-Emotive and Cognitive-Behavior Therapy* 18:1 (Spring).

———. 2004. *Rational Emotive Behavior Therapy: It Works for Me—It Can Work for You*. Amherst: Prometheus.

———. 2005. *The Myth of Self-Esteem: How Rational Emotive Behavior Therapy Can Change Your Life Forever*. Amherst: Prometheus.

———. 2010. *Evolution of a Revolution: Selections from the Writings of Albert Ellis, PhD*. Fort Lee: Barricade.

Ellis, Albert, Ralph Brancale, and R. Doorbar. 1956. *The Psychology of Sex Offenders*. Springfield: Thomas.

Ellis, Albert, and Debbie Joffe Ellis. 2010. *All Out! An Autobiography*. Amherst: Prometheus.

———. 2011. *Rational Emotive Behavior Therapy*. Washington: American Psychological Association.

Ellis, Albert, and Robert A. Harper. 1975 [1961] *A New Guide to Rational Living*. North Hollywod: Wilshire.

Ellis, Albert, and John M. Whiteley, eds. 1979. *Theoretical and Empirical Foundations of Rational-Emotive Therapy*. Monterey: Brooks/Cole.

Ellis, Albert, Janet L. Wolfe, and Sandra Moseley. 1966. *How to Prevent Your Child Becoming a Neurotic Adult*. New York: Crown.

Ellis, Ralph D. 1995. *Questioning Consciousness: The Interplay of Imagery, Cognition, and Emotion in the Human Brain*. Amsterdam: Benjamins.

Ellis, Ralph D., and Natika Newton. 2010. *How the Mind Uses the Brain: To Move the Body and Image the Universe.* Chicago: Open Court.

Engel, Jonathan. 2008. *American Therapy: The Rise of Psychotherapy in the United States.* New York: Penguin.

Epictetus. 1983. *The Handbook (Encheiridion).* Indianapolis: Hackett.

Epp, Amanda M., and Keith S. Dobson. 2010. The Evidence Base for Cognitive-Behavioral Therapy. In Dobson 2010.

Esterson, Allen. 1993. *Seductive Mirage: An Exploration of the Work of Sigmund Freud.* Chicago: Open Court.

Estés, Clarissa Pinkola. 1995 [1992]. *Women Who Run with the Wolves: Myths and Stories of the Wild Woman Archetype.* New York: Random House

Eyer, Diane E. 1992. *Mother-Infant Bonding: A Scientific Fiction.* New Haven: Yale University Press.

Eysenck, Michael W. 1992. *Anxiety: The Cognitive Perspective.* Hove: Erlbaum.

Fancher, Robert T. 1997 [1995]. *Cultures of Healing: Correcting the Image of American Mental Health Care.* New York: Freeman.

Feldman, Gail Carr. 1993. *Lessons in Evil, Lessons from the Light: A True Story of Satanic Abuse and Spiritual Healing.* New York: Crown.

Fensterheim, Herbert. 1971. *Help Without Psychoanalysis.* New York: Stein and Day.

Frank, Jerome D. 1961. *Persuasion and Healing: A Comparative Study of Psychotherapy.* Baltimore: Johns Hopkins Press.

Frank, Jerome D., and Julia B. Frank. 1993 [1961]. *Persuasion and Healing: A Comparative Study of Psychotherapy.* Third edition. Baltimore: Johns Hopkins University Press.

Frankl, Viktor. 1984 [1946]. *Man's Search for Meaning: An Introduction to Logotherapy.* New York: Simon and Schuster.

Fransella, Fay, and Peggy Dalton. 1990. *Personal Construct Counselling in Action.* London: Sage.

Franz, Marie-Louise von. 1998 [1984]. *On Dreams and Death: A Jungian Interpretation.* Chicago: Open Court.

Freud, Anna. 1966 [1936]. *The Ego and the Mechanisms of Defense.* Madison: International Universities Press.

Freud, Sigmund. 1958 [1953]. *The Standard Edition of the Complete Psychological Works of Sigmund Freud.* 24 volumes. London: Hogarth.

Gardiner, Muriel, ed. 1971. *The Wolf Man and Sigmund Freud.* New York: Basic Books.

Gellner, Ernest. 1996 [1985]. *The Psychoanalytic Movement: The Cunning of Unreason.* Evanston: Northwestern University Press.

Glasser, William. 1965. *Reality Therapy: A New Approach to Psychiatry.* New York: Harper and Row.

———. 1985 [1976]. *Positive Addiction.* New York: HarperCollins.

———. 1998. *Choice Theory: A New Psychology of Personal Freedom.* New York: HarperCollins.

———. 2002. *Reality Therapy in Action.* New York: HarperCollins.

———. 2003. *Warning: Psychiatry Can Be Hazardous to Your Mental Health.* New York: HarperCollins.

Gopnik, Alison. 2009. *The Philosophical Baby: What Children's Minds Tell Us about Truth, Love, and the Meaning of Life.* New York: Farrar, Straus, and Giroux.

Gopnik, Alison, and Andrew N. Meltzoff. 1997. *Words, Thoughts, and Theories.* Cambridge: MIT Press.

Gopnik, Alison, Andrew N. Meltzoff, and Patricia K. Kuhl. 1999. *The Scientist in the Crib: Minds, Brains, and How Children Learn.* New York: Morrow.

Grosskurth, Phyllis. 1986. *Melanie Klein: Her World and Her Work.* New York: Knopf.

Grünbaum, Adolf. 1984. *The Foundations of Psychoanalysis: A Philosophical Critique.* Berkeley: University of California Press.

Handlbauer, Bernhard. 1998. *The Freud-Adler Controversy.* Oxford: Oneworld.

Harmon, Katherine. 2011. The Changing Mental Health Aftermath of 9/11: Psychological 'First Aid' Gains Favor over Debriefings. *Scientific American* (10th September).

Harris, Judith Rich. 1995. Where Is the Child's Environment? A Group Socialization Theory of Development. *Psychological Review* 102.

———. 2006. *No Two Alike: Human Nature and Human Individuality*. New York: Free Press.

———. 2009 [1998]. *The Nurture Assumption: Why Children Turn Out the Way They Do*. New York: Free Press.

Henle, Mary. 1986. *1879 and All That: Essays in the Theory and History of Psychology*. New York: Columbia University Press.

Hobson, J. Allan. 1994. *The Chemistry of Conscious States: How the Brain Changes Its Mind*. Boston: Little, Brown.

———. 2005. *13 Dreams Freud Never Had: The New Mind Science*. New York: Pi Press.

Hook, Sidney, ed. 1959. *Psychoanalysis, Scientific Method, and Philosophy*. New York: New York University Press.

Holmes, D. 1990. The Evidence for Repression. In Singer 1990.

Horney, Karen. 1937. *The Neurotic Personality of Our Time*. New York: Norton.

———. 1939. *New Ways in Psychoanalysis*. New York: Norton.

———. 1942. *Self-Analysis*. New York: Norton.

———. 1945. *Our Inner Conflicts*. New York: Norton.

———. 1950. *Neurosis and Human Growth: The Struggle toward Self-Realization*. New York: Norton.

Huelsenbeck, Karl Wilhelm Richard. 1991. *Memoirs of a Dada Drummer*. Berkeley: University of California Press.

Hunsley, John, and Gina Di Giulio. 2002. Dodo Bird, Phoenix, or Urban Legend? The Question of Psychotherapy Equivalence. *Scientific Review of Mental Health Practice* 1.

James, William. 1950 [1890]. *The Principles of Psychology*. Two volumes. Mineola: Dover.

Janet, Pierre. 1971 [1924]. *Principles of Psychotherapy*. Freeport: Books for Libraries.

Janov, Arthur. 1970. *The Primal Scream*. New York: Dell.

Jouvet, Michel. 1999 [1993]. *The Paradox of Sleep: The Story of Dreaming*. Cambridge: MIT Press.

Jung, Carl G. 1965. *Memories, Dreams, Reflections*. New York: Random House.

Kahn, Michael. 2002. *Basic Freud: Psychoanalytic Thought for the Twenty-First Century*. New York: Basic Books.

Kelly, George. 1955. *The Psychology of Personal Constructs*. Two volumes. New York: Norton.

Kihlstrom, John F. 1987. The Cognitive Unconscious. *Science* 237:1445–1452.

Krafft-Ebing, Richard von. 2011 [1886]. *Psychopathia Sexualis: The Classic Study of Deviant Sex*. New York: Arcade.

Lear, Jonathan. 1998. *Open-Minded: Working Out the Logic of the Soul*. Cambridge: Harvard University Press.

———. 2000. *Happiness, Death, and the Remainder of Life*. Cambridge: Harvard University Press.

Ledoux, Joseph. 1996. *The Emotional Brain: The Mysterious Underpinnings of Emotional Life*. New York: Simon and Schuster.

Lieberman, E. James. 1993 [1985]. *Acts of Will: The Life and Work of Otto Rank*. Amherst: University of Massachusetts Press.

Lilienfeld, Scott O., Steven Jay Lynn, and Jeffrey M. Lohr, eds. 2003. *Science and Psuedoscience in Clinical Psychology*. New York: Guilford.

Lilienfeld, Scott O., Steven Jay Lynn, John Ruscio, and Barry L. Beyerstein. 2010. *50 Great Myths of Popular Psychology: Shattering Widespread Misconceptions about Human Behavior*. Malden: Wiley-Blackwell.

Loftus, Elizabeth, and Katherine Ketcham. 1996 [1994]. *The Myth of Repressed Memory: False Memories and Allegations of Sexual Abuse*. New York: St. Martin's.

Macmillan, Malcolm. 1997 [1991]. *Freud Evaluated: The Completed Arc*. Cambridge: MIT Press.

Mahony, Patrick J. 1982. *Freud as a Writer*. New York: International Universities Press.

————.1986. *Freud and the Rat Man*. New Haven: Yale University Press.

————.1996. *Freud's Dora: A Psychoanalytic, Historical, and Textual Study*. New Haven: Yale University Press.

Marineau, René F. 1989. *Jacob Levy Moreno, 1889–1974: Father of Psychodrama, Sociometry, and Group Psychotherapy*. London: Tavistock.

Maslow, Abraham H. 1982 [1968]. *Toward a Psychology of Being*. New York: Van Nostrand.

Masson, Jeffrey Moussaieff. 1984. *The Assault on Truth: Freud's Suppression of the Seduction Theory*. New York: Farrar, Straus, and Giroux.

McNally, Richard J. 2005 [2003]. *Remembering Trauma*. Cambridge: Harvard University Press.

McNally, Richard J., Richard A. Bryant, and Anke Ehlers. 2003. Does Early Psychological Intervention Promote Recovery from Post-Traumatic Stress? *Psychological Science in the Public Interest* (November).

Mlodinow, Leonard. 2012. *Subliminal: How Your Unconscious Mind Rules Your Behavior*. New York: Random House.

Mosak, Harold H., and Michael P. Maniacci. 1999. *Primer of Adlerian Psychology: The Analytic-Behavioral-Cognitive Psychology of Alfred Adler*. New York: Routledge.

Nathan, Debbie. 2011. *Sybil Exposed: The Extraordinary Story Behind the Famous Multiple Personality Case*. New York: Simon and Schuster.

Obholzer, Karin. 1982. *The Wolf-Man Sixty Years Later: Conversations with Freud's Controversial Patient*. London: Routledge.

Offshe, Richard, and Ethan Watters. 1994. *Making Monsters: False Memories, Psychotherapy, and Sexual Hysteria*. New York: Scribner's.

Paris, Bernard J. 1994. *Karen Horney: A Psychoanalyst's Search for Self-Understanding*. New Haven: Yale University Press.

Paris, Joel. 2000. *Myths of Childhood*. Philadelphia: Brunner/Mazel.

Percival, Ray Scott. 2012. *The Myth of the Closed Mind: Understanding Why and How People Are Rational*. Chicago: Open Court.

Perls, Frederick S. 1969 [1946]. *Ego, Hunger, and Aggression: The Beginning of Gestalt Therapy*. New York: Random House.

———. 1969. *Gestalt Therapy Verbatim*. Lafayette: Real People Press.

Perls, Frederick S., Ralph E. Hefferline, and Paul Goodman. 1951. *Gestalt Therapy: Excitement and Growth in the Human Personality*. New York: Dell.

Peterson, Christopher, Steven F. Mair, and Martin E.P. Seligman. 1993. *Learned Helplessness: A Theory for the Age of Personal Control*. New York: Oxford University Press.

Popper, Karl Raimund. 1968 [1934]. *The Logic of Scientific Discovery*. New York: Harper and Row.

———. 1983. *Realism and the Aim of Science*. Totowa: Rowman and Littlefield.

Pratkanis, A.R. 1992. The Cargo-Cult Science of Subliminal Persuasion. *Skeptical Inquirer* (Spring).

Rank, Otto. 1952 [1924]. *The Trauma of Birth*. New York: Brunner.

Reich, Wilhelm. 1978 [1942]. *The Function of the Orgasm: Sex-Economic Problems of Biological Energy*. New York: Pocket Books.

———. 1980 [1933]. *Character Analysis*. New York: Farrar, Straus, and Giroux.

Roazen, Paul. 1975. *Freud and His Followers*. New York: Knopf.

Rofé, Yacov. 2008. Does Repression Exist? Memory, Pathogenic, Unconscious and Clinical Evidence. *Review of General Psychology* 12:1.

Rogers, Carl R. 1942. *Counseling and Psychotherapy: Newer Concepts in Practice*. Boston: Houghton Mifflin.

———. 1961. *On Becoming a Person: A Therapist's View of Psychotherapy*. Boston: Houghton Mifflin.

Rowe, David C. 1994. *The Limits of Family Influence: Genes, Experience, and Behavior*. New York: Guilford.

Russell, Bertrand. 1971 [1930]. *The Conquest of Happiness*. New York: Liveright.

Russianoff, Penelope. 1988. *When Am I Going to Be Happy? How to Break the Emotional Bad Habits that Make You Miserable*. New York: Bantam.

Sartre, Jean-Paul. 2001 [1943]. *Being and Nothingness: An Essay in Phenomenological Ontology*. New York: Kensington.

Schacter, Daniel L. 2001. *The Seven Sins of Memory: How the Mind Forgets and Remembers*. New York: Houghton Mifflin.

Schaler, Jeffrey. 2000. *Addiction Is a Choice*. Chicago: Open Court.

Schilpp, Paul A., ed. 1974. *The Philosophy of Karl Popper*. La Salle: Open Court.

Schneider, Kirk J. 1993. *Horror and the Holy: Wisdom-Teachings of the Monster Tale*. Chicago: Open Court.

Searle, John R. 1992. *The Rediscovery of the Mind*. Cambridge: MIT Press.

Seligman, Martin E.P. 1998 [1990]. *Learned Optimism: How to Change Your Mind and Your Life*. New York: Simon and Schuster.

———. 2002. *Authentic Happiness: Using the New Positive Psychology to Realize Your Potential for Lasting Fulfillment*. New York: Free Press.

———. 2007 [1994]. *What You Can Change and What You Can't: The Complete Guide to Successful Self-Improvement*. New York: Knopf.

———. 2011. *Flourish: A Visionary New Understanding of Happiness and Well-being*. New York: Free Press.

Sharaf, Myron. 1994. *Fury on Earth: A Biography of Wilhelm Reich*. New York: Da Capo.

Sharf, Richard S. 2004. *Theories of Psychotherapy and Counseling: Concepts and Cases*. Third edition. Pacific Grove: Brooks/Cole.

Sharot, Tali. 2011. *The Optimism Bias: A Tour of the Irrationally Positive Brain*. New York: Random House.

Simon, Julian. 1993. *Good Mood: The New Psychology of Overcoming Depression*. La Salle: Open Court.

Singer, Jerome L., ed. 1990. *Repression and Dissociation: Implications for Personality Theory, Psychopathology, and Health*. Chicago: University of Chicago Press.

Smith, Michelle, and Lawrence Pazder. 1981 [1980]. *Michelle Remembers*. New York: Simon and Schuster.

Stein, Murray. 1995. *Jungian Analysis*. Second Edition. Chicago: Open Court.

————. 1998. *Jung's Map of the Soul: An Introduction*. Chicago: Open Court.

Steele, David Ramsay. 1994. Partial Recall. *Liberty* (March).

Still, Arthur, and Windy Dryden. 2012. *The Historical and Philosophical Context of Rational Psychotherapy*. London: Karnac.

Summers, Christina Hoff, and Sally Satel. 2005. *One Nation Under Therapy: How the Helping Culture Is Eroding Self-Reliance*. New York: St. Martin's.

Swales, Peter J. 1982. Freud, Minna Bernays, and the Conquest of Rome: A New Light on the Origins of Psychoanalysis. *New American Review* (Spring–Summer).

Szasz, Thomas S. 1976. *Karl Kraus and the Soul Doctors: A Pioneer Critic and His Criticism of Psychoanalysis*. Baton Rouge: Louisiana State University Press.

————. 1988 [1978]. *The Myth of Psychotherapy: Mental Healing as Religion, Rhetoric, and Repression*. Syracuse: Syracuse University Press.

Tavris, Carol. 1989 [1982]. *Anger: The Misunderstood Emotion*. New York: Simon and Schuster.

Tillich, Paul. 1952. *The Courage to Be*. New Haven: Yale University Press.

Timpanaro, Sebastiano. 1976 [1974]. *The Freudian Slip: Psychoanalysis and Textual Criticism*. London: New Left Books.

Victor, Jeffrey. 1993. *Satanic Panic: The Creation of a Contemporary Legend*. Chicago: Open Court.

Wakefield, Hollida, and Ralph Underwager. 1994. *Return of the Furies: An Investigation into Recovered Memory Therapy*. Chicago: Open Court.

Watson, Patricia J., Melissa J. Brymer, and George A. Bonanno. 2011. Postdisaster Psychological Intervention Since 9/11. *American Psychologist* 66:6.

Watters, Ethan, and Richard Ofshe. 1999. *Therapy's Delusions: The Myth of the Unconscious and the Exploitation of Today's Walking Worried*. New York: Scribner.

Webster, Richard. 1995. *Why Freud Was Wrong: Sin, Science, and Psychoanalysis*. New York: Harper Collins.

Wiener, Daniel N. 1988. *Albert Ellis: Passionate Skeptic*. New York: Praeger.

Williams, Mark, John Teasdale, Zindel Segal, and Jon Kabat-Zinn. 2007. *The Mindful Way through Depression: Freeing Yourself from Chronic Unhappiness*. New York: Guilford.

Wilson, Colin. 1981. *The Quest for Wilhelm Reich*. Garden City: Anchor.

Wilson, Timothy D. 2002. *Strangers to Ourselves: Discovering the Adaptive Unconscious*. Cambridge: Harvard University Press.

Winnicott, Donald W. 1958. *Collected Papers: Through Paediatrics to Psychoanalysis*. London: Tavistock.

Wolpe, Joseph. 1958. *Psychotherapy by Reciprocal Inhibition*. Stanford: Stanford University Press.

———. 1969. *The Practice of Behavior Therapy*. New York: Pergamon.

Wolpe, Joseph, and David Wolpe. 1981. *Our Useless Fears*. New York: Houghton Mifflin.

Yalom, Irvin D. 1980. *Existential Psychotherapy*. New York: Basic Books.

———. 1990 [1989]. *Love's Executioner: And Other Tales of Psychotherapy*. New York: HarperCollins.

———. 2008. *Staring at the Sun: Overcoming the Terror of Death*. San Francisco: Jossey-Bass.

Young, Jeffrey E., Janet S. Klosko, and Marjorie E. Weishaar. 2003. *Schema Therapy: A Practitioners Guide*. New York: Guilford.

Ziegler, Daniel J. 2000. Basic Assumptions concerning Human Nature Underlying Rational Emotive Behavior Therapy (REBT) Personality Theory. *Journal of Rational-Emotive and Cognitive Behavior Therapy*, Vol. 18:2 (Summer).

Index